DETERMINED TO CONQUER
The History of
THE SALVATION ARMY
·CARIBBEAN TERRITORY·

BY ALLEN SATTERLEE

Crest **Books**

Salvation Army National Publications

Published by Crest Books
The Salvation Army National Headquarters
615 Slaters Lane
Alexandria, VA 22313
Phone: (703) 684-5523
Fax: (703) 302-8617

Major Allen Satterlee, Editor in Chief and National Literary Secretary
Judith L. Brown, Crest Books Coordinator

Available from The Salvation Army Supplies
and Purchasing Departments
Des Plaines, IL – (847) 937-8896
West Nyack, NY – (888) 488-4882
Atlanta, GA – (800) 786-7372
Long Beach, CA – (847) 937-8896

Printed in the United States of America

Cover and interior design by Type E Design
Cover photo by Major Allen Satterlee
Other photos courtesy of The Salvation Army USA National Archives
Department, The Salvation Army International Heritage Center
(London) and The Salvation Army Caribbean Territorial Archives

ISBN: 978-0-9831482-5-8
Library of Congress Control Number: 0201293368

DEDICATED TO

The Salvation Army Officers and Soldiers

of the Caribbean Territory.

May God continue to bless His Army.

———∞◦)◦(◦∞———

Contents

————∘∘∘━❯❮❮◉❯━∘∘∘————

I have read of men of faith
Who have bravely fought till death,
Who now the crown of life are wearing;
Then the thought comes back to me,
Can I not a soldier be,
Like to those martyrs bold and daring?

CHORUS
I'll gird on the armour and rush to the field,
Determined to conquer, and never to yield;
So the enemy shall know, Wheresoever I may go,
That I am fighting for Jehovah.

I, like them, will take my stand
With the sword of God in hand,
Smiling amid opposing legions;
I the victor's crown will gain,
And at last go home to reign
In Heaven's bright and sunny regions.

I will join at once the fight,
Leaning on my Saviour's might,
He is almighty to deliver;
From my post I will not shrink,
Though of death's cup I should drink;
Hell to defeat is my endeavour.

Will you not enlist with me,
And a valiant soldier be?
Vain 'tis to waste your time in slumber;
Jesus calls for men of war
Who will fight and ne'er give o'er,
Routing the foe in fear and wonder.

Blind Mark William Sanders
(1862-1943)

FOREWORD

TWENTY-TWO YEARS (1865 - 1887) after The Salvation Army was founded by William Booth in London, England, it established its mission in Jamaica and in subsequent years throughout the Caribbean. Ever since, the Army's evangelical message, based on biblical precepts, has been disseminated across all barriers including those of race, religion, culture, gender and age in almost every island of the Caribbean. Never daunted by challenges, the Army's work in the Caribbean has grown during the past 125 years, is growing today and will continue to grow.

Determined to Conquer tells the wonderful story of the history of The Salvation Army in the Caribbean from its inception until the present day. Through its pages, Major Allen Satterlee astutely tells the story of our movement in the region, highlighting the determination of the pioneers and of today's Caribbean Salvationists in spreading the gospel and fighting the war against all social ills. The early days of the Army in the Caribbean were not without difficulties. Soul winning is always costly. In almost every corner, the Army has had to face challenges that have sometimes resulted in our work being closed down. The Salvationists were determined to hold on to the end and God has always crowned their determination with success and victory. They were determined to fight to the end, believing that the Army was God's blessing to the people of the Caribbean—and still is today.

I recommend this progressive version to all readers. This history book is a record of superb achievement of Salvationists throughout the years. It has been written by one of our most outstanding and distinguished writers. As you read *Determined to Conquer,* thank God for our Salvationists who have faithfully fought and continue the good fight of faith with courage, dedication and determination. Thank God for every Soldier who has reached out and continues to reach out with compassionate hands to the hurting, despised, forsaken, outcast and disadvantaged throughout the region. We thank God for the Reinforcement Personnel (officers and lay Salvationists) who have left their homelands to render their service to God and man here. Their outstanding contribution has helped the work to grow rapidly and continue to grow today. Thank God for every person liberated and made whole through the power of the Holy Spirit. Our testimony is that the gospel of our Lord and Saviour Jesus Christ has been proclaimed and lived out through the faithfulness and enthusiastic witnessing of Salvationists in the Caribbean. May it continue to be so.

Colonel Onal Castor
Territorial Commander

ACKNOWLEDGMENTS

I AM DEEPLY HONORED that The Salvation Army leadership has entrusted me with the task of writing this history. I was first approached to write it by Commissioner Raymond Haughton. The faith he showed in me was confirmed by his successor, Colonel Onal Castor. I also appreciate the great support and help given by Lt. Colonel Lindsay Rowe who has served as chief secretary.

I felt immediately challenged by the difficulty of writing such a history and acknowledged my handicaps. First, I am not a Caribbean and so have struggled to find the Caribbean voice in my writing. The reader will have to be the judge as to whether I was successful or not.

My second challenge was that my wife and I had at the same time leadership of the Western Jamaica Division. We considered it a high privilege to work with the officers and soldiers of this most wonderful place. I often felt I was not giving them my best because of the time and effort that necessarily was needed to write this book. But the people were wonderfully understanding and supportive. I thank them for that as well as for members of the divisional staff who also were supportive: Majors Emmerson and Carolinda Cumberbatch, Major Joliker Leandre, Captains Emmanuel and Edeline Supré as well as my secretary, Miss Shadene Ricketts.

I especially thank my wife, Major Esther M. Satterlee, who filled in for me many times while I was absent from the Western Jamaica Division. She was also generous in her praise and encouragement, honest in her assessment and helpful in every way she could be.

Whether I was qualified or not, the task was mine and an enjoyable one it was! So I set to work nearly three years ago.

Writing history is a bit like putting together a massive jigsaw puzzle. Besides the absolute complexity of fitting the pieces together, the historical writer finds that the pieces are scattered across the whole landscape. He can either try to find it all himself or take advantage of the services offered by those who are only too willing to help him. I chose the latter approach.

I would like to acknowledge my indebtedness to the various archives. They are as follows:

The Bahamas Government Department of Archives
Belize Archives and Record Service
Department of the Archives - Barbados
Jamaica *Gleaner* Archives
The National Archives, Antigua
The National Archives, Guyana
The Salvation Army International Heritage Centre (London)
The Salvation Army USA National Archives Department
(Alexandria, Virginia, USA)
The Salvation Army Caribbean Territorial Archives
(Kingston, Jamaica)
Antigua Division
Bahamas Division
Barbados Division
Belize Region
French Guiana Region
Guyana Division

Haiti Division
Suriname Region
Trinidad and Tobago Division

I would like to especially acknowledge Major Doreen Hobbs. Major Hobbs wrote the first history of the Caribbean Territory, *Jewels of the Caribbean*. Her work was done without any computers or use of the Internet. She not only did a stellar job but she freely shared with me her notes and observations.

Many people consented to allowing me to interview them. Although I did not directly quote from all the interviews, each in its own way was immensely helpful in the record of fact, background information or getting the feel of a situation beyond what can be gathered from just reading about something. In the References section at the end of this book I list each one. Thank you for sharing openly and honestly with me.

I received some excellent help with the manuscript itself by those who consented to review it. Helping me on yet another literary project was my best friend and fellow writer, Major Frank Duracher. Major Lester Ferguson shared insightful observations on a number of items. Members of the Territorial Cabinet at the Caribbean Territorial Headquarters filled in many gaps and gave a great assessment which helped shape the manuscript. To all these I express my sincerest appreciation.

Finally, I give glory to God who always sustains me and who blessed me so abundantly with the voices of testimony from the long departed as well as the ones living today. It is exciting to write about what every Salvationist would acknowledge to be a record of His faithfulness. Always, to God be the glory!

PRELUDE

THE ISLANDS AND COASTLINE of the Caribbean Sea rested in tranquil beauty for untold centuries. That all changed when Christopher Columbus, intent on finding a passage to India from Europe, "discovered" the islands. It wasn't long after this that gold was found in Mexico and South America, and assuming that gold was everywhere in the Caribbean Basin, conquistadors and other opportunists soon overran the native people living there. Subjecting them to slavery, the Tainos, Arawaks and the Caribs were wiped out by the twin threat of unrelenting cruelty from the European conquerors and the diseases they brought with them. Finding no gold, the Spaniards, French, English and Dutch noted two other treasures to be found there.

First, the islands of the Caribbean were strategically placed to allow the capture and plunder of gold being shipped from Mexico back to Europe. In that the European powers were either at war or on the brink of war with each other constantly, coupled with the nations' insatiable appetite for gold, the Caribbean was strategically important. There could be no more perfect place to launch raiders to steal the gold, or for the Spaniards to have fleets stationed to protect the gold. The raiders operated with and without national sanctions. Independent ocean-going entrepreneurs were known as pirates; the ones under a nation's contract were called privateers. Their exploits and their depravity became the stuff of legend.

The second treasure of the Caribbean and Latin America was the abundant and rich farming land. Although not as exciting as the forays on the high seas, the lands of the Caribbean lent themselves to raising sugar cane, bananas, coconuts, rice, nutmeg and a host of other valuable commodities. But these were crops that were labour intensive and with the native Caribbean population now extinct, a cheap source of labour had to be found. The answer was slavery.

Led first by the Dutch but then entered into with equal abandon by the English and French, the trade in human souls was highly profitable—and excessively brutal. Captured in Africa by rival tribes, African slaves were boarded on ships that maximized space and minimized comfort. A rank racism convinced the slave traders and their various nations that the Africans were something less than human and besides, they reasoned, if they were so easily conquered, why would their rights be on par with Europeans? The voyage from Africa to the Caribbean was gruelling and marked with multiple deaths with each passage. Upon arriving at the destination, any vestige of dignity was stripped away by the whip or weakened by near starvation.

If the voyage was difficult, little comfort could be taken in finally reaching land again. Families were separated by the considered auction value of each member. Like a farmer buying a new horse, men were inspected to judge their suitability to work the fields. Some women were judged fit to be domestics but most were sent to the same fields with the same expectations of men. Young children were considered more of a nuisance than anything else until they could be pressed into similar service. With people owned like farm stock, it was not hard at all to breed people as one did cattle. After all, a strong laborer born among the slaves saved the purchase price of a new one.

The result for the slaves was the destruction of almost all vestiges of self-respect and their home culture. Sparse shreds of past lives remained in African rites and rituals as found in obeahism and voodoo—two folk religion forms. Languages soon disappeared with only hints found in Patois and Creole. Old rivalries from Africa were swallowed up in a new misery shared by all, a common lot of bondage and chains.

Added to slavery's humiliation was the difficulty just to survive. The strains of malaria and yellow fever found in the Caribbean differed from the ones found in Africa. They took a fearsome toll as thousands upon thousands succumbed to disease, their death hastened by bodies pushed to exhaustion. Although slavery was a horrible institution to the north in the United States, it was even more sinister in the Caribbean, where the gruelling labor of the cane fields dwarfed the harvesting of cotton in the American South. Survival was more by accident than by design, as death randomly stalked the strong and the weak alike. The only consolation that the slave might take is that his white masters suffered a greater percentage of deaths to tropical diseases than the slaves did. But another man's end hardly made the shackles feel lighter.

Finally in 1832, England outlawed slavery. Other nations soon followed. While it was wonderful for the slaves to be liberated, the European legislators gave little thought to what the slaves would do once freed: no plan, no help for the emancipated men, women and children. They were left to their own devices, not prepared in any way to assume control of their lives or to chart the course of their destinies. The plantations were bankrupted or nearly so by the loss of slave labor, unable to hire the freed slaves that now wandered the roads of the colonies. Poverty had a death grip on the ethnic African peoples of the Caribbean. Schooling was largely withheld, the vote denied them. It was as if the colonial powers were punishing the people they had enslaved for daring to breathe free. Seeing little difference between them and those in Mother Africa, the Europeans called the ethnic Africans of the Caribbean and Latin America "natives," a strange term since they were forcibly brought to foreign lands they did not choose.

But still the colonial powers wanted the riches of these colonies to feed the mother countries. So the British exploited an unholy alternative to slavery by introducing indentured servants. Almost entirely from India, the indentured servants were engaged for a specific period of time to work in the Caribbean. At the end of that time they were free to return to India or, if they elected to stay, they were promised a plot of land as a reward. Rosy pictures of the indentured servants' life resulted in tens of thousands of Indians relocating to the Caribbean. But the recruiting picture and the reality were two different things. Called "coolies," they suffered a fate little better than the slaves but, because they were under contract, they had some defined rights that offered limited protection.

For the freed slaves the introduction of the Indian indentured servants only made their plight more desperate. If there was any hope of hiring themselves out to the plantations for labor, they found the Indian servants there already. In order to be employed, the poor had to accept wages that were severely depressed, reasoning that some work at a low wage was better than no work at all. Added to that, the market fluctuated wildly for sugar and other farm products. No one escaped suffering.

Although the nations of the New World under colonial rule suffered greatly, there were benefits to colonialism as well. With the European powers came funds to develop infrastructure that included roads and ports. In time the infrastructure expanded to railroads and airports. The stationing of garrisons of military bolstered the local economies, which in turn provided entrepreneurial opportunities for ethnic Africans, Indians and Chinese.

Systems of law brought order to the colonies, not only defining criminal acts but affording protections to its expatriate as well as local citizens.

Economies were benefited by often favorable market protections in the mother country and among those who shared in the colonial family of the European powers. The strong currencies of the mother countries also provided stability and reliability. And there were those among the colonial powers who had genuine affection and who greatly esteemed the people who had formerly been slaves and indentured servants. Mostly from Christian evangelical denominational and Roman Catholic efforts, schools were established aimed not at the European population but at the ethnic African and Asian children. And the colonial citizens were allowed to travel freely not only to the home country but to other colonies scattered across the world. The opportunities were there if the local people could only get the help they needed to access them. It was that lack of access, or when available, the difficulty in meeting the requirements to have access that perpetuated poverty, illiteracy and a hopelessness that became deeply ingrained over time.

Misery was found not only in the Caribbean. Although London was considered by many to be the greatest city of the world, like all great cities then and now, it had a dark underside. That underside could be found on the east side and in the collection of lost neighborhoods; none was bleaker than Mile End Waste.

The mass of humanity crowded in tenement flats and whose bodies littered the sidewalks and gutters gave testimony to the hopeless despair that marked daily life. Jobs, when available, paid wages at the lowest of levels because laborers were abundant and employment scarce. Here it was that boarding houses rented their bunks in shifts with beds always warm because when one man got up to go to work the next renter rolled into it to sleep amid smells of stale urine and mildewed decay. Cleanliness was a luxury, a memory from a distant day before the city consumed them. They had come in waves of hundreds and thousands to find work and prosperity. Instead, they were greeted with suffocating poverty and unrelenting wretchedness.

Mile End Waste positioned itself in stark contrast to other parts of the city that boasted the stately halls of Parliament and the grandeur of Buckingham Palace. Its drab and lifeless buildings stood in shambles against the majesty of St. Paul's Cathedral and Westminster Abbey. The pomp of the changing of the guards could scarcely be held in the same mind that stepped across scurrying rats that ruled the streets. Sonorous tones of parliamentary debate set themselves against the screams of a beaten wife, the cry of an always hungry baby, the foul cursing of a once gentle man who surrendered to brutality. Mile End Waste was more than London's dark nightmare: it was the shadow of hell against the glory of the Empire's heaven.

Despite the choking fog of gloom that ever clung to Mile End Waste, shafts of light forced their way through. Here and there messengers braved the sights, sounds and danger to speak an eternal message of unfathomable hope. They lifted their voices proclaiming that Christ loved the world, and no matter how ugly they had become, God still loved them. And if they turned to Him, in the senselessness that was their life, they could be born again.

It was here that in 1865 William Booth, an itinerant preacher, met a group of likeminded evangelists preaching in front of the Blind Beggar Pub. Stirred by God through the sights, sounds and smells of East London and the rich field for evangelism, he went home to his wife, Catherine, and said, "I have found my destiny." The destiny found that day was born in East London but it spread across the world in a matter of years. The little group named itself the Christian Mission but infused by God's Spirit, its innate militancy took over and it morphed into The Salvation

Army. By the time it reached the lands of the Caribbean Sea, the trademark uniforms, ranks, lively meetings and unorthodox methods were not only fully a part of its personality but had made this strange little religious body well known far beyond the countries where it actually worked. Newspapers trumpeted this or that event with The Salvation Army. Letters to the editor in countless newspapers sometimes praised but more often condemned General William Booth and his Army. But whether people aligned themselves as its enemies or sided with it as one of its friends, all admitted that The Salvation Army was big news and what it did—and how it did it—was fascinating reading.

Like the colonies, it was the more positive aspects of the British Empire that helped the Army in its early expansion. The widespread use of the English language, the common law and citizens' rights, the common currency and the ever vigilant protection of the British military forces allowed the early Salvationists to cast a worldwide vision. It was as if a great highway was built that the old Salvation Army chariot could take until the message of salvation was spread to every land. It was that road that one day in 1887 brought The Salvation Army to Jamaica.

Each took the other into its fold, learning to joy together in the dance of salvation.

THE BATTLE IS JOINED

BORN A SLAVE IN JAMAICA in 1820, "Mother" Foster was taken to England where she eventually met The Salvation Army. Taken by the free style of worship, she loved the excitement of the meetings both indoors and out in the streets. She witnessed the change in people who seldom experienced salvation in Christ as some quiet, reflective decision. There was a joy in salvation and in turn there was joy in The Salvation Army.

Mother Foster herself was saved at the South Shields Corps[a] in England and soon enrolled as a Salvation Army soldier[b]. Witnessing that she had been "born in the Army fire," it wasn't long before she could withhold no longer and she preached with passion.

[1]Known as the "Coloured Special," Mother Foster longed for the Army to open in her homeland. She believed that the churches needed a baptism of Holy Ghost power because thousands would not listen to a message that was preached with formal, if not proper, tones. Leaving for Jamaica in 1883, her

---

[a] In keeping with its quasi-military nature, a corps is the name for a Salvation Army worship center that has reached a certain stage of development. A new worship center is initially called an outpost until its membership allows it to be upgraded to corps status.

[b] A soldier is a full-fledged member of The Salvation Army who has demonstrated a consistent Christian life, accepts The Salvation Army's doctrines, pledges to live a holy life and support The Salvation Army. In addition, soldiers are not permitted to use alcohol, illegal drugs or tobacco or to be involved with pornography.

officer[c] daughter remained in England.

Upon arriving home she took her message out to the streets of Kingston, her booming voice hard to ignore. Converts were won and soon she had a mission going with many joining her informal Salvation Army. She told anyone and everyone that this was the opening foray of a full scale invasion. And when it came, she would once again be found in The Salvation Army, and these missioners like her, would be Salvationists.[2]

Meanwhile, a young Englishman and his wife lived in the country district of Bluefields. Coming into contact with Mother Foster, he was taken by her lively approach to soul-winning. He and his wife had already joined the Baptist church but they wanted a more active Christianity in their lives as well as for the people of Jamaica. W. Raglan Phillips and his wife Agnes recalled that, "we wrote International Headquarters,[d] asking them to send out officers. When this leaked out we were much opposed. But this tended to push us forward and we at once commenced aggressive Christian work on entirely new lines, preparing as we openly said, for the advent of the Army."

Raglan Phillips relates that they "soon drew large crowds of people who had never before heard a woman preach. And the promised 'signs' followed, for many vile sinners and a few respectable men, too, got converted . . . Perhaps considerable of this success was due to persistent visiting in the surrounding villages. 'If you don't belong to anywhere else, you belong to us.'"[3]

The first official note that anyone was listening came in the Army publication *All the World*[e] when it was noted that volun-

---

[c] Officers are the clergy of The Salvation Army. Asserting the equality of sexes, from the beginning both men and women have been ordained.

[d] International Headquarters is located in London, birthplace of The Salvation Army where The Salvation Army General oversees Salvation Army work around the world. The next level below that are territorial headquarters overseen by a territorial commander. A territory can be comprised of several countries, a single country or a portion of a larger country determined by the strength and concentration of Salvation Army forces.

[e] *All the World* is The Salvation Army's international magazine that highlights Salvation Army evangelical and social work from the various countries and colonies in the world.

teers were sought to answer the call for workers in Jamaica.[4]

Finally something happened. While celebrating Guy Fawkes Day with his family, Colonel Abram Davey received a telegram that read "FAREWELL IMMEDIATELY AND PROCEED TO OPEN THE WORK IN WEST INDIES."[5] Scarcely ten days later on November 15, 1887 the Davey family set sail for Jamaica via New York. Included in their invasion force were five children and Blind Mark Saunders, a gifted musician and songwriter on the SS Servia.[6]

The Daveys made wise use of the stopover in the United States. With the help of the Army's national leaders in America, Commander and Mrs. Ballington Booth, special meetings were arranged to allow the pioneering party to raise much needed capital for the new advance. They conducted meetings in New York City, New Brunswick, Brooklyn and other places. In speaking about his destination, Colonel Davey laid out his initial plans to an interviewer from the American War Cry:[f] "We have one or two auxiliaries at Bluefields on that island who have made repeated requests for the establishment of a corps at Bluefields. They have offered us a hall and printing press, and we have accepted them; and although that town is my destination, yet I hope to establish headquarters in Kingston, the capital of the island."[7]

As the time drew near for the Army to actually come to Jamaica a stir was created. At its best, it was high anticipation and at its worst, sheer terror that the island would be overrun by overzealous revivalists of questionable moral standing. Trying to make a pre-emptive strike, Raglan Phillips wrote a letter to the editor in which he said:

---

[f] *The War Cry* is The Salvation Army's official publication. It is issued in each territory where The Salvation Army works under that name with only a few exceptions.

I find a great deal of both interest and ignorance amongst many of the people of this city (Kingston) regarding the "greatest religious movement of modern days"—The Salvation Army. Misleading and absurd statements have been published from time to time, one of which was to the effect that in England and elsewhere the Army has been regarded as a combination of thieves and characters!

...(Charles) Spurgeon[g] says that if The Salvation Army were wiped out of London 5,000 extra policemen could not fill its place in the repression of crime and disorder.

The masses of Jamaica are unreached by the existing religious organizations. Four hundred and fifty thousand of our people belong to no place of worship at all. Surely there is ample room for The Salvation Army, and every right thinking man should wish them God-speed.[8]

News of the Army's intended invasion had already stirred up great interest in Kingston. *Gall's Newsletter* optimistically predicted that The Salvation Army would be successful. "Now among those who know anything of the lower strata of Jamaica society, there can be no doubt that a military organization like The Salvation Army is just what will please and attract the great mass of our people, and it is this means for gathering these together, and it affords the opportunities for religious instruction, who will commend the promoters . . . the officers of The Salvation Army have trouble in getting a discipline and orderly organization before the public; but with time and patience they will succeed. We must not be in a hurry to condemn that which is new and strange to us."[9]

After departing from New York on the *S.S. Alene*, on December 15 the assault force arrived. They were greeted on the dock by Mother Foster, Raglan Phillips and a crowd of followers.

---

[g] Charles Spurgeon was a famous Baptist preacher, pastor of the Metropolitan Tabernacle, then the largest Protestant church in London. He was known as the "prince of preachers" because of his eloquence and Bible expositions.

"Thank God, you've come at last," they said. "We've been looking for you every mail (ship) these two years and now you really have come."[10]

Hoping to have a private briefing with Mother Foster about the work she had carried on as well as what preparations were made for the Army to officially open fire, Davey found instead that nearly 300 people thronged the hall. With that many people anxiously awaiting them, the Salvationists launched into an impromptu meeting that included the singing of Salvation songs, vocal solos by Blind Mark, who accompanied himself in turn by concertina and cornet, as well as what was described by one newspaper reporter as a "powerful and eloquent" discourse by Colonel Davey. Davey reported that the West Indies version of *The War Cry* would soon be published and that he expected to deploy 40 officers across the island with Kingston as headquarters.[11] The first official meeting was held the following Sunday at Myrtle Bank Hotel, loaned to the Army by Mr. and Mrs. Gall after the mayor, viewing the Army as a group of holy hooligans, refused to let the Army use the town hall. Despite the snub by the city, a crowd of around 6,000 showed up to hear the Salvationists, with four responding to the challenge to come forward to seek salvation. "In faith, the Salvationists regarded these four new souls as the vanguard of a great multitude to follow."

Soon after, Colonel Davey announced in *The War Cry*, "Roll the old chariot along! We want a hall in this city capable of holding 6,000 people. Who will help us get on?"[12] Later that year the Army managed to acquire a more modest building than Davey had called for when it purchased the former Christian Chapel at 48 Church Street.[13]

Although Davey concentrated his efforts in Kingston where he undoubtedly thought there was the most promise, he did not forget the lone corps in the parish of Westmoreland. Accordingly, it was reported by Raglan Phillips that, "After a few days in Kingston we got orders to open Bluefields. We left Kingston on March 20th and after a ride of one hundred miles by the mail coach, which was rather shaky, we found ourselves on the 22nd in Bluefields."[14]

HISTORY IN THE FIRST PERSON

Colonel Abram Davey

THE WAR CRY JANUARY 2, 188 | CHRISTMAS SUNDAY

Sunday, the 25th was a blessed day. We commenced by holding a meeting at 7 o'clock in the morning at Myrtle Bank, when a good number came out to consecrate their lives to God's service, and to seek the blessing of a clean heart. The afternoon meeting at the same place was well attended, although held when most people were eating their Christmas dinners, after which we marched off with our drum and other instruments, a large crowd following us until we reached the piazza of a friend's house in West Queen Street where we must have had three or four thousand of the very poorest people gathered together without the meeting having been previously announced, and notwithstanding the fact that there were special attractions in the various churches and chapels in the way of flower decorations, anthems and hymns. Those we addressed were evidently not on their way to any place of worship, although we are informed that many go on a Christmas Day who remain away the rest of the year. It was a tremendous meeting and the Holy Ghost was indeed present in mighty power. One after another poured into the crowd some red-hot gospel truths, and Blind Mark read a passage of Scripture with his fingers, and afterwards sung his wonderfully popular song, "Gird on the Armour."

God seemed indeed to come down in a wave of mighty power, and to sway the people to and fro. It was the most powerful and spiritual meeting we had yet had on the island, and at the close a good number sought salvation. Hallelujah! We feel sure that had we been in a large building scores would have come forward, but it is hard for the penitents to push their way through the crowd and kneel down in the street to seek salvation. We are praying and believing that God will incline the hearts of some who have it in their power to send us the money necessary to get a building large enough for the crowds who are anxious to know the way of life.

The Army seemed to polarize the people of Jamaica from the start. On the one hand, especially in its early days, the Army was met with a warm welcome from most of the religious leaders who made their pulpits available to Army leaders and who often attended many Army functions.[15] But acceptance was not universal. *All the World* reported that the Jamaica newspaper, *The Budget*, feared the Army was teaching a highly emotionally charged version of Christianity that they termed "revivalism." They warned that it would "drive the people to frenzy, and cause them to neglect their industry, their social duties, their homes and families, and give themselves up to excesses that level them to the condition of the brute."[16]

The appearance of the Army signalled more than forcing Jamaicans to become accustomed to uniforms. The swinging, free and expressive style of worship that marked Army meetings had horrified many around the world. It had been readily embraced by the poor, however. That free and easy style that dispensed with formalities and customs that were more rooted in English culture than the ethnic African one that dominated Jamaica, made for some interesting clashing of cultures. Colonel Davey immediately recognized the value of the ethnic African culture, warmly embracing its musical styles, allowing for the swaying and dancing that celebrated the joy of salvation and incorporated the unique sounds and rhythms of Caribbean drums. It was The Salvation Army that brought a Christianity that sang its experience, not through the staid tones and lofty words of hymns but in the festive sounds of celebration. It was The Salvation Army that introduced the tambourine that now is used by scores of independent churches and denominations. It was The Salvation Army that allowed for cultural expressions such as dance—sanctified of course! Colonel Davey was wise to let the Army be truly Caribbean and not another pale imitation of proper English church.

This was shocking to most of the established clergy and churchgoers. They accused the Army of vulgarity while ignoring the evidence of changed lives that this approach brought forth.

What was not overtly stated but remained thinly veiled was the fear that the ethnic African people of Jamaica would find in the Salvation Army style of Christianity a freedom from the manipulation used by the wealthy white business owners and government officials that kept them in elite positions over a dependent population of former slaves and their descendants. The empowerment of the majority ethnic African population was something to be feared by those who ran the colony. They had successfully minimized the freedom from slavery that existed earlier in the century by keeping the ethnic Africans in abject poverty, denying them almost any means of empowerment, including education.

The Salvation Army had no respect for the evils of this established system. The ruling class of Jamaica was well aware of the freedom of access given to even the most ignorant in Salvation Army meetings in other countries. That the ethnic African population would find their voice in religion would mean that they might also find their voice in other areas of colonial life. Over the next few decades many of the extremely vicious attacks on The Salvation Army had an undercurrent of fear that the racial hierarchy might be endangered.

While later in the year antagonism would explode upon the Army, the first half of 1888 seemed like a fairy tale. As noted above, the Army had widespread support from most of the churches, enjoyed favorable press and saw the work progressing at an encouraging pace. In addition to the purchase of the property on Church Street, it was announced that a Training Home for women officers was to be opened with another one for men to be opened soon after.[17]

One action particularly garnered widespread approval for

the Army. Blind Mark Saunders had astounded many Jamaicans by his ability to read through his fingers using Braille. In a meeting led by Reverend Alexander McCauley at The Salvation Army Temple, Kingston's blind were invited to a dinner to hear Blind Mark speak.[18] At that time, when a person was blind he was written off that he would ever be useful, or for that matter, educated. To realize a blind person had a means to read and to accomplish as much as Blind Mark had amounted to a startling revelation. In its efforts to reach those on the margins of society, The Salvation Army held out a beacon of hope to the blind. But in the coming days any promise that this beginning held was forgotten. At least for that generation of blind in Jamaica, life would go back to the bleak existence it had been before.[19]

There was no way that Colonel Davey could have foreseen the consequences the morning he mailed off an article to International Headquarters about the work in Jamaica. Written for The Salvation Army international publication, *All the World*, the article was written under Davey's name but not by him, a common practice in that day. It was written instead by Raglan Phillips, although the true authorship remained unknown for quite some time.[20] The article was not unlike others that appeared in *All the World* except that it took some liberties with the truth. One of Davey's consistent faults was his penchant to exaggerate. When the newspapers reported crowds of 300 or 400, Davey reported them to Army publications as 2,000 or 3,000. That flare for the dramatic, with truth being the casualty, is what lay behind the trouble that followed.

What motivated Colonel Davey to even submit such an article? At this time The Salvation Army was rapidly expanding all over the world. Many of the places it went were quite exotic compared to the consistent, if not at times boring, life found in Mother England. Encounters with African tribes and the castes of India made for lively writing by Army pioneers. Although the

Army work in Jamaica was moving apace at good speed and despite the fact that it was filled with challenge, it would seem Colonel Davey was carried away a bit. Beyond that, it is inconceivable that he would allow anything going out under his name which did not reflect his own opinions. By his own admission, he "somewhat perused" the article before sending it, although he was certainly familiar with its content.[21] Whatever his motivation might have been, he could not have expected what would follow in the wake of its publication.

Following the publication of the article in *All the World*, it was reprinted in the Canadian edition of *The War Cry*. A copy reached Jamaica, outraging the readers on the island. The warm friendliness that marked previous relationships with the press evaporated overnight. Particularly aggrieved was Mr. Gall, who so enthusiastically supported the Army previously. He made it a point in his newspaper, *Gall's Newsletter*, to lead the attack against the Army in general and Colonel Davey in particular.

The article entitled, "Jamaica: Past and Present" contained the following points of contention:

1. It was stated that the Army was not well received by other churches when in reality the Army was welcomed and supported by most religious bodies and seen as a partner in the proclamation of the Christian message.
2. The article described a 75% incidence of children born to unwed parents. The real number was still high at 60%, but the higher figure was an inflated number.
3. The article spoke of widespread idol worship. In fact, outside of the small number of Indian indentured servants who were Hindu, idols were virtually unknown on the island.[22]
4. It was reported that there was no meaningful religious influence from the existing churches and that until the Army came, proclamation of the Gospel was virtually non-existent. However, quite a number of churches carried on meaningful evangelism as well as visitation to hospitals and jails and other acts of mercy.

A violent reaction resulted. *The Daily Gleaner* reported:

> About three hundred men, women and boys assembled on Thursday night at The Salvation Army Temple in Church Street, and literally sacked the building, on the ground that Colonel Davey, who is the head of the Army here, had written falsehoods against the island in *All the World*. The Colonel had just commenced his discourse on the duty of Christians, when they had suffered wrongs (as mentioned in St. Matthew) when he was stopped by the people with words to this effect—"Down with Colonel Davey! Down with him!" while others called him an immigrant. Several constables were in the building but they failed to preserve order. When the Colonel signified his intention to preach at Myrtle Bank, the people all protested, and boldly advised him not to go back there. The Colonel was unable to raise a hymn or say a prayer. The people took possession of the temple, when some of the lights were put out, some lamps smashed, while benches, chairs and everything they could lay hands upon were broken.
>
> A general striking with sticks ensued. One of the collectors was knocked down while engaged in taking up the usual collections. Mrs. Davey received a blow, and owing to the excitement of the mob the Colonel and his officers had to retreat. The constables who were there succeeded in reaching the street where they were strengthened by others. Some time after they succeeded in clearing the street, and order was restored. Over five hundred persons again congregated inside and outside of the Temple last night, and when several speakers attempted to make an explanation exonerating Colonel Davey from blame, they positively refused to listen, and shouted, "Down with Davey!" The building was frequently stoned, and the whole proceedings interrupted. The result was that Colonel Davey was compelled to break up the meeting at about nine o'clock, and were it not for the presence of a strong squad of constables of Inspector Wedderburn and Sub-Inspector Porches, heaven only knows what the infuriated people might have done.[23]

Following this violence, the affairs of the Army suffered greatly. No amount of explanation or apologies seemed to have any effect upon public opinion. The Army was definitely on the defensive and losing ground quickly. Davey tried to stand his ground. In a letter to the editor in *Gall's Newsletter* he said, "I have come to Jamaica to live or die for God and souls, and am not going to be asked to be removed ... Upon one thing I am resolved, that is to trust God to supply our needs instead of taking up collections. We shall not then have it said of us that we are money hunters. God forbid that we should ever be that."

Had *Gall's Newsletter* never taken the matter and stormed so against Colonel Davey, it is doubtful that the article would have done much more than raise a few eyebrows. Unfortunately, the massive good that was done across the island was pushed aside. Even while the storm was raging in Kingston, The Salvation Army continued to advance, continued to win souls and continued to engage the poor with the good news of salvation.

HISTORY IN THE FIRST PERSON

Commissioner William Davey

PERSONAL REMINISCENCES

The first sign that something was brewing was an unruly crowd at the back of the Hall, booing and cat-calling and generally disturbing the proceedings, which up to then had always been so respectful, reverent and well behaved. This went on for several nights, getting worse and worse. Then stones were thrown at those taking part on the platform, which seemed to be the signal for a riot. The roughs began to smash up the seats and to pile them into the center of the Hall to set fire to them and burn the place down.

Extra police were sent for and a posse arrived with the Inspector, and ultimately cleared the Hall. The converts went out the back way and, after closing up, we went upstairs. The crowds outside refused to go away. There was a large pile of stones on the far side of the street to be used for road mending. This provided the mob with ammunition with which they stoned the building until every window glass and lattice was smashed.

We were forced to shelter in an inner room that only had a roof light as a continual hail of stones was pouring into all the other rooms and the Hall, both back and front. When the mob found we were in this room they began to throw stones on the roof. Some came through the skylight and one hit Blind Mark. We children were very scared and terrified lest they should set fire to the place.

My eldest sister, Kate, had a convulsive fit and nearly died, but it was impossible to get the doctor to her. My eldest brother, Frank, during a lull in the stoning climbed out of what had been a side window and went for the doctor . . . We were marooned in the building for three days and nights with a menacing crowd in the street, which was being kept on the move by the police. Some order was restored, but everything was strained and under a cloud.

Adding to the Army's woes, their finances also suffered calamity. Colonel Davey sought but was denied relief from paying property taxes on the Temple. Further complicating matters was the insistence from International Headquarters that the work in Jamaica should be self-supporting and also that they were to pay the traveling costs of reinforcement officers that were sent from England.[24] During rosier days, Davey had optimistically committed the Army to a number of financial obligations, including the mortgage on the Temple building. With the fallout from the article, public support had practically dried up. The result was something of a fire sale. Soon his horse and carriage and nearly anything else of value was gone—even the violin belonging to his son, William. Eventually the Temple was auctioned but the Army was still left with a staggering debt of £200, a crushing amount in the 1880s. The Salvation Army was fast falling apart.

This seemed to many in Jamaica to be the end of The Salvation Army. Not that this was a disappointment to those who found the Army's methods to be offensive, particularly the powerful who were against its desire to reach the lower class.

In recording what it thought was the Army's obituary, the newspaper *Weekly Budget* wrote, "We could not certainly be in accord with its methods of working. The interspersing of addresses with allusions and incidents, having apparently no purpose but to create amusement; the hasty exaltation of converts possessing a fatal fluency of speech, or power of song into 'officers' and entrusting them with the responsibility to teach; the pushing of the sale of a newspaper at the religious services, and this on the Lord's Day; the creating of an occasion for money-making out of a marriage ceremony . . . the exacting of a particular kind of dress from adherents and carrying on a trade in supplying them; the seeming capitalizing on the infirmity of one of the leading officers; and the depreciating references to minister of other churches, whose labours have wrought mightily in the improvement of the people, and creating in their minds the very sympathy to religious truths which gives the Army the measure of popularity it enjoys—these are features with which we never could be brought to sympathize."[25]

Word of the financial woes of the Army became widely known, only adding to Davey's trouble. He seemed to find a scapegoat in Raglan Phillips while also blaming the people of Jamaica. Called into account by the Army's Chief-of-the-Staff, Bramwell Booth, Davey defended his conduct in a letter, writing, ". . . in my last letter I gave you intimation that a storm would be likely to burst upon us and it has come in very deed . . . I was immediately warned against Phillips but he impressed me favourably, and he had done much to get the Army here . . . I have found him to be what people said he was. I paid his debts to hide his shame and have done all I could for him . . . I have dismissed him. I did so two days before the storm burst . . . Many of the people of this country do not know how to respect faithful teaching and they prefer to pay well to be dabbed with interspersed mortar . . . I told the people I would ask the General to recall me, but so many friends have rallied round me and when I said it in the congregation, the congregation sobbed . . ."[26]

The view from London was that conditions and prospects in Jamaica were growing increasingly grim. It was decided to farewell[h] Colonel and Mrs. Davey to serve in Miami, Florida (USA). Refusing his orders, Davey instead resigned. While he sent his wife and children back to England, surprisingly he decided to stay on in Jamaica in order to do independent evangelistic work. But soon he, too, retired from the field and went back to England. He eventually had a bicycle repair shop but remained a Salvationist the rest of his life.

It was announced that his replacement would be a Major Carter, but it seems these orders were rescinded.[27] Instead, Captain and Mrs. Derracot were sent to try to reorganize the shattered Army forces. But the Derracots found the situation in Jamaica overwhelming. First, they could not adjust to the change in climate and soon fell sick. Beyond that, the situation on the ground was far worse than anyone at International Headquarters had been led to believe. In less than two months time, the Derracots returned to England.

William Booth was now called upon to make a decision he never before had to make. *Gall's Newsletter* announced the decision: "The General says he is now in possession of the actual facts of the case. He has been driven to withdraw his mission from Jamaica. This is the first time in the history of The Salvation Army that General Booth has been under the painful necessity of beating a retreat."[28]

In making the announcement of the Army's closing, Captain Derracot advised the Salvationists to return to other churches. But in reply, one Salvationist voiced the feelings of

---

[h] When an officer is "farewelled" or receives his "farewell orders" it means he is being sent to another Salvation Army location and/or into new responsibilities.

many others, "I can't go back to the church for I never belonged to any, and none of them ever tried to save me when I was going to Hell. The churches don't want poor people like us, for we can't afford to wear fine clothes like them. If there is no one else to lead The Salvation Army in Jamaica, I'll lead it myself."[29]

While the Army fire may have appeared extinguished in Kingston and to the rest of the world, an ember continued to burn in Bluefields.

FROM SMOLDERING EMBER
TO FULL FLAME

WHEN THE SALVATION ARMY officially withdrew from Jamaica in 1889, the Salvationists left behind spent little time mourning the loss. It might have seemed among the people in Kingston that the Army had been thoroughly discredited. However, among the poor who comprised almost all Salvation Army forces, the validation for the continued existence of the Army was in the changed lives of their converts. What this or that newspaper said made little difference to them. Few of them could read and fewer still could afford to buy newspapers. Being looked down on was nothing new to them, so the stigma of the official disapproval did not affect them.

Back in Bluefields, Captain John Gordon noted the official withdrawal of the Army from the island but continued his work unabated. He was soon joined by Raglan Phillips. Although dismissed by Colonel Davey, he did not allow that to end his service to the Army, stating, "The officers may go, headquarters may refuse to recognise us, but Jamaica shall not lose the Army. We have the dear old flag. We will be the Army and Salvationists shall stay in Jamaica."[30]

Under the unofficial direction of Raglan Phillips, the Army not only sustained the work in Bluefields but it spread throughout the island, particularly in the parishes of Westmoreland, St.

Elizabeth and Manchester. An edition of *The War Cry* was produced with some regularity and a training home for officers opened in Savanna-la-Mar.[31]

Reports of this unofficial Army reached London through a Reverend Hathaway, formerly of Jamaica but now living in Ipswich, England.[32] Soon after in 1892, Raglan Phillips made contact to discuss the re-entry of the international Salvation Army and bringing over the forces that he had raised in the Army's name in the interim. With encouragement from International Headquarters, Raglan Phillips left for England to meet with General William Booth and his Chief-of-the-Staff, Mr. Bramwell Booth. While there he had seven separate interviews with them where he described the work done thus far, the prospects for the future and how the integration of his forces with the international Army might best be accomplished. For his faithful service with no external support, Raglan Phillips was given the rank of Adjutant. At the same time he was assigned as the ADC to Major and Mrs. James Cooke who had been appointed to re-establish the work in the West Indies.[33]

In May 1892, Major and Mrs. Cooke, Ensign Bates and Ensign and Mrs. Alexander, accompanied by newly commissioned Adjutant Phillips, made their way to Jamaica.[34] Stopping briefly in Barbados for seven hours on the way, they walked through Bridgetown. They were gratified and challenged by the greetings received. "Oh, Salvation Army, have you come to stay? When are you coming?" Before leaving they held an impromptu meeting at the public market.[35] Although they soon left, Barbados was never far from their minds. The Army would be back.

Upon arriving in Jamaica, Major Cooke was presented with some astounding figures as to the strength of the Army since its official closing. He reported, "Adjutant Phillips has made out a schedule showing three divisions[i], 110 field officers, 9 staff officers, 77 corps and 69 outposts. There is one staff brass band and we have about one hundred candidates and eight thousand soldiers (it is estimated) . . . I suppose it is safe to say that we have one hundred drums, if not more."[36] Territorial headquarters was first established at Savanna-la-Mar but because of the oppressive temperatures it was moved to Bluefields and then later relocated to Mandeville.[37]

Wishing to reclaim Kingston, officers were quickly appointed to open the work there. A building was bought at 96 Orange Street. With the purchase, territorial headquarters was once again moved to Kingston. The building also served as a training college for women and the Kingston #1 Corps.

There was great excitement with the Army before Cooke arrived but it increased even more once international recognition was given. Recruits for officership readily came forward. Adjutant Phillips was approached by one young man, someone he barely knew.

"I want to be an officer," he said.

"Prove to me, then, that you can get men and women converted," said Phillips, "Go and get the people in your neighborhood—in your own street saved." He quickly went on his way and in a couple of weeks returned.

"I've got seven men and women saved, and I've brought them to give their testimonies."

The young man was commissioned on the spot. When he returned home someone threw a rock at him so he turned and chased him down. Catching him, he prayed with him until the man was sobbing, crying out for God's mercy. In a matter of months the new officer had over 200 converts in his corps.[38]

---

[i] A division is a collection of corps and outposts in a specific region. It is commanded by a divisional commander from divisional headquarters.

Elsewhere in Jamaica at Clarksonville, it was reported that 2,888 soldiers were enrolled with that many more expected soon.[39]

But intrusions into the devil's kingdom invite his response. The problems first appeared internally and then externally.

HISTORY IN THE FIRST PERSON

Captain W. Steer Rose

AS TOLD TO RAGLAN PHILLIPS | *THE WAR CRY* (USA) AUGUST 7, 1899

I think a storm lamp had something to do with it.

I was a bad one, I was. Somebody told me one day that the likes of me would never get into Heaven. I used to drink hard, swear, gamble and live in a sinful way. I could take part in any kind of vice with the next person and I would make a boast of it.

My attention was drawn to The Salvation Army by seeing an energetic little black woman, who was captain at Falmouth, trying to preserve order at one of her meetings. I threatened to knock down those who were making a noise and when the collection was taken up I threw a shilling into the tambourine.

"Won't you be a subscriber to our beautiful *War Cry*?" the captain asked me the question with such a sweet, winning smile that I dare not refuse. So I let her set down my name. Then she wanted a storm lamp for the open-air meetings, and asked me to purchase one for her. I did, and promised to keep it supplied with oil.

"I hear you've joined the Army," said a friend to me one day, "I thought you had more sense. Take care you join 'em altogether," he said with a mocking laugh.

"I have joined to a certain extent," I said, "I subscribe to the *War Cry* and have given the captain a lamp. Look here, Robert, you know as well as I do that it would be a good thing for both of us if we joined; so don't bring none of your interference to me, or I'll use you." So he went away, poor fellow, and I continued to attend the meetings, and to supply oil for the lamp.

"When are you going to give your heart to God?" she asked. "Don't you know that I am interested in your soul?" It was those words—especially the last six, that knocked me over. She interested in my soul, I said; then why am I not interested in it myself?

From that moment I got under conviction and by believing prayer got deliverance next day. It was Tuesday morning. That night I went to soldiers' meeting and gave in my name to be a recruit.

"I've been a bit of scaffolding all the time, but am now going to be a part of the building," I said. I got into uniform a few days after, and was enrolled by Ensign Charlie Smith before the month was up. Later on I volunteered for the field, was accepted, and served my cadetship at headquarters, Kingston. I was converted in January 1896, and became an officer in July 1896, "and have not got weary yet."

During the period when there was no official Salvation Army in Jamaica, most of the work was directed by Raglan Phillips. But with no clearly defined central headquarters, it seemed that anyone who fancied that he was a Salvationist or even an officer could independently open his or her own corps and declare himself or herself an officer with a rank of that person's own choosing. Naturally, the discipline and consistency of witness varied widely. Still, when Major Cooke arrived it seemed that even these wildcat corps were anxious to be included in the fold.

As would be expected, Major Cooke started to enforce certain Salvation Army standards. No Salvationist was allowed to live immorally or to use alcohol, for instance. Beyond that, the individual Salvation Army corps had accumulated land, built buildings and bought instruments in the name of The Salvation Army. These needed to be turned over. The other issue involved the placement within the Army of those who called themselves officers. Many were not officers in the sense of true clergy but were rather like local officers[j] who maintained regular jobs and lived in their own homes. For them, to lose their titles wounded their pride.

A further disciplinary requirement was moderation in the

---

[j] Local officers are lay leaders who serve within a local corps.

late hours of meetings and the use of the drum. Quite a number of people were indignant at the indiscriminate and loud use of the drums into the wee hours of the morning. Major Cooke felt that this was a valid complaint and ordered that while drums should be played with typical Caribbean abandon, they should not be used late at night nor when marching past other churches that were holding services. Many resented this restriction, feeling that they should be allowed to exercise drum playing as they saw fit and where they wished. Coupled with this was the loud singing and shouting that came from Army buildings. Again, Cooke felt that the style of worship should be free and flowing but understood that when meetings were conducted very late at night it could be distressing to those who lived or worked close to Salvation Army buildings.

While most accepted the requirements to be included in the larger Salvation Army, two individuals led Salvation Army factions of their own away from the parent movement. John Gordon, who had been the officer to hold on at Bluefields when the Army withdrew a few years earlier, led one faction away, proclaiming himself to be its General. His headquarters was at Brighton, near New Market in the Parish of Westmoreland. This did not last very long at all, soon disintegrating. Many of the corps that belonged to his faction simply ceased to exist or continued on as independent operations, while others sought to be admitted into the parent Salvation Army.

The other split was led by Mathias Monroe. Styling itself as the Baptist Salvation Army, this faction distinguished itself from the international movement by including adult baptism by immersion as well as observance of communion. Headquartered in Clarksonville (near Cave Valley) in St. Ann's Parish, the Baptist Salvation Army was also known as the Black Salvation Army and seems to have been better organized than Gordon's splinter group. They also sought to distinguish themselves from the parent movement by wearing a band on their hats and bonnets with the initials "B.S.A." But the Baptist Salvation Army suffered the same fate as the other group, formally disbanding in 1897.[40]

The problems with the splinter groups multiplied the already difficult situation facing Major Cooke. Feeling that he needed to clear the Army name, he labored to pay off the indebtedness left by Colonel Davey.[41] The splinter groups as well as the independent "Salvation Army" corps scattered across the island complicated matters as Cooke had no control over their actions, but still found the Army blamed for what they did. Cooke complained to a reporter from the USA *War Cry,* "The country is by no means free from bogus armies and other organizations assuming the name of The Salvation Army which makes it doubly difficult for our people to win their way."[42]

Typical of the complaints are excerpts from letters to the editor below:

Quite a number of companies are about in this parish (Manchester), under the appellation, which I understand is merely borrowed, as they have no connection whatever with The Salvation Army of England.[43]

In a recent issue of your paper it was reported that Mr. Allwood said of The Salvation Army in Jamaica that "they were a set of demi-savages and a curse to the country." Of course, I know that Mr. Allwood had in his mind the people that call themselves Salvationists, and many of whom are no doubt guilty of great excess ... We know nothing of them, nor did we ever acknowledge them being Salvationists.[44]

For many years it has had a very bad name and has been credited with carrying on its work in a manner not altogether reputable ... There is one Salvation Army and a host of Salvation Armies...[45]

Making matters worse was the advent of the Church Army, a part of the Anglican Church. Formed in 1882 in England after

a failed attempt to integrate The Salvation Army into the Anglican Church, the Church Army continues to exist today as an
evangelistic part of the Anglican Communion.[46] It was formed
in Jamaica in 1892 to counteract the effects of The Salvation
Army and to integrate people into what the Anglicans and many
others considered a more acceptable organization. It was hoped
that it might actually drive the Army out of Jamaica.[47] The Anglicans in particular seemed to have objected to the advent of
the Army in Jamaica but even among their number, there were
those who were favorably disposed toward The Salvation Army.
A constant point of discussion among the Anglicans was
whether the appearance of the Church Army accomplished
what was hoped or if perhaps it muddied the waters even more.[48]
After making a valiant effort, the Church Army ceased operations in Jamaica in 1897. It eventually returned in 1958, not to
compete with The Salvation Army but to serve alongside it and
other Christian organizations at work on the island.

The Church Army and other Salvation Army imitators created complications beyond measure. The general strategy from
territorial headquarters was to open no new corps where the
other Salvation Army groups had opened theirs. This was done
to avoid confusion for the general public as well as possible
conflict that would naturally result from a rivalry situation.
This problem persisted for decades with the last reported imitation Salvation Army active as late as 1920. The newspapers
used the term "real Salvation Army" for the international
movement, considering the other work done in The Salvation
Army's name to be illegitimate. These later groups were
termed the "bogus Salvation Army." While it provided much ir-
ritation and some amusement to the people outside of The Salvation Army to see all this, it required a very delicate dance for
the Army. The Salvation Army was careful not to publicly condemn any other group regardless of the trouble it made for it.

But it remained frustrating to work around them while still trying to move forward.

The disdain for The Salvation Army, however, was not just because there were splits and offshoots. People genuinely did not like The Salvation Army and some seemed to find their greatest eloquence in denouncing it. Railed one writer in *The Daily Gleaner*, "We have established among us a moral plague spot, I mean the so-called Salvation Army. It makes the still hours of night fearful and hideous, with its hooting and howling and beating of drums, etc. 'Order is Heaven's first law.' Can the Great Ruler of the universe that did not allow the leader of His chosen people to see His face accept this outrageous and demoralizing display of worship?"[49] Another correspondent reported the dedication of a corps building in Clarksonville noting, "There was a large number of the people who have become members of that body, merely from an infatuation to don the red cloth. It is incredible to see the number of young girls and boys who joined the Army, on the move day and night, revelling in their midnight orgies with drum, concertina and brass horn, deserting their parents' homes and protection, to become castaways, or religious fanatics, inmates for the Lunatic Asylum ... The sooner the Army is disbanded the better."[50]

In Lucea, an anonymous man complained that, "The Salvation Army of Jamaica still carry on their wretched howling and drum beating and instead of doing good, they appear to be causing a deal of harm."[51] While in Mandeville the writer bemoaned the fact that "The Salvation Army is spreading like wildfire in Manchester, and stations are taken up quite near the town of Mandeville. It is a grave pity to see the many stalwart young black boys, who have entirely given up honest labour to follow this idle and villainous pursuit, which can never under present auspices tend to reform or raise a standard of religion amongst a community. The meetings ... are of the most disorderly and uncivilised character and consist of outrageous dancing timed to the beating of a great drum ... We hope that these young men will soon awake to a right sense of their error and turn again to the machete and hoe which will gain for them the sobriquet of honest and useful members of society."[52] A writer who named himself "Pickwickian" wrote from Savanna-la-Mar, saying, "It is an acknowledged fact that recruits for the Lunatic Asylum are for the most part drafted from The Salvation Army, which is not a beautiful picture to look at, nor hopeful prospectively for Jamaica."[53] And another grumbled, "The Salvation Army, a caricature of Christianity, is becoming a perfect nuisance to the more intelligent members of the community living in the environs of the P- Church. When this hideous drum-beating, yelling (singing), and other symptoms of savagery and barbarism commences, civilised reflection ceases. I think the police should see that those who are not so sunk in ignorance, should be protected from this type of torture."[54]

More refined condemnations stung nonetheless. The *Presbyterian* censored the Army, saying, "The Salvation Army . . . whether it is the original Army or its imitation . . . is unsuited to the passionate people of this country . . . The drum and not the cross is the focus of the Army. Were it not for the drum the Army in Jamaica would be practically non-existent."[55] An editorial in the *Daily Gleaner* reached a similar conclusion: "We are inclined to believe that Jamaica—the West Indies generally—is not a proper sphere for the work of the Salvation Army. It is dealing here with a comparatively primitive people lacking in the fundamental attributes of character . . . They are emotional to the last degree . . . The result is that after the excitement is past the reaction carries those affected further back than ever."[56]

Sometimes derision came at a price. Adjutant Raglan Phillips told of one such occasion:

A circus company had come to Kingston, and sought to add to their "attractions" by showing "the Salvation Army in action." On the night announced some performing dogs were made to kneel down before a long box, which was stated to be the penitent-form.[k] The clown sought to show that these Salvationists as he termed the dogs, would not stop praying until he, the leader of the meeting, said "Amen!"

The clown did his part, the dogs did theirs, and the people looked on and applauded.

The next day that clown was taken ill. On the following night nobody in the hotel where he lodged could sleep, for he was bawling out for mercy, and yet cursing himself and cursing God. He became quiet as the morning dawned, or rather his body did, for his soul had gone to meet its Creator. No sooner was his body buried than a girl to whom he was engaged took sick, and the company, dreading another death, at once took the steamer to New York.[57]

It wasn't just the written disapproval of the citizens and the mockery of circus acts with which the Army had to fight. Now the police forces came to bear against them with numerous arrests across the island. Likely the most interesting arrests occurred in Savanna-la-Mar where the authorities overnight locked up the drum and the Salvation Army flag, returning them the next day to the officers' quarters.[58] On another occasion the Salvationists were hauled into jail because someone saw them marching on an isolated stretch of country road where they were singing and playing the drum. They were spotted by a man gazing through his telescope who indignantly turned them over to the police to be arrested.[59]

When arrests occurred, if the Army officers and soldiers were found guilty they typically refused to pay the fine. An appeal was made and almost without fail the conviction was over-

---

[k] A penitent form is usually a piece of furniture that is in front of the pulpit where people are encouraged to come to pray about their spiritual needs or to make a spiritual commitment. Usually an invitation to come and kneel occurs at the end of most public meetings.

turned.[60] Such an arrest was made in St. Ann's Bay and the decision of the appeal became a benchmark ruling for the Army when further arrests occurred. Still, arrests were so numerous that the authorities had to make special provision for them in the jails. It was reported that, "Salvation Army cases are for the first time treated as a separate class and not classed with ordinary prisoners. The object is to provide a treatment less severe and degrading for persons convicted of offenses not involving moral turpitude or criminal intent."[61]

Despite the opposition and interpretations of its many enemies, The Salvation Army continued to grow and to make an impact on Jamaica. In 1893, a men's training garrison was opened in Porus to supplement the one for women already opened in Kingston.[62] Meetings were crowded beyond the building capacity. One former missionary officer remembered that people had to fight their way into the buildings because the atmosphere of joy and spiritual power was so great that people considered it a loss to miss the meeting.[63]

But the Army had suffered setbacks from the splits and persecution. What started out as 8,000 soldiers in 1892 was down to 1,000 by 1896. The number of officers was half of what it had been and finances were, as always, a deep concern.

Despite this, the optimism of the Army was undiminished. Writing to *All the World* the territorial commander spoke confidently about the future. "The West Indies lies before us . . . We want to open Barbados, Cuba, and many more islands great and small."[64]

Opposition was expected but the Salvationists were convinced that victory was sure. The march was on and before the end of the century the Salvation Army flag was planted in three more colonies.

INDIGENOUS INVASION

AFTER HE WAS SAVED in a Methodist chapel in Grenada, Samuel Marshall traveled to Jamaica. While there he was given a copy of *The War Cry* and was so taken by what he read that he made up his mind to have The Salvation Army in his native land of British Guiana. A cobbler by trade, he told people he was interested in mending both "soles and souls."

Brother Marshall didn't know how long it would take the Army to reach the colony. His solution was to become a one man Salvation Army until the real one arrived. He sent off for a Salvation Army cap and jersey. Standing often alone at night in the open-air with his kerosene lamp, he began preaching the salvation that had become so real to him. But if The Salvation Army in other places was ridiculed where it showed up in strength, the sight of this old man on his solitary watch made him the object of scorn, especially by the street urchins who found him an easy target. Occasionally a Salvationist sailor, Brother Coburn, would be in port and join him, often bringing him Salvation Army ribbon, Song Books, instruments and other things to help him and his Army. But for the most part it was his solitary witness that, like his little lamp, sought to dispel the darkness of Georgetown. Despite the ill treatment he received, he was known to all not only by his familiar uniform but his gentle greeting: "God bless you, my beloved."

One of those who had stood with him, a steward on a ship based in England, decided to go to International Headquarters and report the one man warfare being conducted in Britain's solitary colony on the South American continent. In the meantime, Marshall sent yet another letter pleading for officers to come to take over the work he had started and get the Army on the proper footing for the people he labored to save.

His nine year vigil came to an end when Adjutant and Mrs. Widgery set sail from England on April 10, 1895. When they arrived Brother Marshall quickly turned over the converts he had gathered, pledged his loyalty to the incoming officers and gladly accepted his position as the corps sergeant-major.[65,1]

Despite the problems going on in Jamaica at this same time, the reception in Guyana was decidedly more positive from both the public and the government. Staff Captain Widgery was able to report, "The authorities are very favourable and each of the three Georgetown papers, on our arrival, continued to refer to us. The *Chronicle*—owned by government printers—said, 'The Salvation Army will "open fire" on Sunday in the colony.' We have noticed *The War Cry* flying around town, and everything is apparently ready for a rousing time. *The Echo* prophesies a great future for the Army in Guyana; and the *Argosy* views our appearance with interest."[66]

Officially the Army opened fire on May 12, 1895, its advent into Guyana sparking a revival with impressive results. Within six months 200 soldiers had been enrolled with more enlisted as recruits.[67] Lt. George Walker gives a rollicking account of what was happening:

---

[1] Corps Sergeant-Major is the highest lay leader in a Salvation Army corps. It is a volunteer position although the person may carry responsibility for the entire operation of a corps or outpost, especially if there is a shortage of officers.

Thank God, many of the devil's good servants, some of his call-birds, and big and little sinners are getting saved in British Guyana. May all the music of hell soon be stopped!

The influence of The Salvation Army is being felt through the town. During the last six weeks the weekly average of souls saved has been about fifty real good cases, many of these properly broken down and weeping their way to Jesus. One of the most interesting and beautiful things about the soul-saving here is the numbers in one family who follow one another to Jesus. One night two brothers, another two sisters, another night one woman and the next night her two sisters, husbands and wives, sons and daughters, brothers and sisters, fathers and mothers come one after the other, until in several cases almost all in the family are saved. Salvation does indeed make home happy.

Alas! There is a dark side, and salvation appears in some cases to bring enmity and a sword. One dear woman had a black-eye given to her by her unfaithful husband. Another had to choose between home and God; another had to leave her husband and home when she dared to go to the penitent-form; but, of course, we expect to see the devil attack when he sees his kingdom beginning to crumble. Almost every convert has a very interesting testimony, and it would take a very big volume to chronicle all that God has done. One dear fellow used to get drunk and then go home and knock his wife about.

Since he has got saved he goes home and kisses her. Thank God for a salvation that makes kissing husbands! Another comrade was a very good fiddler and much in request for weddings, and such like; now, both he and his fiddle are well saved. A colored man who got saved in Liverpool over three years ago, but on coming home was led astray by old friends, has again found the peace he once enjoyed, and we are also praying for a young man who was once a soldier in New York, but, also through the influence of companions, backslid.

Men who have been convicted since the first week we were here are at last yielding, and night after night some more of the devil's dupes are having their eyes opened. The sisters, too, are not going to be left behind. Invitations to dances are being returned and the world is losing its charm and nervousness and timidity are breaking down.

Last Sunday we had our second swearing-in. The town hall was gorged, and eighty-four men and women vowed to be true to God and the dear old Army, and what a sight it was to see their faces glow, as they sang, "We'll be conquerors forever, for we never shall give in."[68]

Open-airs were held in places with colorful names such as "Light House Alley."[69] Until the Army could secure a meeting place of its own, indoor meetings were held principally at the town hall. When the rent for the town hall proved difficult for the Army, it applied for relief to the City Council. The rent was reduced from $161 to $9 because, they said, there was, "no mission in the colony where the services are so orderly as those of the noisy Salvation Army."[70]

In both Jamaica and Guyana a pattern was already emerging of indigenous and spontaneous beginnings of Salvation Army work. Mother Foster and Raglan Phillips were the real pioneers in Jamaica; Brother Marshall was the true pioneer of Guyana. The Salvation Army only recognizes those sent by International Headquarters or one of the territorial headquarters, but in many instances in the history of the Army in the Caribbean, they merely assumed control of work already begun. The spontaneous beginning of Army work was to be repeated in St. Lucia, Suriname, French Guiana, Saint Maarten, Haiti, Dominican Republic, Cuba, Venezuela and Panama. Much of this work was started by transplanted Salvationists who longed for the Army of their homeland where they now lived. Other work was begun that was so close to The Salvation Army as to be easily grafted in. The unplanned openings that were done on the mega-level of opening nations and colonies were repeated multiple times on a much smaller scale in the opening of corps and outposts.

This was a remarkable development that shows the great initiative shown by the Caribbean people. It should be remembered that while most of this work was being started, the whites in power were saying that the Army did not fit in the Caribbean, that it might work elsewhere but not among the poor. But the poor people of the Caribbean, mostly ethnic African, were the reason that the Army took root in the region. Had it not been for them and their holy entrepreneurial spirit, the Army would have never seen the development nor flourished as it did.

This was no more clearly demonstrated than in the opening of St. Lucia.

A young man in Britain's military forces was stationed at the garrison in St. Lucia. Feeling he needed to take his stand for Christ among his military comrades, he resolved, "I must be one thing or the other; as I have given my life to God there's only one way open and that is to be as out-and-out for Him at Santa Lucia as I was at home." Although not a Salvationist, he had read of the Army and was deeply moved by what it represented, believing that its warlike tactics were the best approach in his new surroundings.

An ethnic African woman named Mrs. Grant came by daily to sell her basket of fruits and vegetables. Although she made good sales and needed the money, she dreaded going there because of all the verbal abuse hurled at her by the soldiers. One day she sold her fruit to this new British soldier but was surprised when he stayed around to talk to her. Finally he got to his point, "I wish that you knew what it is to have the love of Jesus in your heart. It would brighten your life—even this big basket would not seem so heavy."

Mrs. Grant was not impressed. "Oh, don't tell me nothing about it. You white gents don't show me much of that. It ain't for poor people like us."

He was quick to answer. "Oh, yes it is. As much for you as

for me. And you can get it the same way I did."

Mrs. Grant was caught off guard, but interested. The two arranged for the soldier to come to her cottage where he made several visits explaining the gospel. His love for God and for her broke through her resistance and she believed that God's mercy was for all races. Soon she bowed her head in submission to Christ.

Others believed and a nucleus formed. By now feeling that with his new convert he must establish some kind of work, he decided it simply had to be The Salvation Army. He sent to London for a Field Officer's book and a concertina and launched his unsanctioned Army. With his small pay he rented a small building, ordered and sold two dozen copies of *The War Cry* each week, and commissioned Mrs. Grant as the corps sergeant-major. Finding an Articles of War in the Field Officer's book, the soldier signed his name to it and in his mind at least, that made the work official.

After a while the soldier was ordered to return to England, leaving Mrs. Grant and the small group of converts to their own devices. Two years passed before another British soldier arrived who was not only a Salvationist but a Sergeant in the Salvation Army's Naval and Military League.[m] While walking one day he was stopped by a woman who anxiously asked him, "Are you a Christian?" When he answered that he was, she followed with another more startling question, "Are you Salvation Army?"

"Yes, I am a Salvationist, but what do you know about the Army here?"

"I'm Salvation Army, too! I've signed the Articles of War." With no chance to recover from this surprising meeting, Mrs. Grant pulled him away to see her home and the room set aside

---

[m] The Navy and Military League provided recreation and fellowship for members of the military to avoid the vices often found in port cities.

for the "corps" that was in operation. She then told him of how the Army started there and how she had kept the meetings up on her own. The Salvation Army was alive and well in St. Lucia.[71] This unofficial work was started in 1895. Officially, The Salvation Army would not open in St. Lucia until 1902 by Staff Captain and Mrs. Morris.[72]

The forward march of The Salvation Army soon reached the island of Barbados. Since Colonel Davey stopped there on his way to Jamaica in 1892, Barbados had been targeted for opening. A brief visit was made by Commissioner McKie in December 1895 when he held three meetings with overflow crowds.[73] He reported back to International Headquarters that Barbados was decidedly ready for opening and that the work should commence as soon as possible.

At this time Barbados, along with the rest of the West Indies, was going through a severe financial crisis due to plummeting sugar prices. Property prices fell sharply adding to the huge losses. As a result, there were massive layoffs of cane workers with a follow on effect in other labor sectors as well. In the countryside there were widespread reports of starvation. This led to a huge increase in thievery as people took to stealing in order to survive.

The result was social unrest, resulting in volatile situations across the region. No labor unions existed among the workers to allow them to have a reasoned way to address the issues of the unemployed or the working conditions of those who had jobs. In the next decade there were riots of all sorts in many places, a good deal of them extremely violent. The Salvation Army's work among the lower classes was viewed both positively and negatively. On the positive side it was thought that religious influence would help keep in check the frustrations of poverty. On the negative side, the emotion displayed in meetings was viewed with suspicion. How hard was it, reasoned those in power, for a Salvation Army march to an open-air to quickly turn to something more sinister?[74] As Hilary Beckles notes, in Barbados the Army was one of the churches that "captured the imaginations of the black poor who, throughout the island, built their own churches, threw up their own preachers and managed their own affairs. This self-leadership was in direct contradiction to the traditional practice of blacks congregating under the white clergyman on Sunday mornings."[75]

Despite the bleak economic and social climate, the Army forged ahead with the opening of Barbados. The *Barbados Globe* announced, "We are expecting a battalion of The Salvation Army by the mail (ship) on Monday. They pitch their camp on High Street at Wilhelmina Hall which theatre they have taken for one month from that date at the paying rate of $15 a night. 'Tis an ill wind indeed that blows nobody good. No doubt the Army will take in Barbados; in a very short time the list of recruits will be enormous; the music and dress will be pressing incentives, and there are so many dissidents so awfully unsettled that they are sure to enlist in large numbers."[76] In speaking about the Army, the *Barbados Advocate* noted, "The knowledge of a drum and tambourine may draw some hardened sinners to the service, but, on the other hand, it often provokes quite decent people to swear."[77]

Despite the fears expressed in the newspapers, the Army landed on April 30, 1898. Staff- Captain and Mrs. Widgery, the pioneers from Guyana, now led the way in Barbados. The new Army quartered itself temporarily on Nelson Street, proclaiming it as divisional headquarters for a field that did not yet exist.[78]

Within a few days the Army held its first meeting at Wilhelmina Hall on May 2.[79] As so direly predicted by those who feared its arrival, the Army did indeed grow rapidly. A meeting was covered by a reporter from the *Barbados Globe/Adviser* who couldn't resist making a double dig at the Army's appeal for funds and a woman speaking: "Last night a full exposition of their financial circumstances was made with an urgent appeal by one who evidently knows how to beg for support to carry on their glorious work. Mrs. Widgery possesses the old fault; there is no stopping her tongue."[80] The same newspaper chronicled the growth. "The Salvation Army is apparently growing by leaps and bounds. They have pitched their camp at Wilhelmina Hall where their first intended settling and crowded meetings are gathering on each occasion. An old woman who evidently possesses some experience, thinks them better than the mission because 'in the barracks all day they continue the same way.' This is a typical Barbadian old woman; there are dozens of these to be gathered in every hundred; yet another instance of a new broom sweeping clean. The beating of the drum and the unfurling of the flag is a greater inducement by far than all the oily gabble Army officers are able to offer them."[81]

Then came something absolutely dumbfounding the Army's critics. Quite unexpectedly, the Anglican Church approached The Salvation Army about taking over a Soldiers' Home on Bay Street. The Army quickly accepted the offer and opened it as a branch of The Salvation Army Navy and Military Home, a haven for members of the British forces stationed in Barbados as well as for sailors visiting the port.[82] The home would operate for many years under the Army's superintendence and in that time serve tens of thousands of members of the British armed forces.

Despite this coup, opposition to the Army was still very much alive. It boiled over on June 1 during an open-air meeting. A police officer approached and ordered the Army to stop the meeting and disband. Widgery refused, resulting in the arrest of him and his wife. When brought before the judge, the officers were fined but refused to pay. Both were put in jail.

In the trial that followed, Corporal Lawrence, the arresting officer, reported that the Army was making noise by "beating a drum and shaking a tambourine." He stated that 300-400 people were in attendance who added to the noise by loud singing. The police officer seemed to be disturbed that one of the Salvationists was praying for "the Lord to have mercy upon the prison warders and police who locked up people and were malefactors generally." He reported further that he pulled Staff-Captain Widgery aside to tell him that it was unlawful to gather in such a way and they must disburse. Widgery, he said, replied that since this was a British colony he would not do so. Further testimony was given by a Mr. Clarke who apparently called the police, relating, "The beating of the drum was such an outrageous thing that as I heard it I immediately sent a policeman to stop it." Widgery countered their testimony, sharing that, "While we were singing the first verse the same policeman who seemed much agitated returned; and rushing into the ring attempted to seize the drum, but I stood in front of it and forbade him touching it."[83] After hearing the testimony, the judge upheld the charges against the Army, leaving the fines intact.

All of this made great theater for the Army. In order to raise funds for their expenses as well as capitalize on the publicity, meetings were held. Mrs. Staff-Captain Widgery made quite an impression by appearing in the meetings wearing her prison clothes and describing her prison ordeal. A fee was charged: eight cents for reserved seats, four cents for general admission.[84]

The Army was no worse for the wear. In fact, within weeks it conducted its first enrollment of soldiers that was so large they were divided into three groups. The Number 1 Corps took 54 of the new soldiers; the Number 2 Corps took 68; and a group of 12 Queen's Soldiers formed the third corps, all of them in Bridgetown.[85]

On September 10, a ferocious hurricane hit Barbados leaving 112 people dead while destroying the homes of 10,000 workers. More died later from outbreaks of typhoid and dysentery.[86]

Though still only months old, the Army swung into action distributing food, clothing and blankets as well as offering spiritual comfort. The previously critical *Barbados Advocate* commented, "the Salvationists ... are thoughtful not only of the souls of people but also the bodily wants."[87]

At the end of nine months of salvation warfare in Barbados, Staff-Captain Widgery reported that close to 1,000 had knelt at a Salvation Army penitent form. There were 310 soldiers, 380 recruits[n], 156 junior soldiers[o], 99 Band of Love[p], a Young People's Legion[q] of 40. He also reported a weekly Bible class that averaged 80 in attendance and five candidates[r] for training.[88]

Meanwhile back in Jamaica, life had settled into a rhythm. The Army felt some gratification to learn that the Jamaican government had officially recognized it as a religious denomination.[89] In 1896 it was able to report strength in Jamaica alone of 1200 soldiers and recruits, 102 officers, and 65 corps and outposts.[90]

Corps work continued to progress across the island, albeit under difficult circumstances. Most of the meetings were conducted in the open-air, whether this was in the country or in the city. Corps buildings were often little more than palm tree poles with thatched roofs and bamboo woven into walls. Benches were crude and backless, often nothing more than a log sawed in half lengthwise with legs attached. When it rained it was not unusual to get as wet in the building as out.[91] There were no lights in the corps—these were brought by the people when they came.

---

[n] A recruit is someone who has declared their intention of being a Salvation Army soldier and is in training until ready to be enrolled.
[o] Junior soldiers are junior members of The Salvation Army. Believing that children can have a saving knowledge of God, a child can become a junior soldier at the age of seven.
[p] Band of Love was a youth group that met during the week where Bible stories were shared and recreational activities were held.
[q] Young People's Legion was similar to Band of Love but for teenagers. It also was used to train youth in public prayer, Bible reading, leading meetings, preaching and soul-winning.
[r] A candidate is someone who witnesses that he/she has heard a call from God to be an officer and seeks to enter The Salvation Army training college.

An illustration of this is an account of a meeting in Bluefields that was described by a guest that night. Sitting in almost
total darkness at the corps they waited and then, "We see before
and behind numbers of small lights dancing through the bush,
these, we discover, are the lamps carried by the people to light
their way to the Hall. By the way, they serve a double purpose,
for these are the only lights we have to light our building. Can
you picture the scene? One minute the Hall is almost dark and
then dozens of small lamps are brought in by the congregation,
some of whom hold them in the hand whilst singing, in order
to see the words in the Song Book."[92]

Spending the night, another visitor described another feature of country corps: "After a good Sunday's meeting I retired
to rest; shortly after midnight I heard a terrible boom. There
was silence for a few seconds and then another solemn boom;
and this kind of thing was repeated until I fell asleep. It was our
old friend the drum. The officer informed me next morning
that a sergeant of the corps had gone to his reward during the
night, and the drum beats were to announce the fact to all and
sundry."[93]

Corps work in the country was carried on by means of "circle corps." There was one main corps where the officers lived
and primarily worked. They would go a distance of eight to ten
kilometers to visit various districts where other corps and outposts would be found. Because few country people owned
clocks, meetings were announced by standing at the door of the
corps and beating a drum until people started to arrive.[94] Haddo
and Moneague were prime examples of circle corps in the
mountains of the island.

Officers' meals were simple. When the territorial leaders
visited one corps they described their meal, the best the officer
could offer: boiled root and a little salt butter.[95] Another visitor
described the meals as "hot water sweetened with molasses

sugar, boiled with a little mint to give it flavour . . . A bit of roasted plantain answers for bread and a little fine salt for butter! Breakfast at 11—boiled herring or salt fish, boiled yams, cocoas or breadfruit. Dinner at 6—the same with some variation of a little fresh fish or goat's mutton."[96] When traveling to headquarters, officers often had to depend on the goodwill of friends for overnight accommodation because the Army quarters were almost exclusively single room huts. One such billet was offered by the Sangster family in Mountainside, who counted among their children Donald Sangster, future Prime Minister of Jamaica.[97]

HISTORY IN THE FIRST PERSON

A Salvation Army Wedding

THE DAILY GLEANER | OCTOBER 21, 1902

It is not remarkable that the unusual sight of a Salvation Army wedding of two popular officers attracted a crowd which the Town Hall could hardly accommodate.

Ensign Percy B. Richardson was the bridegroom and Captain Annie Howell the bride. Both are very well known and popular in Salvationist circles, and both are devoted and capable officers. The bride was dressed in her ordinary Salvationist uniform, with a white sash inscribed with the motto, "God with us." Her bridesmaid, Captain Gowers, was similarly dressed. As Commissioner Cadman said, Salvationists do not believe in having any foolish frippery or extravagance about their weddings, or in "marrying a debt."

The service was a long one, lasting over an hour. Commissioner Cadman conducted it on the well known Salvationist lines, and in the course of his refreshingly original talk remarked that the Army had a book of rules and regulations which provided for the conduct of life from the "cradle to the grave." Even "courting" was regulated, and the officer who desired to become engaged had to obtain the sanction of his commanding officer. "I wish," added the Commissioner, "that the courting of all of you was regulated, and then there would be less irregularity about it, and fewer mistakes."

Adjutant Naden performed the wedding ceremony proper, which was brief and impressive, in its perfect simplicity. Unlike most Salvationist ceremonies, it was very quiet. There was simply an interchange of vows, based largely on those in the Church of England service even to the phraseology. But the most prominent feature in the ceremony was the emphasis laid on the wedding as a new consecration for Salvationist work. Bride and bridegroom solemnly swore not to allow their union to hinder their zeal in the cause, but rather to find in it fresh enthusiasm and fresh willingness for self-sacrifice.

The bride bore herself very bravely before the large crowd. It was no small test of her courage, especially as she had to make a speech before the meeting ended. How many brides could do that? Mrs. Richardson came through the ordeal admirably. She is a very pretty and sweet-looking girl, evidently imbued with a deep and abiding enthusiasm for her work.

The great popularity of Mr. and Richardson among their comrades was shown by the hearty cheers which greeted them when they first came on the platform and, after the conclusion of the wedding ceremony, and it was testified to in brief speeches by their brother and sister officers.

Later in the evening there was a wedding feast at the Conversorium, to which the general public were admitted on the payment of a shilling.

The quarters were simple as well. The furnishings consisted of a bed which was made out of scrap lumber. Next to it was a small table, a chair and a couple of soap boxes. A personally owned trunk held the clothing while a bench was there for any visitors to sit on.

Visitors from The Salvation Army International Headquarters were taking note of the Army that stood in Jamaica. Commissioner George Scott Railton declared, "Oh, for such drums and drumming in England! These drums are almost all homemade, and can stand proper use. But the drumming I despair of describing. It is in splendid time to our fast choruses; but it is more like the continuous work of a steam-hammer, coupled with the rattle, say, a long luggage train than anything else I can think of."[98]

When Commissioner Edward Higgins visited Jamaica in 1896, an officers' council was held. He described how the attendees arrived: "I was very much struck with the amount of luggage almost all seemed to carry. They came with trunks on their heads, and large parcels under their arms, and on inquiring whatever induced them to bring so much for so short a visit, I was told the boxes contained the food which they would require during their stay in Kingston and the parcels—in addition to perhaps an article or two of clothing—consisted of a pillow and a blanket or two, which would be required in being billeted at the barracks of the corps. And further, knowing something of the inconveniences of travel from various parts of the island from whence many officers would have to come, I was informed that many of them had walked many, many miles."[99]

The first Christmas social work in the Caribbean was done in Kingston in 1899. A description of these efforts as well as Salvationist celebration of the holiday is noteworthy as described in *All the World*.

> Salvationists were among the earliest arrivals at the market, and after a brief halt in the open-air our comrades marched to their Hall nearby and held a crowded service at 4:30 am for the people. Later, they gathered 400 poor children and marched them all behind the band to the Hall, where they were regaled with sweet drinks, buns, candy and fruit.
>
> Boxing Day...This is a day when local Salvationists have their outing in the fine private grounds near the famous Constant Springs Hotel. What fun the jolly Jamaicans have on that day! Their quaint native games afford them much pleasure and the stranger considerable interest; while a Salvation Army Brass Band discourses sweet music, and efforts are made by our comrades to turn the thoughts of the merry-makers to the real meaning of Christmas.[100]

All these good efforts in the face of harsh criticism and out-right persecution led to the Army winning more admirers because of their self-sacrificial service. A letter to the editor of the *Daily Gleaner* by a man who called himself "An Old Wesleyan" commented on another officers' gathering in Savanna-la-Mar. "What struck me most was the fine band of native officers that has been raised up, and I believe there are about 100 of them. If anyone had told me twenty or thirty years ago that it was possible for our common people to so improve themselves I never could have believed it . . . When I listened to them and remembered that none of them had received any college education and none received any salary but many live lives of self-denial and go about 'doing good', and telling the story of God's salvation, I confess that the tears came to my eyes and I said to myself, 'Of a truth these are the people of God—the weak things that God hath chosen to confuse the mighty.'"[101]

4

—∞∞◦━◦❁◦━◦∞∞—

OF INDIANS
AND EARTHQUAKES

BECAUSE OF THE rapidly expanding work in the Caribbean Basin, International Headquarters decided that there should be a new territory established: the West Indian Territory.[102] Brigadier Thomas Gale was named the first territorial commander. One of his initial decisions was to move headquarters from Kingston to Bridgetown, Barbados.[103] At the same time it was announced that the Army was drawing up plans to open work in Cuba, St. Lucia (officially), St. Vincent, Costa Rica and Nicaragua.[104] Because the Army had further ambitions beyond these for extension to the other northern colonies and countries of South and Central America, it seemed like a reasonable decision to put headquarters in Barbados. The work in both Barbados and Trinidad was going extremely well, making a territorial center all the more attractive. But it didn't last. For reasons not clearly recorded, after a year it was decided to move the territorial center back to Kingston.[105] The training home that had been opened in Barbados remained there, functioning several decades alongside the one in Kingston.

Although the Army had dabbled a bit in social work in Jamaica, it received a major boost in providing meaningful services when a citizen of Kingston gave a major donation. The *Daily Gleaner* announced, "The Salvation Army in Jamaica is shortly going to undertake social work among the 'submerged tenth' on the lines made familiar by the 'Darkest England' scheme.[s] A start will be made with a soup kitchen. The Army has obtained Mrs. Denniston's premises on Orange Street which has been used as a Sailors' Home and will establish a kitchen there. Work on a more ambitious scale will be undertaken as opportunity permits."[106] A more detailed plan was announced a month later declaring that beyond the soup kitchen, the Army intended to operate a night shelter for men, a reading room and a temperance bar. They also were working to take in prisoners recently released from jail.[107]

The food depot opened in September where the Army offered a breakfast tin of coffee and bread for a penny. A plate of food for lunch would cost 1½ d consisting of salt fish, rice and peas, stewed beef, beef soup and yams.[108] In describing the importance of the Army's social work effort, Brigadier Gale said, "There is as much religion in giving shelter to a poor man, or finding work for a worthless man, or visiting prisons and hospitals and helping outcast persons as there was in the most eloquent sermons that were preached from any of the pulpits. That is the distinguishing feature of Salvation Army social work."[109]

Although the public was rallying around the Army for this foray into practical expressions of ministry, the church leaders largely snubbed the Army. All of the clergy in Kingston were invited to the opening of the food depot. Only one showed up. With the failure of the Church Army to take root as an answer to The Salvation Army, the Anglican Church still did not want to voice approval of the Army. At a meeting of the Anglican Church's Kingston Parochial Council there was deep concern

---

[s] The "Darkest England Scheme" was based on General William Booth's hallmark book, *In Darkest England and the Way Out,* which outlined a massive plan of social work aimed for what he termed the "submerged tenth." Although never fully implemented as he planned, it nonetheless became The Salvation Army's blueprint for its social work and took the Army into the field of social redemption to supplement its evangelical work.

about the Army's continued growth in Jamaica. The body issued a statement to the press that said, "While this Council of clergy and lay representatives appreciates the value of the social work and the general intentions of The Salvation Army, it deprecates the methods of its religious work, and the interference with the beliefs and practices of Church people."[110]

And still there seemed to be sport in making fun of The Salvation Army. A popular if not curious musical piece performed in orchestral concerts in Jamaica, was a composition known as "Fantasia – The Advance and Retreat of The Salvation Army."

In 1901 the oldest Salvation Army soldier was "Promoted to Glory."[t] Nearly one hundred years old, Mother Sterling had been born into slavery during which time she was beaten so badly the scars were clearly visible on her back. When the Army opened in Bluefields, she was among the first to step forward. Asked how to spell her name she replied, "I can neither read nor write, but I can read my title clear to mansions in the skies."[111]

Meanwhile, on August 7, 1901, Captain Luther Atkins was appointed to Port-of-Spain to clear the way for the opening of Trinidad. Later, Ensign and Mrs. Glasspool and Lt. Lillian Bailey arrived as reinforcements. They reported to *All the World* that they had "claimed Trinidad for God."[112] They experienced fierce persecution resulting in Lt. Bailey receiving injuries serious enough for her to be hospitalized.[113] Despite the difficulty, the Army gained a foothold and expanded from there. It was able within two years to open a sailors' home on Queen Street.[114]

On the island of Grenada, which was also opened in 1901, Captains Morris and Grant reported on their opening: "Our small but energetic band of Salvationists are determined to be true to God and the Army even when the volcanic showers and erup-

---

[t] Promoted to Glory is a Salvation Army euphemism for death. It is believed that the Salvationist who has remained faithful to Christ until death is not lost but has received a promotion "to Glory."

tions of Satan threaten to overwhelm us . . . We have . . . enrolled five more comrades under the Blood and Fire[u] flag, and by ones and twos we rejoice to report that sinners are being converted."[115]

Despite the best of intentions, however, sometimes the sterling efforts of Salvationists backfired. Such was the case in Montego Bay in 1902. When a popular leader among the townspeople was arrested, a large mob gathered in protest. Becoming more restive, there was a violent confrontation with the police until both sides temporarily backed away. Adjutant Simons, the corps officer, felt that the Army might be able to help calm the rioters. Marching out with his band to where about 2,000 of the rioters had gathered, with the Army band he managed to lead them from the city square to the train station. It seemed that all was going well as Adjutant Simons urged the people to disburse.

The police knew nothing of this. They heard the sound of drum and brass instruments and decided they needed to investigate. Just as the police inspector rounded the corner, Adjutant Simons had the band strike up "Onward Christian Soldiers." But the rioters, seeing the face of their enemy, apparently took the marshal strains to be divine approval for their cause. The mob gave chase with the police inspector running for his life to the police station. There they pelted the station with rocks and the riot was on again. Afterwards an inquiry was done, and though there were some differences in the accounts offered by the rioters, the police and Adjutant Simons all agreed that the timing and the unfortunate choice of "Onward Christian Soldiers" only inflamed an already tense situation.[116]

A more positive note was struck in Cuba. Brother Alexander Hay, a Salvationist from Jamaica, started meetings in Santiago at a house loaned by Mr. Robert Dixon. When the Army had to

---

[u] Blood and Fire is the motto of The Salvation Army. It stands for the blood of Jesus Christ and the fire of the Holy Spirit. The motto is inscribed on The Salvation Army flag as well as on The Salvation Army crest.

relocate to Santa Cecelia, he traveled to Guantanamo where a local businessman first loaned a tent and then a building to hold meetings. The work was done only in English among Jamaican and other West Indians with no apparent outreach to the local Cuban population.[117]

In 1902, Barbados suffered a great crisis when smallpox swept through the island. The situation was dire as the island was quarantined with ships barred from entry or exit. Responding to the growing crisis both on the health front and economically, The Salvation Army started a free distribution of food. But the crowds were so desperate and the need so great that police had to be assigned to keep order.[118]

Yet another unexpected opening for the Army occurred when Captain and Mrs. Grant, serving in Jamaica, went back to their home in Antigua with their five children for furlough. Because they were wearing their uniforms, they were approached by the locals to conduct Army meetings. The whole family were musicians and, desiring to see the Army established in their homeland, they began holding meetings. The first was an open-air under a Tamarind tree in the town of Parham. Despite no official sanction of their work, they nonetheless had meetings around the whole island, enrolling soldiers and commissioning local officers.[119] When the Grants returned to their appointment in Jamaica, they reported on the success they had, claiming 250 converts during their furlough. One hundred more were awaiting enrollment as soldiers. Soon Captain W. Martin was dispatched to officially open the work.[120]

Elsewhere, the positive effects of the Army could be found in different ways. In Guyana in 1903, the Comptroller of Customs' yearly report showed a decrease in the rum duty of $5,942. He said this was for two reasons. First, people were drinking less because times were hard and second, the influence of The Salvation Army.[121] And in Port Antonio, Jamaica, a man loaded a revolver to kill one of his enemies, intending when he finished to then turn the gun on himself. Hearing the corps officer's cornet at an open-air, he turned aside to hear Captain Critchlow say that there might be someone in the crowd who intended to shoot someone. The would-be killer was seized with conviction and came crying for mercy. Handing the revolver to the captain, he abandoned his murderous ways, eventually becoming a soldier of the corps.[122]

In Guyana, a most significant work was begun among the East Indian people, most of whom were indentured servants. The period of indenture lasted five to seven years. At the end of that time they could return to India or accept a plot of land set aside for them in the colony. But some chose a third option—to drift into Demerara to seek work there. They went to a city without family, a job, or a place to live, and nowhere to sleep except for the pavement. They huddled together at night over a small open fire to cook their one simple meal of the day. Many fell sick. Obviously their situation became quite desperate.[123]

HISTORY IN THE FIRST PERSON

Adjutant Ghurib Das

GUYANA | ALEXANDER ALEXANDER

Before I was saved I worked in a large sugar-mill factory outside of Demerara. They generally give overseers a run in the factory and when my turn came I fitted so well I was never let out. One morning I was looking for a problem in one of the machines. I stuck my head in and for a few minutes I thought I was going to die. I couldn't pray; God shut my mouth. I thought three minutes would see me in eternity. I thought that. My head was awfully cut. No one thought I would live. God showed me one great truth there for I saw how awfully earnest a man can be at the gates of hell, and how careless afterward.

My employer gave me three months' leave of absence to go home and recruit myself. I believe if I'd been a manager three months longer I'd never have been saved. I was just getting with the money. It's an awful job for a rich man to get saved. My, my, so hard! I never thought I'd any love for money till God showed me my heart.

My favorite sister had been saved and I went to the Army meetings with her. I felt kind of strange, something new was happening in me. I decided it was religious fever. But I couldn't stay away from the Army. I could not rest. I talked about religion to everyone I met. At last one night a soldier got me on my knees before God. There were people all around me. All the people were excited but I was as cold as I could be. There was not a tear in my head nor a piece of sorrow in the heart of me. I felt my need for a Savior but I had no depth of repentance. Everyone kept telling me to believe but no one helped me to understand that I needed to repent. I went home and prayed but it was no use. I got up the next morning and prayed again but still nothing happened. But everyone told me to believe I was saved so I went back to the Army hall the next night and said, "I thank God I am saved and mean to go out and show all the people in Demerara that I am saved." Then the light came in! God changed my heart and filled it with joy. All the world looked different.

A month or two later I sailed back to Demerara and even the town looked different to me. The rich planters who before I envied, now I saw them as God did in the pride and sin, drifting straight down to hell. I saw my old friends and they were headed to hell but no one was warning them. I saw the blacks, who were slaves before with men but now were slaves to sin. But what bothered me the most were the coolies from India who shook off the restraints of their old religion but did not gain the knowledge of Christ.

My first Sunday back I went with my brother to another estate. "You can't go and begin to preach on a strange estate," the devil said to me. But I felt bad for not doing so. But already people were seeing that I was different. They could not believe that a manager wouldn't swear and storm at the coolies. They knew I used to be one of the worst at that.

The next Sunday I went out of my house and said to the first man I saw, "Go and tell the people I am going to preach on the bridge by the rum shop." About a hundred people were there. I wore some Army ribbon and my S's . I spent the afternoon with the coolies and that is how I got started. A few months later I was due to go back to England. I knew that I couldn't go back to what I was doing before so I showed up at the British Guyana headquarters and begged them to make me an officer. I decided not to wait on headquarters. I was sure God called me so I gave my employers a month's notice and came to England to enter the Training Home. I returned to Demerara as an officer and got to work.

Let me tell you about Demerara. It's cultivated along the sea and riverside for the sake of shipping the sugar. Each estate averages about a thousand people—proprietor, overseers, coolies and all. The inhabitants of each live in a village which clusters round the factory, so they are perfectly easy to get together for preaching. The nature of the congregations one would get depends largely on the language you use. There are lots of Portuguese shopkeepers. Half the population is what they call, "natives," but are really ones who are descended from slaves. They all speak English.

But it's the coolies who mostly laid on my heart. They are mostly from Bombay, Madras and Calcutta and keep their caste *pretty strictly*. They'll have to be gone for on native lines, as in India. Only the Englified coolies speak English, so it will be easier than India. How did I work? Well, my hardest working Sunday would be like this: Out from seven to ten among the coolies—taking hold little open-air meetings around the huts. Open-air at eleven among the blacks. Then I used to go to church at half-past twelve. In the afternoon, I used to set off to get the coolie children into Sunday school. I generally got from ten to twenty; but it was impossible to interest them in ordinary Sunday school doings. One needed to use their instruments and their *ways*! Then I'd go off on my bicycle to some village for open-air and perhaps preach at night.

The planters who ran the estates were known for their rough handling of the East Indians. As a group they saw the indentured servants as inferior and showed them little compassion, providing the bare minimum for them while exacting the maximum amount of work. One of these planters was a young Scot named Alexander Alexander. After being injured in an accident, he went home to Scotland to recover. Finding his sister had become a Salvationist, he agreed to attend the meetings where eventually he was saved. His transformation was complete, so much so that he could not think about going back to his life as a planter again. He also found that the callousness of his heart toward the East Indians had completely changed. Now he longed for them to know Christ.

He heard about Commissioner Frederick Booth-Tucker,

who when he opened the Army's work in India, abandoned Western dress and lifestyle to live like the Indian people. Alexander felt that this was the correct approach and so determined to do the same when he went back to Guyana. Alexander Alexander took the Indian name of Ghurib Das, meaning "servant of the poor." He wore the East Indian *baba*, walked barefoot and spoke Hindi. He chose to live in a hut measuring 12 feet by 8 feet with a dirt floor, surviving on a diet of rice and plantains. Moving out of Demerara, he chose to live as one of the poor in one of their villages.[124] The planters all remembered him when he was among them and seeing his change of lifestyle were convinced that Alexander was demented.[125] On his own Alexander opened a cheap shelter in Demerara for the East Indians. But soon he offered his shelter and services to The Salvation Army.

When he married in 1901, he insisted that his bride, Mary Howell, wear a *sari* at the ceremony while he came in *dhoti* and barefoot. Mary's proper English mother was horrified that her daughter would do this but Mary shared her new husband's love for the Lord and the East Indian people. For her it was not a hard decision. To help raise money for their work, tickets were sold for the wedding.[126]

To support the work further, twice a year Das mounted a bicycle and crossed the length and breadth of Guyana on a collecting tour. By now there were multiple Salvation Army shelters opened to care for the East Indians and at one point there were four corps for East Indians in Demerara. Das provided Army schools for their children and the problem of former indentured servants wandering aimlessly around Demerara was over. There were few converts to Christianity and fewer still who became Salvationists but Das labored on. This won him the respect of the ones who used to call him demented because the validity of his decision was undeniable.[127] For his outstanding service to the East Indians, in 1921 Adjutant Ghurib Das was awarded The Salvation Army's highest honour: the Order of the Founder.

One story from Das's work among the East Indians typifies his service as told by General Frederick Coutts in his book, *Down in Demerara*:

> With the ever-open door which he kept, it was inevitable that now and again a shady character would worm his way into one of the shelters. One who did so was an Indian who had to be turned out because of his questionable habits.
>
> One morning this same man was found lying at the back of the shelter with his throat cut, and a bystander called the police, who at once took him to hospital. In an attempt to clear himself, the would-be suicide accused the East Indian in charge of the shelter, with his assistant and also another Indian, of trying to murder him. The motive behind such an accusation was so obvious that Alexander never dreamed that the police would proceed with the case. His amazement changed to indignation, and indignation to controlled fury when a verdict of "guilty" was returned against these men and all three were sentenced to hang.
>
> Alexander then went into battle himself. He was angry, but it was not a blind anger. Hitherto he had left the case in the hands of a lawyer whom the Indians themselves had engaged, but in the appeal he so shook the Supreme Court that the sentence was committed to one of penal servitude for life.
>
> Still he was not satisfied. These men were innocent. Forthwith everyone in the colony was made to realize it. The Governor, the Crown lawyers, the Bishop, the Chief of Police were waylaid by Alexander in turn. Like the importunate widow, he wearied them by his continual coming. The authorities responsible for the verdict disliked what they styled his interference, and tried to silence him. But Alexander had not been in Demerara since the age of twenty-one for nothing. By this time he was one of the best known men in the colony. His plantation colleagues, who had once thought him mad, now swore by him as a man whose daily motto was "I serve" to such good effect that one morning the three men were abruptly released and though neither explanation nor com-

pensation was offered, Alexander was content with so signal a victory of justice over prejudice.[128]

Construction on the Panama Canal had begun two decades earlier, but by 1904 the United States took over the Panama Canal Zone. The work to finish the canal was now being done in earnest. Tens of thousands of West Indians poured into Panama for jobs. For The Salvation Army this created both a problem and an opportunity.

With so many men leaving, especially from Jamaica, the corps was stripped of much of their leadership when many of the local officers went to work on the canal. This slowed the expansion in Jamaica considerably while it weakened existing corps. But with so many transplanted Salvationists, it wasn't long until they had banded themselves together and begun holding Army meetings, complete with open-airs, in Panama. Hearing of yet another spontaneous opening of the Army in another country, territorial headquarters dispatched Staff-Captain Leib to investigate not only the work that was going on but the prospects for establishing the Army permanently in Panama.[129]

Staff-Captain Leib came back with a glowing report of what was being done along with the enthusiastic response from local leaders to the Army's advent in Panama. Within a few months Staff-Captain Leib was joined with Adjutant and Mrs. Jackson, a Jamaican couple, to establish the work in Panama. Staff Captain Leib returned to Jamaica, leaving Adjutant and Mrs. Jackson to pioneer the work officially.[130] They immediately experienced a problem when the police arrested them when they first appeared in public in uniform. They were released when they finally got them to understand that they were not part of any earthly military but messengers of peace and goodwill.[131]

The work in Panama had hardly gotten started when Captain Eduardo Palaci pioneered the work in Costa Rica. In Limon he counted 21 converts and had a building given to the Army for its use. The shortcoming with this work, however, was that it was done only in English among West Indians. When the Panama Canal was completed the work quickly came to a halt as there was a great reverse migration back to the West Indian home islands.[132]

In 1905 the work of the Army further expanded to St. Vincent.[133] Commissioner Elijah Cadman had visited the island in 1902 in the midst of an eruption of the volcano, La Soufriere. He was going to turn back, but a local minister offered him his church for a meeting, begging him to come over. He found that the people were very keen on the Army opening there.[134] This was reported back to International Headquarters but it took a few more years to become a reality. Official work also began in St. Lucia that same year.[135] And in 1905, Staff-Captain Leib was sent to British Honduras (Belize) to explore the possibility of opening there. Although an optimistic report was given regarding the Army's prospects, it would not occur for a few more years.[136]

In 1905, Antigua was officially opened on March 15. Within a month they were able to report that 56 people had been saved.[137] The Antigua *Standard* soon noted: "The number of cases of a certain class which used formerly to crowd the courtroom and fill the books has been very considerably reduced since the advent of The Salvation Army to this island . . . We have noticed a distinct change for the better in the singing of street songs. In place of vulgarity we have almost *ad nauseum* the popular airs sung by the Army."[138]

Meanwhile, back in Jamaica further advances were seen. In 1905 a men's "metropole" was opened in Kingston to provide inexpensive shelter. A women's shelter was opened as well, offering rooms and meals for women. A reporter for the *Daily Gleaner* reviewed the shelter on its opening day. "What The Salvation Army can do for a small payment is surprising. For the trifling sum of 3d a night a poor woman can secure a comfortable canvas cot, with sheets and pillows, in an upstairs room having only one other occupant." The reporter was favourably impressed, not only with the price and the provisions, but that there was a feminine touch in what was clearly an institution.[139]

Responding to a specific need, the Army opened a children's home called "The Nest" in Kingston in 1905. There was at that time a leprosarium near Spanish Town. Although parents were afflicted with leprosy[v], it was noticed that children were born without it. There was no facility to care for these children, so the government approached the Army about opening a children's home specifically operated for the children of lepers.[140]

A rather novel approach was offered by Adjutant Richardson to a social problem. He appealed to the public to donate gold rings and pieces of clothing. He explained, "As you know the illegitimacy question is a burning one in Jamaica ... We are not so much concerned about the cause of it as the fact that it is there ... Our investigations up to the present convince us that there are many well-intentioned people who are living together in this state who would welcome any means of honourably recognizing their union. They are poor. They tell us that they cannot afford a carriage; the man cannot get a fine suit of clothes, the woman has no wedding garments, and what is even of greater importance she has no ring, and the man is unable to buy one however desirous he might be to make the woman his wife."[141] It is unknown whether many donations were received or any marriages performed as a result of this appeal.

The Salvation Army experienced a great tragedy on December 3, 1905 when Lt. David Watson was killed during labor riots

---

[v] At the time it was still thought that leprosy, or Hansen's Disease, was little understood. We now know it is a bacterial infection that if left untreated can disfigure the sufferer. Recent scientific research points to its spread through respiratory droplets, similar to tuberculosis infection. It is not surprising that the children were not infected at birth but their vulnerability to infection made their removal from their parents the only safe course at the time the Army established The Nest.

in Demerara, Guyana. Local newspaper reports are not clear on how exactly this came about or even the details of exactly how events unfolded. The riots began when cane workers, unhappy with pathetically poor wages, marched on Demerara carrying their cutlasses. The police and militia were called out, eventually supported by British naval forces from ships in the harbor. After a couple of days of tense confrontations which amounted to little more than name calling and a few rocks being thrown, shooting erupted, leaving several people dead. Later reports said that only the militia and the police did any shooting. But at the time it was reported that Lt. Watson was likely killed by a sniper hidden in a window where the mob had gathered. No one was ever brought to justice for his murder.

There are several questions raised by the whole incident. While the police arrested and the courts sentenced a host of people for offenses in connection with the riot, no one was ever arrested or prosecuted for the numerous deaths that occurred. This is all the more surprising during a time when people were arrested and received jail time for public profanity or petty theft. The likelihood is that all the deaths were caused by the wild and admittedly inaccurate shooting of both the police and the militia. It seems that they were aiming at the mob leaders but they never hit any of them, instead hitting those in the crowd behind them.[142]

So how was Lt. Watson was killed? In all likelihood he was in his uniform because the newspaper immediately identified him as a Salvation Army officer. As such, he would have clearly stood out from the rest of the people who would have been dressed in farm clothes. Clearly he was not leading the people, nor would he have joined in any of the lawless behavior that they may have been involved in, nor was he accused of anything of the kind.

From the newspaper accounts, we know that the Anglican

priest as well as other clergy tried to calm things with the rioters. No one would have had more sway with the poor than a Salvation Army officer. And seeing the danger that the people were in, the show of force by the militia and the police with their superior arms and training, it is almost certain that Lt. Watson was seeking to turn them back for their own protection. His shooting was without doubt accidental and most likely not the result of a sniper but of an errant bullet from the militia. Nonetheless, he died in service to his Master and the people he was called to serve. It is proper to consider him a martyr. Lt. Watson was only 21 years old, having served as a Salvation Army officer for only eight months.[143]

In Jamaica further advances were made in its ever expanding social work. A huge step forward was the opening of Wakefield Farm in 1906 at Bog Walk. Originally part of a sugar estate, it was established in order to take in men who were released from prison so that they could learn trades and reintegrate into society. The government as well as the Discharged[w] Prisoners' Aid Society heartily endorsed the plan.[144] Released prisoners were sent to Wakefield where they were allowed to receive a gratuity for their work which increased over time as they continued to do well. Sugar cane was raised as well as chickens, hogs and cows for milk production. In fact, it was said that the best milk in the city of Kingston came from The Salvation Army farm.[145]

Monday, January 14, 1907 was an otherwise peaceful and beautiful day in Kingston. At 3:32 in the afternoon, everything came to a halt by the deafening sound of an earthquake, described like "a train roaring through a tunnel." The shaking of the earth for twenty seconds left the city of Kingston in ruins.

---

[w] The Discharged Prisoners' Society was organized by private citizens to aid former prisoners. Many former convicts returned to crime because they had no other options when set free. The society sought to remedy this and in the Army's early days of prisoner and probation work they often worked hand-in-hand with the Army.

Sir Frederick Treves and W. Ralph Hall Caine reported they saw "solid brick walls bulging and collapsing, carriages being lifted up and flung through the air, telegraph poles swaying like leaves in the wind, and great structures, whether made of iron, wood or stone, crumbling. People were simply picked up and tossed while struggling to maintain their balance . . . Those individuals who managed to make it out to the streets were quickly enveloped in a thick yellow fog punctuated by the sound of crackling and tumbling walls . . . Within twenty minutes fire blazed through the streets of Kingston and lasted for up to four days . . . It was not long before looting broke out . . ."[146]

The Salvation Army was not spared any of the chaos or destruction. *The War Cry* reported that when the quake hit, "Cadet Palaci . . . amid falling beams and bricks picked up Mrs. Lofthouse in a dazed condition and carried her to a place of safety. Captain Lofthouse was away from home visiting the matron of the hospital who was sick and when the shock came he happened to be in the room. As the walls began to totter, with an effort the captain got the matron to the street, the house collapsing behind them. Thus he was saving another person's life at the very moment God had sent Cadet Palaci to look after Mrs. Lofthouse's safety."[147]

Another narrow escape was also described. "One of our oldest soldiers was walking down a narrow lane in the city when the shock occurred. She immediately lifted her hands in silent prayer and then stepped forward hurriedly. Before she could take a second step a heavy wall crashed down in front of her, and while she hesitated a house fell within a few feet to her rear . . ."[148] Somehow, no officers were wounded or killed although the child of Staff-Captain Leib received a serious head wound when their house caved in.[149] An unknown number of soldiers died in the quake.

Brigadier Charles Smith

JAMAICA | *THE WAR CRY* OCTOBER 21, 1933

———◦✕◦———

At about 3 pm on the Monday there was a peculiar sound like thunder under the earth and in a moment the ground began to shake. The mountains overlooking Kingston seemed to sway and the earth heaved, and then, with a crash, the walls of the buildings caved in, roofs, losing their support, collapsed in great heaps of masonry into the roadway, and falling beams lay in all directions. Screams of horror and groans of death sounded on every hand, as thousands of people in stores and houses were killed. Many were unable to extricate themselves and were burned in the fire which swept the town, following the shock. Kneeling figures could be seen, for many thought the Day of Judgment had come and hundreds prayed for God to have mercy on them.

The Army, together with other organizations, immediately set to work to give help to the distressed and homeless. Hundreds who escaped ran to the Central Park, carrying chairs and other articles of furniture which they had managed to snatch up in the rush for safety. The park was crowded with people, who slept out in the open and officers were busy for days helping to provide food and other comforts.

Some of our officers had narrow escapes and many soldiers lost their lives. The result of this visitation was a great revival of religion. Our Halls were packed and hundreds of seekers were found at the Mercy Seat.

My life was saved through a clerical error. At the time of the earthquake I was Honorary Secretary to the School Board. The denominational schools had been amalgamated by the government and made into a government school with a committee of ministers and laymen. My duty was to keep the minutes and call the regular meetings. We used to meet in a church on a Monday, at 3 pm. This church was built of square masonry, and we used to sit under the south gable, where a table was fixed to do the business. I sent out the usual notice, intending to say that the School Board would meet at three o'clock on Monday but in error I put Tuesday. The mistake delayed the meeting and on Monday the church where we would have been sitting came down with a crash, the seats and table we used being smashed and buried under huge squares of stone.

Lt. Colonel Bruno Friedrichs

JAMAICA | *THE WAR CRY* MARCH 2, 1907

Looking from the sea upon the green sun-bathed landscape, stretching from the green seashore up to the peaks of the mountains, shrouded in fleecy clouds, one discovers no trace of the fearful havoc played by the recent earthquake. We had left New York a few days before in a hurricane of snow and icy wind. Now we look upon extensive plantations, graceful palms, and the luxuriant tropical growth that is only seen in a land of perpetual sunshine.

After coming within sight of land we sailed in the beautiful bay of Kingston. The neat brightly-painted buildings of Port Royal, with their red roofs in a setting of coconut palms and banana trees, with the distant background of hills and plantations, gave no indication of recent disturbances, except that the coastline is marked by a number of half-submerged trees.

Kingston, the metropolis of Jamaica, is as yet hidden from view but as we approach the wharf we can see the large warehouses in ruins, walls partly fallen, roofs smashed and other signs of destruction. It is not, however, until we enter the streets, after stepping ashore, that the full extent of the disaster dawns upon one. All the descriptions read in newspaper pale before the cold facts. Street after street through the entire business district, as far as your eye can reach, is a mass of ruins. Portions of ragged walls, heaps of bricks and tangled wires; burnt stumps of trees and heaps of debris are seen everywhere. Only two per cent of Kingston's buildings escaped and those are chiefly little wooden frame structures, which swayed with the motion of the earth, twisted perhaps, but still held together. A few scorched palms stretch their crown tops towards a glowing sky, like hands petitioning for mercy.

Officers were in a position to directly assist many very urgent and special cases requiring food and clothing and they are still giving meals of soup daily to a number of destitute families. Several officers have also assisted in doing guard duty.

Our meetings have not yet recovered from the disorganization of the life of the city. Number III Corps was fortunate in keeping its hall, which escaped damage, and meetings are held there regularly. The other corps have held an occasional open-air, but now they are organising regular open-air meetings, to continue until a building can be erected. The financial loss to the Army has been very great.

All but two Salvation Army buildings in Kingston were destroyed. The lone remaining structures still standing were the Number 3 Corps and the Women's Industrial Home. The home became a refuge for officers and soldiers. People slept out in the open areas on whatever they could find to avoid the masonry that continued to fall from the aftershocks and because there was a universal fear of being inside buildings that might collapse.[150]

The Army immediately set to work to help with the relief efforts. The territorial commander, Colonel Lindsay, was off the island on a tour of the territory when the earthquake hit. It was some days before he knew whether his wife was safe or the state of affairs with the Army. The Jamaica *Telegraph* noted the Army's response even while they themselves were suffering, reporting, "Mrs. Colonel Lindsay and Mrs. Major Clifford are daily at the hospital rendering aid to the wounded . . . Ensign Garbutt with five officers of the Salvation Army are to be seen every day at their posts handing out salt fish, yam, flour or vegetables with the same energy and enthusiasm as displayed in their normal religious services."[151]

Salvationists began clearing the debris away from the men's shelter, salvaging lumber to make repairs so they could provide shelter space for those who needed it. The mayor and the Anglican archbishop asked the Army to serve as part of the relief committee and as a result, were assigned a place at the horse track to care for those who were previously homeless or had no one else to turn to. The railway granted the Army rights to issue passes to people who wished to leave Kingston to stay in other parts of the country. This provided help not only to the victims but relieved pressure for the already overstretched resources in the city.[152]

The spirit of cooperation and selfless service would long be remembered. Father Mulry, a Jesuit priest, related how the

Army offered to help his priests to distribute food. For a time he also supervised the Army. He later said, "I have but one doubt and that is my getting there myself, and if I do go to Heaven I shall shake hands with the captain and his Army."[153]

Not forgotten was the tremendous loss sustained by the Army to its buildings and to its officers in the city. Chief-of-the-Staff Bramwell Booth sent out a notice to be posted in all Salvation Army publications worldwide: "Our officers were providentially preserved; but, I fear, many of our soldiers must have perished. We have sent £500 from International Headquarters but £500 will not go far, and I am, therefore, making a special appeal to every reader of *The War Cry* to come at once to the help of Jamaica."[154]

Despite all the problems, the determined officer at Kingston Number 2 Corps meant to carry on. Her corps and her quarters were both in ruins. Salvaging a framework from a nearby yard and scavenging for old posts and other lumber, she covered the framework with coconut fronds. Not only did this result in her keeping her soldiers together but the corps doubled in size from others who began to attend. A contemporary report says, "Following a procession through broken streets, the drums and cornet giving a weird effect amidst the devastation, the march turns into a lane and then single files into the yard where the temporary booth is packed. People are seated on an upturned hen-coop, kerosene box, broken tree stump, and on the bare dusty ground. Visiting the corps in this setting the territorial commander, Lt. Colonel Lindsay, swore-in 14 recruits and promoted Lt. King to captain."[155]

From this unspeakable disaster, the Army literally picked itself up, dusted itself off and set to work again. And there was plenty of work to do.

5

———∞◦}◎{◦∞———

FRIENDS AND FOES

THE NEXT FEW MONTHS were fairly quiet ones by Salvation Army standards. The earthquake had not only wiped out most of the Army buildings in the territorial center, but it left the entire country of Jamaica struggling to find its feet again. With the Army grappling with its losses, the forward momentum that marked the rapid spread and progress of the Army in the West Indies Territory was considerably slowed.

The Army had to reassess the use of its various properties in Kingston. In doing so different functions were moved around to make best use of what was available. In addition, donations had slowed because of the economic hardship experienced by the people of Jamaica. The Army had to find the means to not only restore its damaged social institutions but find the funds in order to do so.

What probably appeared to be sound business sense and good stewardship to Army officials unleashed a series of attacks by means of letters to the editor of *The Daily Gleaner*. An anonymous writer who identified himself only as "Citizen" leveled accusation after accusation at The Salvation Army that covered almost every phase of Army life. It seems that the writer was inspired by a highly critical book printed in England entitled *The Salvation Army and the Public: a Religious, Social and Financial Study* by John Manson, published in 1906. Manson's book was a well articulated critique of The Salvation Army—however flawed it might have been as to some of its information. But the anonymous critic took up Manson's points and applied them as best he could to The Salvation Army in Jamaica. For over eighteen months Citizen pressed his case and for eighteen months the territorial commander, Lt. Colonel Maidment, sought to answer them. At times the correspondence bordered on bad-tempered with Citizen especially resorting to personal attacks against Maidment.

The gist of Citizen's complaints were as follows:

1. The Army had vast real estate holdings that it must have purchased with money meant for the poor. He had accused it of engaging in property speculation which seemed wrong for a church to do.
2. A specific property donated by Mrs. Denniston was to be used for social work only but the Army had also opened on the location a training home for officers as well as a corps.
3. The Salvation Army failed to issue a properly audited financial report leaving Citizen to assume it was hiding large sums of money.
4. Salvation Army officers were poorly paid and often experienced great hardship as a result.
5. The Salvation Army had entered into the retail market in the sale of furniture and milk and thus was competing against privately owned businesses.
6. The Salvation Army had been at work in Jamaica for twenty years and should have been farther along than it was.[156]

Most of the complaints were fairly easily answered. Undeniably, the Army did own a number of properties, especially in Kingston, but all were in use for social services, headquarters or as locations for corps. None were bought as investments and were placed in immediate use. As to the financial statements, they were not being issued at the time. Subsequently and largely due to the attacks of Citizen, the Army started issuing public financial statements. Citizen was still not happy with this and continued to complain about it. At any rate, it proved that the Army was not sitting on large sums of money but in fact, suffered from a pretty precarious financial status. As to the compensation to officers being poor, there was no argument, as it was true for most officers around the world. All officers knew that no compensation was guaranteed to those who served in The Salvation Army.

The complaint about the Army competing with local businesses was a twofold issue. Immediately following the earthquake, the Army opened a furniture shop in a space near territorial headquarters. This was done to create surplus income in the wake of the financial crisis created by the disaster. Furniture was in great demand as people rebuilt their homes, so it seemed a reasonable decision. After a short time the furniture store was closed down. However, the Army continued to sell milk and other agricultural products as a means to support the work among former prisoners at the Westerfield Farm. This allowed the farm to be self-supporting and also turned a small profit to be applied to the Army's other social work in Kingston.

The criticism that the Army should have been further along after twenty years was a subjective one at best. In fact, the population in Jamaica in 1910 was 823,000 people. The Army had over 100 corps and outposts operating at that time, making the ratio of corps to population 1:8320. That was a higher concentration of corps and outposts per capita than in Continental Europe, India, Australia or the United States. The Salvation Army at this point was still in its infancy. It would appear that this criticism was hardly warranted.

The most serious of the complaints and the one that Lt. Colonel Maidment had to work the hardest to fight was that the property donated by Mrs. Denniston a few years earlier was being misused and that Mrs. Denniston's wishes were not being honored. The Salvation Army historically has taken donor intent very seriously and so it was that Lt. Colonel Maidment presented witnesses as to what occurred during discussions about the donation, including further clarification from Mrs. Denniston to quiet this accusation. In the end it was her word that mattered most. Maidment reported after meeting with her to review her wishes and the subsequent use of the property by The Salvation Army: "Mrs. Denniston is satisfied with this, and has no wish whatever to place any obstacle in the way of the Army making the best possible use of the property in the interests of its social and evangelical work, and she approves of the present intentions of the Army with regard to the development of the property."[157] There were one or two letters from Citizen after that but finally the siege was over. The property in dispute became the home of the training college, the Central Corps and territorial headquarters.[158]

GLIMPSES

Constructing a Corps Building
ALL THE WORLD, 1909

The plan our comrades adopt to build halls in agricultural districts is somewhat as follows: One of the small land owners will donate a site of land. Others will give a hardwood tree or two, another a cedar tree, the latter is utilized to make roof shingles. The trees are felled and sawyers are called in to saw them up and otherwise prepare the timber for erection. As a rule the Corps has no cash to spend on putting up a building; but the sawyers must be paid, and here territorial headquarters steps in and pays the cost of sawing and other expenses. Salvationists sometimes carry these heavy timbers and shingles on their heads for many miles from the woods to the building site. In some cases the corps officer has a rudimentary knowledge of a hut or shack building; or if he or she has not, then maybe a soldier or adherent has; thus, under proper supervision, now a little, then a little, the work of the building gradually rises. Precious sovereigns are given from the limited exchequer, so that skilled labour may be employed and refreshments provided for the voluntary helpers. Thus the hall materialises. Doors, windows and benches are added as months go by. At times when local help, for one cause or another, is limited, the corps must possess its soul in patience until headquarters can afford to pay for the erection of a frame, and put a floor in and a roof on, and so forth. When this is done nobody will complain of having to wait a few months or even a year, for the completion of the work.

Meanwhile, the sides are temporarily covered with coconut or other palms. As the days or months pass, according to the financial ability of headquarters or the industry of the local corps, this is replaced with ordinary boardings, Spanish wood, or maybe even with wattle and daub. In some districts our comrades have to content themselves with a booth of bamboo frame covered with coconut palm leaves.

Elsewhere in the Caribbean, the Army in Barbados had six moveable buildings constructed to allow them to follow the moving population and quickly set up corps meetings.[159] In Guyana, the work of Adjutant Das among the East Indians saw three East Indian corps established as well as a home for overseers, four cheap food depots and shelters. Meanwhile in Trinidad, a Sailors' Home and metropole opened in Port-of-Spain.[160]

Despite a promising beginning in Cuba a few years earlier, the work closed when West Indies Salvationists migrated back to their home islands. Another effort was announced, this time spearheaded by The Salvation Army in the United States. However, this effort soon sputtered to a halt and the island was abandoned again.

On August 20, 1912 the legendary leader of The Salvation Army, General William Booth, was Promoted to Glory following complications from surgery. Salvationists worldwide mourned the loss of their prophetic and charismatic Founder with memorial services held in every country where the Army operated. In Kingston, the *Daily Gleaner* reported on the local memorial:

As a mark of respect to the memory of the dead founder and leader of The Salvation Army, local Salvationists marched in procession from the North Parade through several of the principal streets of the city yesterday. The procession was headed by Colonel Maidment and Major Souter, and was witnessed by thousands of the citizens, who by their attitude showed their respect for the great and good man, whose body was that day buried in London.

Last night a memorial service, conducted by Colonel Maidment, was held at Coke Church, which was packed to its utmost capacity. At the front of the rostrum, which was draped in royal purple and white, was a picture of General Booth. The ministers of several of the city churches took a leading part in the service and paid glowing tribute to the worth and work of General Booth. He was by one and all acclaimed as one of the great men—the great Christian men—of this or any other age, and confidence was expressed that while the great worker had been called to his reward, his work would go on.[161]

Two years later Salvationists in the West Indies Territory would have another reason to mourn. Their leaders, Lt. Colonel and Mrs. Maidment, were transferred to Canada. While journeying to The Salvation Army's International Congress in London, the ship, *Empress of Ireland*, carrying a contingent of Salvationists including Colonel and Mrs. Maidment, was struck by a Norwegian coal freighter in the St. Lawrence Seaway. Among the 1,073 who died were 130 Salvationists, including Colonel and Mrs. Maidment.[162]

St. Vincent, closed at some unrecorded point in time because of some local problems, was reopened. In the intervening years between official Salvation Army activity, four female soldiers continued the work without interruption, conducting open-air meetings and holding cottage meetings.[163]

In 1914, work in Panama had to be scaled back when, upon the completion of the canal, thousands of workers were repatriated. Despite this, the corps in Colon and Panama City continued to flourish.[164]

In Trinidad the Army received a gracious compliment with a generous gift. The Legislative Council voted to give £250 toward the erection of a new Central Hall in Port-of-Spain because it saved government expenditures by its work in the colony.[165]

In 1914 the First World War broke out. Although affecting primarily the European nations, their colonies in the Caribbean region were stirred to action as well. Military units were mobilized and men were sent to the front. To support the war effort The Salvation Army in Jamaica announced it was collecting 10,000 pennies.[166] Later, dealing with the casualties of war, the Army took over the Queen's Hotel, using it as a hostel for disabled members of the British West Indian Reserve while the men were trained at the technical school in Kingston.[167]

Notwithstanding the war and all the restrictions and hardships, The Salvation Army in the West Indies continued to expand. The next country to be opened was British Honduras (Belize). *The Clarion* on June 17, 1915 happily announced the Army's official arrival:

On Saturday last the SS Sizmala brought to our shores, from Jamaica, a fully accredited representative of the Army, in the person of Adjutant Trotman, who, in the words of the letter of introduction addressed to us by Colonel Ballard, Territorial Commander, "has been appointed to establish the work of The Salvation Army in Belize."

Colonel Ballard adds, "He is a native of Barbados, and has done 15 years of service in the ranks of The Salvation Army and we believe that there is a need for our work in your town. We have sent him to do whatever he can to uplift the masses."

We were very much impressed by the soldierly bearing and evident earnestness and honesty of the bearer of this letter of credit and readily promised to accord him as the Colonel asks, "any assistance that lies in our power."

Anxious to be about the work for which he has been sent the

Adjutant organised an open-air meeting in the Market Square on Sunday afternoon where he addressed a fair sized gathering. On Monday hand bills were distributed inviting the public to attend a meeting on Tuesday night at the C. Us Theatre, kindly lent by the management, when the aims, objects and purposes of the Army would be made known.

Whether one is in full sympathy with the methods employed in carrying on this work, which, commenced some forty years ago by a single individual, has become a great force in the world, one cannot but admit the useful and practical work it has done wherever it has been established, and admire the energy and zeal which has brought about such great results and which other and older religious institutions had failed to accomplish.

The Market Square in Belize City was so much identified with the work of the Army that it is to this day known as Battlefield Park. There are two reasons for this. First, Adjutant Trotman loved to sing the chorus, "I'm on the battlefield for my Lord," often beginning the open-airs with it.

I'm on the battlefield for my Lord,
I'm on the battlefield for my Lord,
I'll never run away!
I'm on the battlefield for my Lord.

Secondly, it was known as the place of battle between the claims of God and the resistance of the devil. The first Prime Minister of Belize, George Price, permanently changed the name of the park to Battlefield Park.

HISTORY IN THE FIRST PERSON

Brigadier Charles Smith

THE WAR CRY NOVEMBER 11, 1933

—◌◯◌—

One of the most thrilling journeys I had was a visit to the Mahogany Camps in the Colony of British Honduras where the best mahogany is cut. In company with the divisional commander we started our journey, taking the first stage on a truck like a jaunting-car. We sat sideways and the truck was attached to a small motor, run on a single line through the bushes. The driver and assistant carried rifles, as there were wild animals along the track. This part of our tour had many exciting moments, especially as we crossed a number of very narrow, primitive bridges thrown across a ravine, and, as we sat sideways, we could only see the great depth below waiting to swallow us if we dropped from our perch.

Having finished our jaunting-car ride we came to the next stage which was on foot. We had to cross fifteen "bridges." They were merely sleepers fixed on to a huge piece of lumber meeting both ends of the ravine. Between these sleepers there were big open spaces, no wall or parapet on which to hold and we could see as we looked down the rushing stream or deep valley. As we stepped across these open spaces at times we became quite giddy and had to proceed on all fours. After a few more miles we came to the camps in the forest, and met hundreds of West Indians, all busy cutting huge trees. At the dinner hour we were able to have a meeting with them.

How these men sang! It was a joy for them to see us and the uniform made them feel that there was still a world outside the camps. These men are in the forest for about nine months a year. The Army provided a hostel for them in Belize, the capital of the colony, but the recent hurricane swept this away.

Our return over the mountain and river was made by means of an aerial trolley. This consisted of a large, square box suspended from an overhead cable. At each end of this great cable is an engine-house which works the wire, pulling the box which is used for bringing the mahogany from the forests, backward and forward. As we moved along the cable suspended high in the air, the sight was magnificent. In the sunshine the whole country seemed ablaze with color. Now and again we passed a new section of the cable and the box would give a terrifying jerk. After half an hour's sail through the skies we made our descent and went inside the screened dwelling of the overseer. Our faces and hands were red and puffed with the bites of a very small fly which sticks on your skin and makes bumps. We were not too comfortable and after applying a solution, we felt a little relief, but we were glad to have been able to carry some cheer and the Army's message to those men in the mahogany camps.

One of the first outreaches in Belize was to work among the lumbermen at the mahogany camps in the interior of the colony. The Army had a thriving ministry among these men until the mahogany forests were nearly exhausted and the economic climate forced the closure of the camps.[168]

The work in Belize moved forward rapidly. It was here that the first Home League[x] in the territory was formed.[169] But if the Army had not endeared itself already to the hearts of the people, it did so in 1916. The worldwide flu epidemic killed more people than fell in battle during the First World War. When it reached Belize the colony was leveled. The officers in charge, Ensign and Mrs. Matchett, visited the sick and dying, trying to provide comfort. But as Ensign Matchett visited he realized that the death toll was much higher than it needed to be because people were not only dying from the infection but also from starvation. They were too weak to get up to get food and lay in bed starving to death, or were so weakened by hunger that the flu easily took them. He went home and said to his wife, "Make them some soup. It might help them fight the disease."

"Soup for the whole district?" she asked. But she set to work by contacting the butchers and produce salesmen to supply the needed food while she prepared batches of it on a kerosene stove in her backyard. As the soup was distributed it had the desired effect and people started to recover much quicker. A lawyer whose cook had fallen ill heard about the effort and calling a meeting at Battlefield Park urged the townspeople to join the effort to wipe out the disease. The city was divided into sections with the Army and the hospital being the main centers for soup distribution. Within three weeks the epidemic was brought under control. Despite all their contact with the sick, neither Ensign nor Mrs. Matchett ever took ill with the flu.[170]

Expansion in the West Indies continued. St. Kitts was opened in 1916 by Staff Captain Rosina Bishop with Cadet Freckleton. *The War Cry* announced, "We have commenced our work on the

---

[x] Home League is a Salvation Army women's ministry that uses a fourfold emphasis of worship, service, fellowship and education.

island of St. Kitts. So far all salvation fighting has been done in the open-air and the appearance of the flag is the signal for the gathering of a huge crowd. Many of the people bring chairs and boxes on which to sit. Already 30 souls have knelt in the open-air and sought deliverance from sin."[171] Still without a hall, the pioneers were able to report that 100 souls had been claimed for Christ, all won while still searching for a building.[172] After a year St. Kitts boasted a hundred soldiers while coping with the happy problem of having such huge crowds attending their meetings that they couldn't get everyone in.

HISTORY IN THE FIRST PERSON

Mrs. Ensign Hortropp

MONTEGO BAY | *THE OFFICER* AUGUST 1917

When we were cadets, my husband and I volunteered for work in Africa. After our training we were appointed with our son Willie to the West Indies. The black people were there too, so it didn't matter.

For nearly two years we worked on the island of St. Lucia and saw many souls saved and people become Salvationists. Then we went to Bridgetown 1 in Barbados where we not only had the corps but we were responsible for training West Indian cadets. But in the middle of this work that we loved so much, a yellow fever epidemic spread across the island. My husband and I were deathly ill. In just four days my husband was Promoted to Glory. I was not frightened by anything like disease because I was called to do this. I prayed to the Lord and felt His comfort and strength and guidance. When my husband and I stood shoulder to shoulder we had promised each other that if one fell, the other would carry on. I determined to go forward in faith with my son at my side.

After a couple of appointments we were sent to Montego Bay. The work was very difficult because we had no hall and no hope of getting one. The people were not poor in the things they needed. The weather is warm so they needed only a few clothes. The ground grew everything they needed so they weren't hungry. But no one had money. Building material had to be imported. However, we had so many people attending our open-air and that encouraged me. We would just start singing a song and Willie would play his cornet and soon a crowd was there. On Sundays, we gathered the children together for a meeting just for them. Willie was such a help to me. He was clever and loved the Lord with all his heart. When he was 15 we found that he needed to have surgery. We had every hope of a speedy recovery but within a few days he went to be with the Lord.

I was all alone now. I prayed in my deep despair, "Dear God, help me in this place to raise a memorial to my son, a hall where we can gather and bless those lost sheep."

Two terrible hurricanes came through Montego Bay causing horrible destruction among the people. Many were homeless and absolutely wretched. I organised relief and did all I could to feed and clothe them. Twice when it looked like headquarters was going to farewell me the people sent a petition to leave me there.

I continued to pray and work as hard as I could, believing that God would provide for us a hall as well as an officers' quarters. For four years I kept the salvation of the people and the building of this hall uppermost in my mind and God be praised! We dedicated a new hall before I farewelled.

I am in England to take a course of maternity nursing at the Mother's Hospital in Clapton. Am I going back? That is my island. Those are my people. I must go back.

The conversion of the corps sergeant major was a notable story. A master carpenter, he worked for the government of St. Kitts. Well paid but thoroughly wicked in his heart, he was known for his wild ways and excessive lifestyle. When the Army came to town he was fascinated by it and faithfully attended until under conviction, he sought forgiveness of his sins and accepted Christ as Savior. Given his former life, his word of testimony and his example made a powerful impact on the people of the island.[173]

A further expansion came with the opening of St. Thomas, Virgin Islands in 1917 by the Belize pioneers, Adjutant and Mrs. Trotman, assisted by Cadet Peter L'Esperance.[174] This United States possession did not long remain under the supervision of the West Indies Territory, soon being transferred to the USA Eastern Territory where it has remained ever since. Sadly, when Adjutant and Mrs. Trotman left St. Thomas for Antigua, in the midst of a great revival, he died suddenly from an apparent heart attack.[175]

In 1918 the countries of Honduras and Cuba were added to the list of countries where the Army worked. The work in Honduras seems to have been short lived but Cuba was a different story. Ensign John Tiner was sent to supervise a work that, as in other times, had spontaneously begun. West Indian Salvationists were meeting at Baragua, a large sugar estate. For a year Corps Sergeant-Major Dean and Corps Sergeant-Major Sysnet from Panama had been holding meetings several nights a week. They were meeting in a room loaned to them but the owner decided he needed it back. They prayed earnestly for the Lord to provide a new place. Within two days they were able to buy a partially finished house for $50 and a supply of lumber for $50 more. They opened their building in July 1918 and realizing that they needed officers, sent an urgent appeal to territorial headquarters to send someone.

When Ensign and Mrs. Tiner arrived they also found a work going at Santa Lucia under Corps Sergeant-Major Comerie from Port Antonio, Jamaica. They were having great success, having had a government school loaned to them. The Tiners decided to open up a third corps in Santiago where they also established headquarters and a day care center in November 1918. The work rapidly spread to San Mauel, Chaparra, Delicias, Florida, Puerto Padre, Banes Boqueron, Preston, Mirandna, Estrada Palma, Marcane and Cupey.[176]

In Trinidad the Army was making progress in several directions. The government appointed the divisional commander and Ensign and Mrs. A. Thompson to probation work.[177] The Army would continue doing probation work in Trinidad for decades, reaching thousands with counsel and practical help. In Port-of-Spain, the spiritual work was booming as well. *The War Cry* shared that sometimes the crowds around the building were so great during meetings that authorities had to send in mounted police to keep the throughways clear.[178] Later when there was a move to restrict street preaching, the police stepped in, pointing out that such a law would prohibit the Army from continuing its efforts on the street. They felt that the Army's presence had become so great a positive influence that restricting them was undesirable. As a result, the Army continued to have full access to the streets.[179]

On the periphery of the Caribbean was the French colony of French Guiana. It was in this colony where the Army would conduct what was undoubtedly one of its greatest offensives in social justice. The place: Devil's Island.

6

—∘∘∘-⊰⊱-∘∘∘—

ATTACKING
HELL'S STRONGHOLD

THE VERY NAME of Devil's Island conjures up images of heartless cruelty, absolute depravity, a three-dimensional horror. Although it has been closed for over half a century its name lives on.

Devil's Island is the northern most island of the ironically named *Iles du Salut* (Islands of Salvation) off the northern coast of the colony of French Guiana. It was made a penal colony by Napoleon III to send his enemies and political prisoners, while at the same time hoping those so banished might also populate the colony. He expanded that to include any prisoners that the French wanted to put far away. Originally, most of those sent were from the French colonies but this was broadened to include the most hardened and desperate criminals from the mother country as well. It was argued initially that the penal colony was supposed to be more humane than leaving inmates to wait out their sentences locked away in prisons. What was created instead was an exquisite death trap that combined physical and emotional pain that would destroy all but a few men.

What made the Isles of Salvation so vicious? The islands were surrounded by shark infested waters and baked under a merciless tropical sun. The air was filled with malaria carrying mosquitoes with insatiable appetites. Those men who worked on the mainland found that if they tried to escape by land they were ill prepared to survive the jungle filled with wild animals and other hidden dangers like quicksand. The favorite escape route was southward to the Moroni River to Brazil. But in crossing the river they were easy prey to crocodiles and piranha. For those who tried to escape but were recaptured, there was the promise of cruel punishments of solitary confinement, iron shackles, increased work and extended sentences. When a man fell sick, he would receive minimal treatment or was simply left to die. Suicide and murder were major killers by those who could not take another hour or stand the sight of another person as wretched as himself. The prison guards quickly became calloused, with many sadistically enjoying the suffering of the prisoners. Life was cheap; rather, it was worthless.[180] Remembering that most of those sent to the penal colony were men in their twenties and thirties, it is all the more startling to realize that the rough treatment resulted in the average prisoner surviving less than five years.[181]

HISTORY IN THE FIRST PERSON

George Senton

THE PEOPLE APRIL 30, 1950

The first twenty years had been good. I was one of the "bright young things" of Mayfair (England), a member of the "upper crust," closely related to a titled family. When I was nineteen, my allowance stopped. With no ability or desire to work I turned to thief. The law—the harsh French law—caught up with me and after various short sentences I was labelled "incorrigible" and made a "Relegué" and sent away to the penal colony at Devil's Island.

I met a Belgian convict named Pierre. He suggested we attempt an escape. I agreed, although I knew the odds were cruelly against us. We decided to trek to Dutch Guiana, about 200 miles away. We should have kept to the paths—to wander from them meant death by exhaustion in the impenetrable jungle. Yet, by keeping to the paths, we would run into

Dutch frontier guards. As we had no papers they would return us to the French. We set out but before dawn we were caught. I was thrown into the prison camp at St. Jean. Once more I carried water and latrine buckets, cut wood and hoed land, while I was cursed, beaten and thrown into the cells for not doing more. The declaration of war in 1939 made things bad for us. Food became scarce, punishments increased and the warders became more brutal.

Our camp held 1,200 men, and an average of five or six died everyday from starvation and ill treatment. Most of the doctors were callous insults to the profession. What human beasts the warders were! There was no decency in any one of them. They could talk only with their boots and their whips. The whippings became so severe that a humane doctor reported the state of affairs to Cayenne and whips were banned. The warders made up for their loss by using their boots with extra ferocity. Apart from men who died from beatings and starvation, many were guillotined for murder. These murders usually happened with a frightening suddenness. All Releagués and convicts were mustered in the open to watch the "entertainment." One morning there were five executions and one of the officers had the heads preserved in his office. He would show them to visiting American officers describing them as "Madame Guillotine's best day's harvest."

With the war on, food became very scarce. The shortage was so desperate that when sent to official residences to work we made straight for the garbage cans. Every scrap of orange peel, banana skin, and half chewed rotten vegetable was gobbled up. We were maddeningly hungry all the time. We stole a number of cats, which were cooked over open fires in the jungle.

In September 1946 after 18 years in that jungle hell, I was once more made a free man—within the confines of the colony. My age was 45. I was freed at the little town of St. Laurent, pushed into the world with a shirt and trousers of cotton, shoeless and hatless. I worked for ten shillings a month as a houseboy and warder.

I slept at the Salvation Army and there I met the only decent man in that colony of corruption and hate—Salvation Army Major Charles Péan, a Frenchman. Charles Péan, with a little band of helpers, worked for years to ease the misery of those left behind. Péan started a restaurant where we could go for cheap food instead of being robbed by warders running their own cafes. He was to open it by giving a free meal to 400 men. But when the great day arrived, Péan found that the Releagué waiters and cooks—trusting by experience no one in that colony of the damned—had stolen the table utensils and most of the food. Finally he convinced them and they helped him all they could. The opening dinner was given.

Despite bullying, obstruction and intimidation by the French officials—one of his assistants was beaten up and given a broken jaw—Péan kept on and on, bringing a ray of light and decency to that graveyard of the living dead. He is a very great man.

Charles Péan wrote, "But *la Bagne*—Convictland—is dreadful enough: not only the physical condition of the convicts, but their spiritual state, the stench of immorality, in which all the vices germinate and grow. Each new arrival in this sad community contributes all that he possesses of vices, diseases, corruption and obscene stories of which he is the hero, often enhanced by an abnormal imagination. The horror of Convictland is the hell in the convict himself. Its torture is due not to the military warder, but to the convict's corrupt nature, with its terrible demands and unquenchable thirst which drive him to the vices he abhors and which in the end destroys in him all that is human."[182]

As if that were not enough, the French legislature enacted a system called *doublage*. Those prisoners sent to Devil's Island for sentences of less than eight years had their time doubled before they were allowed to return home. During the time of their extended sentence they lived as free men on the mainland but were not allowed to leave French Guiana. Those whose sentences were eight years or more would be freed on the mainland but *never* allowed to leave, having to stay in the colony for life.

There were two categories of convicts at Devil's Island:

1. Regular prisoners who were confined to the Isles of Salvation camps.
2. *Libérés*—On the mainland this class of prisoner was allowed to hire himself out to private employers as domestic help. Some were required to return to camp at the end

of the day while others were not. Once they finished their sentence, they could return home if they were able to afford to pay for the passage. These were subject to the doublage system. In many ways, they were worse off than the regular prisoners because when they were "freed" they had no meals or shelter provided for them.[183]

The territorial commander of France, Commissioner Albin Peyron, felt that something must be done about Devil's Island. The approach was twofold: to raise awareness among the French public to pressure the government to close this inhuman form of punishment and secondly, to provide care to the men who were imprisoned there and to those who were freed but unable to return to their homeland. To this end, he wrote to the Minister of Justice in 1910 to offer the Army's services. The letter was never answered. Again, in 1921 he wrote to the French government and this time after some delay there was a positive response.[184]

GLIMPSES

The Mosquito Death Ray

THE TRINIDAD GUARDIAN OCTOBER 4, 1933

A death ray machine has been installed in French Guiana by The Salvation Army which it is believed will wipe out all mosquitoes and bring happiness to hundreds of convicts and colonists in the French penal settlement there. The machine is capable of killing every mosquito within a radius of ten miles, according to Commissioner Peyron, the Commander of The Salvation Army in France and Belgium, who arrived in Trinidad yesterday, from a visit to French Guiana.

In a test made recently in France where the machine was invented by Mon. Gourdon, millions of mosquitoes were killed, and the test was acclaimed to be highly successful, Commissioner Peyron said. The machine is not yet in operation in French Guiana, as a lamp which is needed for its operation has not yet arrived from France. If the machine proves as successful in French Guiana as it did in France, it will practically eradicate malaria, Commissioner Peyron claims.

The installation of the machine is one of the principal features of a scheme which has been started in French Guiana by The Salvation Army to improving conditions of liberated convicts. "We are going to make some experiments there with the mosquito killing machine," he said. "We have not been able to make the experiments yet because of the non-arrival of a special lamp to be used. But the machine is already installed."

Commissioner Peyron explained that the machine sends out waves in the ether that destroy all mosquitoes within a radius of ten miles. The machine, Commissioner Peyron said, is named "Germaine Gourdon," after the daughter of the inventor, who is also a scientist. It cost 13,000 francs, about 620 dollars in Trinidad currency.

Major Charles Péan was selected to spearhead the effort. General Bramwell Booth gave him a charge to "work for the salvation of the convicts; to set up a colony for the libérés; to reunite men and their families when practical; and to organise for the repatriation of those who had completed their terms in Guiana."[185]

In 1928, Péan crossed by ship to the colony to make an initial assessment so The Salvation Army could settle on a strategy. There was only one ship a month in and out of Cayenne. Describing how it felt to arrive, Péan said, "A strange feeling gripped my heart. Now I too was a prisoner in Guiana for a month. No letter could reach me during this period nor could I send one; and if, for one reason or another, I wanted to return to France, I could not, I had the feeling that I, in my turn, had become a convict."[186]

Speaking about his own fears in a place he described as the "gateway to hell," he spoke of what sustained him:

I read Psalm 121, the traveller's psalm . . . this psalm was given me in the station waiting room for my journey. After that I repeated it to myself almost everyday, "I will lift up mine eyes unto the hills"

—but they were hills of difficulty and of obstacles whose height frightened me. "From whence cometh my help?" was the inevitable question, and then the voice of the Spirit would reply to my anxious heart: "Help cometh from the Lord."

While in St. Laurent, where more than six hundred libérés used to wander round without work and without resources, I stayed in a room with seven French windows, none of which could be locked. I was alone with a criminal as an attendant, but this psalm said to me then: "The Lord is thy keeper." Now, in a city full of convicts, in prison and out of prison, who alone profited by the unsettled conditions, the psalm said to me again: "He that keepeth thee will not slumber."[187]

Péan was allowed full access to the prison. The warders spared him none of the stark savagery of the place, somewhat amused that anyone would volunteer to come there. On the mainland and in Cayenne in particular, Péan moved among the libérés, finding some viewed him with jaded indifference or even hostility while others, who had nearly forgotten what it meant to hope, surrounded him, shared with him, followed him and believed in him. When the month was complete and it was time for him to go back to France with his report, many accompanied him to the dock. He recalled, "As the boat pulled out a great cry arose from the quay: 'Come back! Come back!' I waved my hand to them and, in answer, they waved their hats. As the group on the shore became smaller and smaller, they still continued to call: "Come back! Come back quickly! It was the cry of a forgotten people."[188]

But it would take five years for Péan to return. On February 8, 1933, the Minister of the Colonies gave him the all-important authorization for the work to begin. "I duly accredit you to the Governor of Guiana. I am saying to him as well that I want your work to be facilitated in every way, both with the convicts and the libérés."[189] On that same day the *Bureau de Bagne* was established at territorial headquarters in Paris.

Seven officers were chosen to accompany Major Péan—many more volunteered. On July 6, 1933 there was a final consecration ceremony at the Paris Central Hall where the party was presented a Salvation Army flag to unfurl in Cayenne. Upon reaching French Guiana, Péan recalled, "As the *Antille* lowered her gangway my head began to spin. The unbelievable had come true. What looked impossible had come to pass. The Salvation Army was in the *Bagne*. The era of projects and plans was over. Now was the time for action."[190]

News of their arrival spread like wildfire. They never ate an undisturbed meal from that time forward. As they started, they met each morning to review what had happened thus far and to plan the day. They rented a shed for a carpenter's shop and hired two of the *libérés* to start making the furnishings needed. They leased the peninsula of Montjoly, about 12 kilometres outside of Cayenne to be used as a work farm. Twenty of the *libérés* were immediately hired to help. Within three weeks they were selling produce. A hostel in a long abandoned building was opened in Cayenne in the Rue Malouet in the quarter where the *libérés* gathered. The building had 13 rooms with space for a small garden, across from a park which ensured fresh air flowing through the building. Within a month the Army had started to accomplish one of its primary goals: to give the *libérés* a means to earn a living and to begin rehabilitation.[191]

When the hostel opened it was a banner day. But when they started the ceremony they found that someone had stolen the cords to the flagpole, half the tools in the workshop were missing and someone had stolen three bags of charcoal, the cutlery for the restaurant, the meat in the locker and even the chef's cap![192] An earnest plea somehow got through to the thieves resulting in most of the items being returned. The hostel was named *La Maison de France* housing up to 100 men at a time. Despite the endemic hopelessness, the Captain and his wife who were in charge were able to witness some solid conversions among men who showed a total change of life.[193]

One day, a *libéré* named Carlier was washing some dishes by the well when he started waving his arms, dropped the dish in his hand and disappeared. When they rushed to help him they found he had dropped to the bottom of a huge ants' nest. Investigating, they found the network of tunnels stretched to the house next door, 20 meters away.[194]

GLIMPSES

Lacour

THE CONQUEST OF DEVIL'S ISLAND

—◦❭◉❬◦—

One evening the *libéré* Lacour was helping the captain's wife. He himself liked the Army very much, and although he could have employed his time otherwise, he used to help the officers as much as possible. He came from a good family and his education made him an agreeable companion. Yet his crime was a horrible one, and it is hard to imagine how this sensitive man with so gentle a voice could have drowned the child he had had by a maid in his family's employ.

He was serving cold drinks while the captain's wife was giving out the games, books and gramophone records to the fifty or sixty *libérés* present that night, all the time keeping one eye on her baby sleeping in his pram.

"Mrs. Captain," called a boy from the restaurant door, "the Captain is asking for you upstairs."

"I'm coming," she replied and, turning to Lacour she said after a moment's hesitation, "I leave the baby to your care."

Some minutes later she returned. Lacour was on his knees in front of the baby, gazing intently at the child, his own face bathed in tears. "What a wretch I am!" he was sobbing. Through the sleep of the child he understood his own sin. Through the smile of the mother he discerned the pardon of God.

One of the constant struggles the officers faced was the addiction of the men to a liquor called *tafia*, a cheap rum high in alcohol content made from sugar cane. Major Péan told of one man who they tried in every way to help but whose addiction to the drink was very strong. One day one of the officers found him in a tafia den and tried to appeal to him with the memory of his mother. The man sneered, "My mother? I have only one memory of her. When I was a little child she took shoes off my feet in order to sell them to get drunk."[195]

Even with all the Army was trying to do there were men who could not stand the colony any longer. They tried to escape in homemade boats, often feeling that if they perished on the high seas it was no worse fate than rotting in French Guiana. Some of the escapees made it to Trinidad where they were arrested when they landed. The journey took them no less than ten days but often up to thirty. They were so exhausted and emaciated that they posed little threat to the public. The police handed them over to the care of the Army instead of putting them in jail. When the Army officer in Port-of-Spain was asked how he viewed these men, he answered, "The French government must take account of the past and the reason why they were transported to Cayenne. We only see sick and neglected men whom suffering has reduced to a state of collapse. So we welcome them at the request of the authorities, who repay later whatever expenses we have had on their behalf. We treat them as we would anyone else. A man is always a man. Besides, how many are there among the men in our institutions whose past is beyond reproach? If all the guilty people were punished, half the world would go to Cayenne. These escapees have more courage, perseverance and hardiness than any other men I have known."[196]

Péan realized that many of the *libérés* eligible to return home were prevented from doing so because they could not save enough money to pay for the passage back. A plan was devised that would allow a man to earn a ticket to be repatriated in exchange for fulfilling specific requirements. The men had to be in the Army hostel to qualify. The guidelines for the men were that they would be—

1. Fed and lodged free of charge;
2. Given all the advantages of the institution, whose program was such as to make his stay agreeable and assure his physical and moral development;
3. Given a gratuity varying from one franc per day to fifty francs per month, for sundry expenses;
4. Given a coupon for forty francs at the end of each month which he could cash whenever he wished;
5. Dismissed for drunkenness, abuse of trust or disorderly conduct;
6. Given in exchange for twenty coupons a third class ticket for France.[197]

The work of The Salvation Army in both French Guiana and in France to not only address the evils of the penal colony, but to have it closed down permanently, was making an impact. Increasingly the public in France and the French government saw the penal colony for the evil that it was. It was decided that in 1938 Devil's Island was to be closed and, over the next few years, the *libérés* who wished to return to their homes would be repatriated at government expense.

In announcing this, President Paul Matter said, "Is it possible by gentle reforms to change this system which is the object of such just vehement criticism? Have regulations and modifications been able to transform the *Bagne*, not into a paradise but, let us say, a purgatory? I speak about this question with nearly fifty years' service as a magistrate. After all I have seen and read, I say: the *Bagne* must be abolished! . . .

"Punishment should have both deterrent and moral power but the *Bagne* has neither. Thus, being neither deterrent nor edifying, neither preventing crimes nor reforming the punishment of hard labour has not that twofold value which all sentences should have.

Brigadier Charles Palpant

We had amongst the convicts a task of sowing without seeing any spectacular results, although we did see several real conversions. Many men who had appeared to be unreceptive accepted the Saviour as they faced death and departed in peace, testifying to the faith and their pardon gained by Jesus on the cross.

Later, I was to accompany a group of 50, plus about 40 more still serving sentence, whose liberation had been brought forward. The shipping company was nervous about this shipment unaccompanied by police and the guards did not feel capable of taking on this responsibility. Finally, it was to The Salvation Army the authorities turned for help. We held the respect and confidence of the penal settlement population. I was given the job of accompanying and entertaining this shipment in a troop ship with cabins for 40 to 50 passengers and room for 200 to 300 men.

We spent Christmas at sea and it was unforgettable. While the passengers celebrated in their own way, we celebrated in a worthy manner the birth of the Saviour—traditional hymns known by all and sung with all their heart, sermon and proclamation of salvation. Each man received a message by letter in his own language: French, German, Polish, Arab, Indo-Chinese, etc. These letters came to us from Great Britain, carefully written and containing a vital and durable message. The hatchway was open during our celebrations. It was fine weather – we were still in the tropics—and gradually about 50 passengers gathered along the deck and, from above, shared in our joy.

Leaving St. Laurent-du-Maroni we had left behind one faithful employee who stayed with our successor right until the closure of our Home, when repatriation was completed. When the officers left, not wanting to return to France, he took a job as an accountant in a neighbouring saw mill. One day he didn't turn up for work and his boss, thinking he might be ill, sent someone to see if he needed help. The messenger found him, kneeling by his bed, his Bible open—the Saviour had come for him.

"If anyone says to me, 'Do not you, as a magistrate, think about protecting society?' I reply, 'Yes, but replacing the *Bagne* with a regular prison system.' Were it not solely for the convicts, but for all of us, for France and her reputation and for humanity. As an old magistrate who has almost reached the end of his judicial and perhaps his earthly, career, I can sum up my convictions in one sentence: There is no justice without humanity. I am here to express our gratitude to you, officers of The Salvation Army, to you, Péan, and I want to say this one word which will be at once your encouragement and your recompense— Thank you!"

The announcement was made on June 17, 1938. The news was almost impossible for the men of Devil's Island to believe. They praised, they asked for explanations, they asked if it was indeed true that they would be able to leave, be able to rejoin family they thought they would never see again, to be able to hear, taste, touch and to smell the joys of "home." But before the plans for repatriation could become fully operational, the Second World War broke out.

For the entire period of the war no one could leave. Conditions actually deteriorated as supply ships could not come. Finally, when the war was over, the troop ships that had helped bring soldiers to liberate France arrived to take back home the liberated men of Devil's Island.

Some of the men chose to stay. Either there was no one at home waiting or because they came to Devil's Island already abandoned by life, the family back home making it clear that there was no forgiveness and no one who wanted them back. But those who returned were far different men than the defiant prisoners who were sent there so many years ago. A newspaper reported on the last group of *libérés* to return: "The morning after the ship docked the ex-convicts, with their pitiful bundles, stepped ashore amidst crowds of curious dock workers. One man, who 20 years ago killed a taxi driver, was taken straight to the lunatic asylum. Another, a 66 year-old Savoy peasant, hesitated a long time before disembarking. He had spent 34 years in Cayenne and feared that no one in his native village would recognise him. Perhaps the most pitiful of them all was Georges Remy, a petty thief who was shipped out to the prison in 1921. On the way over, he who survived the world's worst climate, caught a chill, and it was on a stretcher that he came down the gangway. He had pneumonia . . . The first batch of convicts number 2,200. In the first years, sickness, the jungle and bad treatment killed 63 percent of them."[198]

The captain and his wife that kept the hostel and who were part of the original seven officers to accompany Major Charles Péan were the last to come home, carrying with them the flag they had been given at their farewell in 1938. The task was done. Two thousand *libérés* returned to their homeland out of 70,000 who had been sent to Devil's Island since the penal colony opened.

A corps in Cayenne made up primarily of these truly free men flourished for a time but because of the needs back in France, the France Territory decided to close down operations in French Guiana. The territorial commander of the West Indies Territory, Colonel Francis Ham, approached the French territorial commander, Colonel W. Booth, about turning the corps over to the West Indies Territory. Booth simply replied that France could spare no more officers and that he was not in favor of it coming to the West Indies Territory. It is not known why he felt that way but the last officers were told to liquidate the corps and come home. After the broad vision of its noble crusade, its work apparently ended because of some unknown and forgotten petty disagreement.

The Salvation Army ceased to exist in French Guiana until 30 years later.[199]

RECOGNITION
AND REJECTION

"IT WAS A PROUD MOMENT for me to think that after so many years, the West Indies was now taking its place among the missionary producing countries," said Mrs. Major Walker in 1920 at the farewell meeting of a party of twelve officers going to open the work in Nigeria. Leading the missionaries was Brigadier and Mrs. Souter, supported by a West Indian officer party consisting of Adjutant and Mrs. C. Wilson, Ensign and Mrs. E. Purser, Ensign and Mrs. E. Ricketts, Ensign and Mrs. Z. Wisdom and Captain and Mrs. Adrian DaCosta.[200]

The idea of a pioneering party from the West Indies to open West Africa was the brainchild of General Bramwell Booth who felt that a group of well trained, accomplished officers could form a nucleus that would result in a successful beginning in a new country. This would allow for synchronized multiple corps openings and also ensure faster recruitment of national officers in Nigeria.[201] Booth also felt that ethnic Africans would have one less barrier to overcome with the Nigerians.

When the West Indian pioneers arrived in Nigeria a great meeting was held at St. George's Hall with the Bishop of Lagos in attendance. The building was overflowing with more people crowding outside the church vying for places by the windows and doors in order to share the meeting. The Salvation Army

flag was unfurled while prayers were raised asking God's blessing on the new venture. This was followed by multiple open-airs
held throughout Lagos with a number of converts. The work
progressed rapidly and, with the opening of a new railway in
Nigeria, new corps were opened all along the new track.[202]

It was in the same year The Salvation Army led the way with
opening probation work in Jamaica when the provincial commander, Brigadier Edward J. Coles, was appointed as probation
officer for the parishes of St. Mary, St. James and St. Catherine.[203] The increasing success of the Army among those who
had criminal backgrounds was evidenced in a story carried by
The Daily Gleaner on March 27, 1920.

> . . . a character whose boast was that he "had not eaten a Christmas
> dinner out of prison for over 40 years." Owing to his frequent so-
> journs at one of the most famous convict establishments he was
> familiarly known as "the Duke of Portland." He was a man of a
> most diabolical character and his frequent attacks on warders
> and his general insubordination had earned him not one flogging
> but many. On one occasion this worthy, while on ticket leave, was
> interviewed by the then Chief of Police Sir E. Henry, and ex-
> horted to turn over a new leaf. His reply was characteristic: "The
> first policeman that speaks to me is going to have a fall—I shall
> have a drop afterwards." In spite of this significant, if cryptic
> threat, he ended his days peacefully under the sheltering wing
> of The Salvation Army, where so many bad characters eventually
> find sanctuary.

The next year probation work began in Trinidad when
Brigadier Edward J. Bax was appointed probation officer.[204] An
even more significant work from Trinidad was begun with the
opening of Army work on the island of Tobago, which got off to
an excellent start.[205]

In 1921, Vere C. Bird entered the Training College in Trinidad.
A native of Antigua, Bird was a charismatic and highly success-

ful officer. Possessing great leadership skills, he only served as a Salvation Army officer for a few short years. He returned to Antigua where he worked with the labor union movement and pushed for the colony's independence from Great Britain. He became the recognized leader of the Antiguan people and when Antigua and Barbuda transitioned from British colony to an independent nation in 1981, V.C. Bird was made the First Premier and First Chief Minister and Prime Minister. He is considered to be the father of modern Antigua.

Even though he left officership, V.C. Bird continued to love The Salvation Army, considering himself to be a Salvationist his entire life. When he became transitional prime minister in 1976, his first Sunday in office he came to the St. John's Corps with his entire Cabinet. He attended the Army the rest of his life at least once a month, always bringing someone with him until failing health prevented him from coming any longer. Each year he asked for his copy of *The Salvation Army Year Book*, reading it faithfully.

When Prime Minister Bird died, he had a "private" Salvation Army funeral that hundreds attended. The regional commander and St. John's Corps officer, Major Keith Graham, conducted the service with the territorial commander, Colonel Dennis Phillips speaking. At the public service at the Antigua Recreation Grounds that followed, The Salvation Army band was one of three official bands. The Army had further participation in the public funeral. Major Graham then performed the committal service.[206] Later the airport was named after him, making it the only airport in the world named after a Salvationist.

When asked why he did not remain a Salvation Army officer, the Prime Minister had replied, "I am quite satisfied with my experience as an officer, a captain in The Salvation Army, the highest point to which I could aspire then. And I was very much impressed with the spirit of service in The Salvation Army."[207]

How is it that The Salvation Army lost a leader like this so early in his life? No one knows for certain how things might have turned out one way or the other had he remained as a Salvation Army officer. However, the reason given for his leaving underscores a problem that persisted within the Army for some time. It is found in V.C. Bird's words, "... *a captain in The Salvation Army, the highest point to which I could aspire then.*" An intelligent young man like Bird could see that an ethnic African West Indian would have limited opportunities for advancement within The Salvation Army regardless of his intelligence, talent or leadership. Despite its forward progress in many areas, The Salvation Army leadership at this time reflected the view held by the colonial powers that was considered unquestioned fact: that the ethnic African race was somehow lesser than the white.

An example of the colonial view toward race can be found in the *Barbados Agricultural Report* (October 1895), which said, "Some book learning is of course essential, but the mistake of conveying to the (black) child the idea that such education as he acquires at school is calculated to make him eligible for the highest honours in life must be avoided."[208] It is not likely that Salvation Army leaders would have subscribed to such a blatantly biased view, but there were undertones of it in the decisions made about leadership.

Although there was a Jamaican divisional commander in the earliest days of the Army, this was the rare exception. It would take over 90 years before there was another West Indian divisional commander, nearly 100 years before there was a West Indian chief secretary and over 100 years before a West Indian became a territorial commander. The key leadership positions were constantly filled by British officers, then later supplemented by leaders largely from Canada and the United States. Even though it was recognized that the Salvationism of the West Indian officers was as good as or superior to that found elsewhere in the world, and in spite of the increased education and training available to Caribbean people, there was a reluctance to let go, to trust the national people with responsible leadership.

Among the Caribbean officers and soldiers it was largely accepted that this was the way it was. Those who questioned it were considered troublemakers by the leadership, the person complaining written off as someone with a critical spirit or who had ambitions for himself. The Caribbean Salvationists appreciated what each expatriate officer brought in knowledge, skill and often, resources. But they wondered when they might be given their chance to lead. There were some, like V.C. Bird, who were not willing to wait for change to come in future generations. One can only speculate how many gifted people were lost to the Army over the years who felt discounted when they were attempting to offer their best service to God through The Salvation Army.

Regardless of the restrictions within The Salvation Army, it remained a tool in the hand of God. At Basseterre, St. Kitts the comrades were conducting an open-air meeting when the miraculous happened. A man known as one of the most debased men on the island had lost his speech due to paralysis, earning him the cruel nickname of "Dummy." When he approached the open-air, those listening knew he was there to make trouble. But they watched in silent wonder as he made his way to the drum turned over to make a penitent form. There he kneeled and, after being prayed with, he suddenly began speaking. His first words were praise to God. Turning to the crowd he said, "God has saved me and given me back my speech and I will ever live to praise Him."[209]

Local leadership on yet another occasion was responsible for The Salvation Army opening up a new country. This time it was the Dutch colony of Suriname on the northern coast of South America. Henriette Alvarez went to Holland to receive her training to be a nurse. Already a Christian, she was attracted to The Salvation Army, eventually to be enrolled as a soldier in 1922. She wrote back to her sisters in Suriname, telling them of The Salvation Army's structure, purpose and doctrines. Her sister, Emily, was meeting with a mission group that was formed along lines very similar to the Army's. When Emily shared the information with the members, they said, "Let the Army come to Suriname and we will become Salvationists."[210] Henriette sent Emily a copy of the Articles of War[y], but when it was returned it had 26 names on it!

GLIMPSES

Harvest at Spanish Town Road Corps

JAMAICA | *THE OFFICER* OCTOBER 1924

Harvest Festival at Spanish Town Road Corps, which has no hall, and did so happily and successfully under what might be considered adverse conditions. The meeting was held in the yard of a kindly disposed friend. At one end of the yard an old sail had been spread for an awning, supported on bamboo poles; beneath this were the platform and a number of tables loaded with harvest gifts. A few chairs and planks supplied a limited amount of seating accommodation and the drum was utilised for the penitent-form. A most attentive crowd filled the yard to its capacity and the meeting was a spirited one.

Really touching was the Altar Service. True, many of the envelopes contained only small amounts but the spirit in which they were given, and the atmosphere and reverence created, were deeply impressive. The meeting closed with four seekers at the drum-head penitent form. Fishing went on just as in an ordinary inside meeting and with other arrangements provided a striking example of what can be done in the open air.

---

[y] The "Articles of War", now called "A Soldier's Covenant" is the document all soldiers (full members) of The Salvation Army must sign in order to become a soldier. Included in the document is agreement with Salvation Army doctrines, a pledge to live a holy life free from alcohol, tobacco, gambling and pornography, and to support The Salvation Army with time and financially for "the salvation of the world."

Henriette wrote to General Bramwell Booth at International Headquarters asking for officers to be sent to Suriname. None were available, she was told. But, the General asked, "Why don't you go?" Even though she was shocked by this response, she agreed to it. Commissioned with the rank of envoy and presented a Salvation Army flag by the territorial commander of Holland, on September 18, 1925 she sailed for Paramaribo with the intention to open The Salvation Army in Suriname. She was surprised and pleased to find that her sister's mission had already become a fully functioning Salvation Army corps.[211]

But Envoy Alvarez still felt that for the Army to really take hold in Suriname, officers were needed. At the end of 1925 she sent to General Bramwell Booth a photograph of the large group of soldiers that had already been enrolled. The inscription said it all: "If you will look in all the faces on these pictures you will see that they all come to you with one desire, to beg: GENERAL, PLEASE SEND US OFFICERS."[212]

Their prayers and petitions were answered when a newly married couple, Captain and Mrs. Josephus Govaars, were sent to officially open the work. When Govaars arrived he knelt immediately on the dock to seek God's blessing. Awaiting him was a crowd of 450 people including 30 who were wearing Salvation Army insignia. In his remarks, Captain Govaars shared that on three distinct occasions God told him he was to go to Suriname so he happily accepted the General's appointment.[213] Govaars then led the Salvationists in singing, "Joy, joy, joy, there is joy in The Salvation Army." They then followed the captains as they paraded through the streets playing his cornet. Crowds immediately formed because nothing like this had ever been seen in the colony. The procession ended when everyone reached the quarters the comrades had prepared for their new officers.[214]

The work in Suriname progressed well. Soon Envoy Alvarez was asked to go to the Dutch colony of Curacao where she and a Corps Cadet opened the work.[215] One of the innovative approaches in Suriname to ministry was described in *The Salvation Army Year Book* (1951): "We also took to the sea. The *De Heilsoldaat* motorboat evangelistic work on distant plantations and settlements, scattered along the rivers of Suriname, was undertaken. In this way many blessings were brought to isolated people and souls saved. (Though when new roads and ferries made road travel possible, very few of our voluntary "Salvation Sailors" begrudged this floating wooden Salvationist retirement.)"[216]

It wasn't long until the government of the Suriname found in the Army a trustworthy friend and helper. In 1928 it was asked to work with them in establishing parole and probation work. Later the governor of the colony requested Salvation Army assistance in meeting the needs of the destitute with a food depot, providing lodging and food for 80-100 men a day. It was at this time that the idea of a playground for children was envisioned by Mrs. Captain Govaars. It came to pass, providing decades of service to the youth in Paramaribo.[217]

The continuing expansion of the work resulted in the splitting of the West Indies Territory into two: West Indies Western Territory with territorial headquarters in Port-of-Spain, Trinidad and the West Indies Eastern Territory with territorial headquarters in Kingston, Jamaica.

The idea for one of The Salvation Army's hallmark services in the Caribbean got off to a rocky start. In 1927, Colonel John Barrett, territorial commander for the West Indies Western Territory, announced in a united holiness meeting that the Army was going to teach blind people how to read and write. The laughter was so long and prolonged that he could not speak for five minutes. When he could at last be heard, he said, "Very well. You shall see!"

Colonel John Barrett

THE OFFICER DECEMBER 1929

Our first students came at the beginning of November 1927 and teaching was commenced at divisional headquarters. To begin with, we sometimes had to seek for the pupils, as many would hardly believe that a blind person could be taught to read.

In order to give the blind, who were mainly poor, some means of earning money they had to be instructed in some handicraft, and thus we had, in addition to up-to-date teaching equipment and a Braille writing machine, two Olivet typewriters, cooking utensils, and three looms on which the boys could weave mats.

We have enjoyed the noble assistance rendered gratuitously by Miss Edna Ferguson, a blind lady, who had been very well educated in the United States. In addition, it was found necessary to train an officer for this work, especially as our stay in the West Indies would not be forever. Ensign Fidelis Lewish, was appointed and is rendering excellent service.

During the first year twelve people learned to read and write Braille; ten learned to sew and eight to weave.

The first Chinese in Jamaica to become a Salvationist was a blind student. When he stretched out his hands to grope his way to the penitent form it was indeed symbolical of a soul groping for light.

Think of a blind boy of sixteen, living in the country, in the darkness and, mentally, "in the shadow of death!" Now he can read and write and has stepped forth from a lonely country home into a vast world of literature and thought. He has had the restrictions of his mind broken down, and has established contact with the world's great thinkers. One can relate such a story in one minute, but will it not take that lad all his life to express the light, gladness, hope and enlargement into which he has come?

Both Colonel and Mrs. Barrett were qualified to teach Braille. Colonel John Barrett learned when his beloved sister's sight failed to the point that it was lost altogether. Setting to work now in Jamaica to address this need, he approached 50 people to give £2 each to raise the £100 needed to make Braille frames. These were special tables made of mahogany with rounded edges to keep the blind from hurting themselves.

Announcing to the newspapers their intentions, it was deflating when they opened the doors on the announced date they found only one solitary student! But later at a meeting at the Ward Theatre in Kingston there were 1,000 people present including the acting governor, to witness an elderly Jamaican schoolmaster who had lost his sight being led to the rostrum. He opened his Braille Bible and announced, "Your lesson for this service is taken from Isaiah 42:15." Then placing his hand on the Bible he read the words, "And I will bring the blind by a way that they know not." The laughter that had greeted Barrett when he first announced that the blind would read had stopped. It was now replaced by reverent silence.[218]

Exploratory work was also done in the openings of both the Santo Domingo (the Dominican Republic) and Nicaragua.[219] In the Dominican Republic, when an officer was appointed to go there the authorities would not let him in.[220] Work in Costa Rica, was also considered, as well as an effort to open Columbia and Guatemala.[221] None of these would last. And yet another attempt was made to establish Salvation Army work in Cuba. Three previous attempts had stalled out, although with promising beginnings. A hotel for West Indians was operating in Santiago but no other Salvation Army work was being done in Cuba at this time.[222]

Brigadier Jose Walker arrived in Havana where he quickly rented two rooms—one for English meetings, one for Spanish—found a friendly Jamaican carpenter who made benches and platforms and re-established the work. Three corps were opened in Havana, with two being entirely Spanish speaking. Mrs. Brigadier Walker set herself to the task of opening *Hogar Evangelina* (Evangeline Home) as the Army's first social service since reopening Cuba. Aimed at neglected children, the

Army sought and was given help by the Rotary Club. In the first three months 280 children received care.[223]

The Army experienced immediate success with its work among the blind, so much so that the new territorial commander, Colonel Cloud, proposed the opening of a School for the Blind to teach Braille and ways for visually impaired people to earn a living. By this time, the enrollment had expanded from the lone student who had initially come to thirty, although all were adults. Eight officers were engaged in the work and the Army was seeking to build a library of Braille books.[224] In preparation for the school's opening, Colonel Thomas Cloud put a notice in the newspapers: "The Salvation Army is very desirous of getting in touch with all the blind, apart from those in the Poor House, specially those who are fifty years of age, and I would ask all sympathetic friends to write regarding all the blind in their immediate neighbourhood, giving their personal address, name and age and circumstances." He continued, "Our effort on behalf of the blind in Jamaica has even surprised us, so much so that we will have to develop our school and apart from teaching to read and write, we are going to introduce industries, and many other phases that will be helpful to them. We are very anxious that all shall be the recipients of the benefits that will come from the efforts put forth."[225] The School for the Blind became a reality, on July 9, 1928.[226]

When the school opened, one of the most memorable moments came when Mr. Cole, a blind student spoke. *The Daily Gleaner* reported, "He said, before he met The Salvation Army in the School for the Blind, he had come to the conclusion that life was not worth living. He was in darkness, and the continual darkness of his blindness made him give up the desire to live. Life was blank and dull, in fact, there was nothing to live for, because his life was in darkness, he cared not what became of him, how he appeared, or what he ate, but now that was all changed through the blessed Salvation Army. 'I am living in a new world.' He said, 'I am no longer in the darkness. My life is no longer sombre and sad. Through The Salvation Army, taking upon its great heart of love the care of us afflicted ones, I see not with my eyes, but through my fingers. I have again come into the light, I live again in a new world. I can read, indeed, it is a noble Army, and I am thankful to God for bringing these people.'"[227]

In 1928, General Bramwell Booth donated a motor van to the West Indies Territory for evangelistic purposes. It had previously been used in Europe, East and South Africa. The vehicle was to be used to drive from town to town to conduct open-airs. Three officers could sleep and eat in the built in, if not cramped, living quarters. It could carry an additional 15-20 people as well.[228] The van started its service in Guyana, and was later transferred to Trinidad and Barbados, finally making its way up to Jamaica.[229]

When it reached Jamaica, Colonel Cloud dubbed it the "War Chariot" and outfitted it for its evangelistic work in Jamaica. But events arose that pressed the van into a different kind of service.

A severe drought had hit Jamaica, centered in the parish of St. Elizabeth. People were literally starving to death as crops withered under an unrelenting sun. The War Chariot was loaded up with food supplied by the Women's Social Service Association and rushed to St. Elizabeth with the first of several loads.[230] Ten depots were established by the Army throughout St. Elizabeth to alleviate the suffering. Brigadier Smith, who operated the War Chariot, described what he saw: "The land looks as if a fire has passed over it, and the crops are absolutely barren and useless. A girl of twelve years of age was carrying a tin of water on her head and someone made her take off her hat to show me in what a condition she was. We saw that she was starving; her arms were bony, her face drawn, her hair matted, and her clothes were the colour of soil. She is one of a large family, and I felt this was a special case, for the other children were almost naked ... When I took a loaf and gave the child her eyes glittered with joy and the people thanked us and said, 'Right, sir!'"[231]

There were problems in Antigua as well. Sugar and other crops had failed. When Captain and Mrs. John Stobart arrived to take command in St. John's Corps they immediately set to work to provide for the needs they saw. They started with a hot lunch for school children in the city. Children marched from their school to the corps where they received a bowl of soup and bread. In the back yard of the corps, milk and biscuits were given to babies and nursing mothers.[232]

When territorial headquarters heard of the effort they sent funds enabling Stobart to double the number of meals. As conditions continued to worsen, the government provided a grant to the Army to expand its work to feed all the needy children on the island. Between 4,000 and 5,000 children were thus fed daily. The Secretary of Education said that attendance at school had dropped to 65% and the children who were attending were performing poorly because of malnutrition. After the Army began its relief efforts, attendance rose to 85% and the children's school performance improved dramatically.[233]

In the city of Georgetown, Guyana, a corps was opened in the almshouse with 45 soldiers composed entirely of inmates. Corps Sergeant-Major Jeremiah Green spent 17 years in charge.[234]

Salvationists across the West Indies were saddened to hear of the death of Reverend Raglan Phillips, one of the pioneer officers of the work in the Caribbean. Phillips had resigned as a Salvation Army officer some years earlier because of a doctrinal disagreement with the Army over divine healing. Although The Salvation Army readily accepted God's ability to heal, it did not feel that it should be the central focus of its ministry. Phillips felt that God had gifted him in this regard and that he should be allowed to exercise the gift freely.

The parting was on friendly terms and Raglan Phillips, although not a Salvationist anymore, remained a staunch friend and advocate for the Army. He eventually started the City Mission in Kingston. Two years before he died, he asked Brigadier Charles Smith if he might be given a Salvation Army funeral which Smith promised to do.[235]

GLIMPSES

The Almshouse Corps

SELF DENIAL | *THE WAR CRY* MARCH 2, 1935

The Sergeant had a grievance. Could he see him (the officer) on an important matter? With almost an injured air the man asked if these converted inmates were not really Salvationists, and if they were, why they were being treated differently from Salvation Army soldiers the world over? The officer protested that he knew of no distinction which had been made nor any reason why there should be. Jeremiah enlightened him.

"Self-denial is on," he said, "and we have heard that Salvationists take part in an Altar Service. Should not we have been asked to do so?"

The officer's throat became dry and too swollen for speech. A great happiness came to his heart with an overpowering emotion.

"I know that you came in here you received a half penny a week," he stammered, "when you had been here for six months 5s. was put in the bank to your credit and after a second six months another 5s., and so on. From so little how could we think of asking you to give to the Self-Denial effort?"

"But you forget that after two years we are given allotments," persisted the Sergeant, "that you helped us to buy seeds and to sell our produce to the hotels. We have means, and we would like to give to the Self-Denial Fund."

On the appointed day an Altar Service was held. It was a most moving meeting. These men, shut away from society, were giving of their poverty in order to help the Army save the world.

He died in 1930. A large procession of Salvationists and members of the City Mission marched from North Parade led by The Salvation Army band before the memorial service at Coke Memorial Church. Eight hundred people crowded the building with hundreds turned away. The territorial commander, Colonel Cloud, in tribute to Raglan Phillips, said, "We are here to do honour to a Christian worker whose early life was associated with our organization, and who sacrificed much in its early development in this island, and we feel that The Salvation Army ought to pay its tribute to one whose work is not only written in the pages of Salvation Army history but in Jamaica."[236]

By this time the Great Depression was tightening its grip on the world. It swept across the Caribbean like a great tsunami. The poor experienced greater levels of desperation as factories closed and mills shut down. Oil prices dropped by the glut created as people quit driving their cars to save money, shipping dropped sharply as goods were not needed in markets where people had no money to buy.

Somehow amid the growing gloom The Salvation Army not only pushed its mission forward but made another major new advance.

8

SHADOWS ACROSS
THE CARIBBEAN

AFTER VISITING BERMUDA and part of the West Indies Eastern Territory, the territorial commander, Colonel Mary Booth, made a visit to The Bahamas. Formerly assigned to Canada, it was only in recent years that it fell under the direction of the West Indies Eastern Territory. Booth's visit was very public, with newspaper reporters following her every move, constantly asking her when The Salvation Army would open in the colony.

The answer to that question was announced in the Nassau *Guardian*: "Commandant William Lewis and Captain James Mottram of The Salvation Army arrived today in the *Lady Rodney*. It is understood that Captain Mottram will be here for a year."[237] Commandant Lewis was only in the Bahamas for two weeks, leaving Captain James Mottram in charge.[238] An open-air was held the night they arrived at Rawson Square where they announced they had come to open The Salvation Army in the Bahamas. Temporary headquarters were established at Aurora Hall on Charlotte Street with immediate plans to purchase or build a permanent building.[239]

Captain Mottram, born in Wales, was known as "Happy Mottram" and had been an extremely popular officer in Bermuda where he served previously. Mottram soon announced that it was the Army's intention to conduct social work as well as car-

131

ing for the blind, the aged and the infirm.[240] True to his word, The Salvation Army soon established a soup kitchen to provide relief for the poor. The only requirement was that recipients had to bring their own bowl.[241]

Hardly had the Army been able to enjoy the victory of this very promising opening than on September 10, 1931 a massive hurricane slammed into Belize. The conditions were perfect for the storm to wreak maximum damage on an unsuspecting people.

September 10 was a national holiday in Belize so the streets were crowded with people who had come to watch the huge parade that marked the annual event. Without the benefit of storm warnings, there was scarce attention paid initially to the darkening clouds or the winds getting stronger. As it appeared that things were getting worse, the parade broke up and most people headed home. Rain came down harder and harder and with it the wind rose to gale force.

The first part of the storm wreaked havoc. But it was when the eye of the storm passed over that the storm took its heaviest toll. When the eye passed, people thought it was over and ventured outside. But some noticed that the water had receded. They could see fish flapping around and went out to pick up this easy catch. By the time they realized the danger they were in it was too late. The water that had receded now came back with an overwhelming surge, carrying anything and everything with it. In horror, those who had been happily gathering fish found they had no traction in the wet sand and the debris scattered about. They never had a chance.

Barges broke from their moorings and acted like steamrollers as they crashed into house after house. Homes that were previously damaged were now finished off. The barges were once again afloat, and drifting through the capital they flattened building after building that irresistibly yielded to the floating battering rams. The dead and dying drifted by while the living clung to whatever they could to keep from being swept away.

Adjutant James Austen

BELIZE | *THE WAR CRY* NOVEMBER 28, 1931

The hurricane struck us on a holiday when various societies, including our Home League, marched in procession in the National Day Parade. It suddenly began to rain so I marched our children back to the Hall, and then hurried home. By the time I again reached the hall rain was falling very heavily. As it did not cease I instructed the teachers to send the children home. We had not gone very far before our zinc sheets, which cover most of the roofs, began to fly in all directions and trees began to fall. On arriving home I found all the roof was saying good-bye to us. Then in came the rain. I tried to get the beds in the dry, but as piece after piece of roofing left, the task became more and more hopeless.

Suddenly there was an ominous lull. I went out to see what damage had been done and found that a few houses had been blown down and that the sea had receded a considerable distance. In about ten minutes I looked again and saw the water was coming back rapidly so I began to run home, getting in just before the water came rushing across the street.

Quicker than it takes me to write, our house was surrounded by a swirling torrent which rapidly rose higher and higher until the whole of the bottom flat was under water. It rose to a height of ten feet and in some parts to fifteen feet. We stood with our backs to the wall while the wind howled and our doors and windows went flying in many directions.

We could do nothing but stand still. Then the house began to sway backward and forward until at last it gave a mighty heave. I thought the end had come, and that we would be flung into the water. The building crashed off its pillars and was actually carried into the next yard.

I had to climb over trees, houses and boats. Barges of 200 tons burden had been flung into the streets as if they were toys. Dead lay all around, many having been drowned as they fled. Others were drowned like rats in a hole, pinned beneath the wreckage. It is estimated that 90 percent of the deaths were by drowning.

After the first day the death toll mounted so high that it was impossible to bury quickly enough, and it was decided to burn the dead. Great fires were started over the town and burned for nearly a week.

Mrs. Major Hazel Pyle

BELIZE | MY MOTHER TALKED ABOUT IT FOR YEARS

My mother was at home with the baby and a four or five year old boy. There was no news to warn us which is why so many died. The first storm came and rocked the house but my mother said she didn't feel it. But my neighbour saw the house and after that first wind, he went over and said, "Katie, I've come to get you out of this house because it is not safe. I noticed when the storm came it was rocking. Give me the little boy and you come with the baby."

He took the little boy and my mother wrapped up the baby girl. By then the sea came in. The sea rolled out and then rolled in again and mounted the wall. She said she was struggling through the water. She had the baby in this hand and using the other hand to go through the waves. Light came down and they were going to the Scot's church for safety.

It was then my mother missed the baby. She cried all night because she didn't know when or where the baby came out of her hand. But the waves were against her and she was struggling and it just washed the baby out of her hand. She said that the following morning as soon as daybreak came and the storm was gone everyone was out looking for their loved ones. So many dead people were on the road and you had to walk over them. She went looking for her baby and she found the baby in a bath full with water. The wave had taken it out to sea and back again leaving it on land and the baby was right there in the water, drowned.

She blamed herself because she couldn't say when or where the baby was taken out of her hand. I was born the following year. And when they told her I was a baby girl, she said, "Well, God give me back my girl." So she was going to give me the same name but the family said, "Don't give her that name! She will die too." She changed the name to Hazel.

When the storm finally passed, Belize City looked like a war zone. Most of the homes were wood—the hurricane left them little more than kindling. Dead people and animals were thrown in trees, buried beneath the wreckage, left laying in the roads and ditches. An untold number washed out to sea, their bodies never recovered. The survivors began their search for the missing. With the noises of the city stilled, the only sound was the wailing of grief stricken survivors when the body of a loved one was found.

But the fear of further death and disease forced the survivors to spend little time in identifying the dead. As bodies were were found, they were piled into great funeral pyres that burned for days. Many victims were washed out to sea, their bodies never recovered. Because of this, no accurate death toll could be tallied.

Major Austen, dressed in an old pair of trousers and a Kimono shirt, his only surviving clothing, set forth to see what he could do.[242] The Salvation Army tried to pull its shattered forces together but found of its many buildings in Belize City only one was left standing.[243] With very little to work with, the Army nevertheless set up a soup kitchen across from City Hall and an emergency aid station at the First Presbyterian Church where it treated more than a thousand people since the storm.[244] The Salvation Army, like the colony, rebuilt and tried to resume life again.

Back in Jamaica, the program at the School for the Blind was continuing to develop. It was decided to expand work to school aged children, splitting the work with a Home for Blind Boys being established at Orange Street while a Home for Blind Girls operated at Church Street. Then it was decided to extend services to include those who were deaf and mute. This latter service continued for some time until another agency was formed to deal specifically with the needs of the hearing impaired.[245]

With the Depression deepening, The Salvation Army opened an increasing number of hostels. In Jamaica, the Bethesda Home for Girls and Women opened to especially target at risk youth. Some came to the city looking for work but had not considered how vulnerable they might be. Others were referred by the courts in order to avoid placing them in jail.[246] An additional home for women, called the Florence Booth Home, was opened.[247] In Trinidad, a series of night shelters catering to men were operated in Port-of-Spain.[248] The government in Trinidad asked The Salvation Army to take over the operation of the Josephine Shaw House in 1932, a hostel for working women in Port-of-Spain.[249] The next year, the government in Suriname approached The Salvation Army requesting that it open a shelter for homeless men, particularly Japanese immigrants. In the first six months, 7,600 men received lodging and breakfast.[250]

But the Depression was affecting Salvation Army operations as well. The bold decision of a few short years before to have two territories in the West Indies, was rescinded. Both territorial headquarters were suffering from a lack of funds, but the West Indies West Territory was especially hard hit. The two territories were once again amalgamated into one in 1932 with headquarters in Kingston.[251]

Work in Curacao evidenced progress with the opening of the island's first public playground in 1933. That same year the former Christian Military Home and Club for company workers was contracted to the Army by the Curacao Petrol Industrial Company.[252] The Shell Oil Company later donated a house and a plantation for a boys' home and farm at Barkkeput, which operated through the war years.[253]

As economic conditions continued to weigh heavily on the nations and colonies in the Caribbean Basin, Brigadier Walker was asked to do something about the homeless people in Havana, Cuba. Similar to the arrangement that had been made with the Army almost twenty years earlier there, a large "concentration camp" was established for those in need. It included

THE SALVATION ARMY

• CARIBBEAN TERRITORY •

1899-2010

1899 | Group of local officers, West Indies.

1907 | Territorial headquarters in Kingston, after earthquake.

1911 | Salvation Army Hall in Savanna La Mar.

JAMAICA

1916 | Opening of new Hall in Montego Bay.

BRITISH GUYANA

1913 | Opening of the Salvation Army in Georgetown.

1953 | Officers' council.

TRINIDAD

1979 | Salvation Army officers.

SURINAME

Christus voor de wereld

1977 | Commissioners Pitcher salute comrades.

1987 | New Home League members enrolled in Eastern Jamaica Division.

JAMAICA

1987 | General Eva Burrows, with Bandmaster Lewis and others in Eastern Jamaica Division.

1988 | Hurricane Gilbert.

1989 | Graduation from basic school (kindergarten) in Falmouth.

JAMAICA

1989 | Delegates, Staff at Brengle Memorial Institute, Kingston.

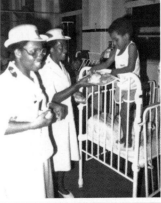

1989 | The Children's Ward, University Hospital, Kingston, Christmas.

CUBA

1992 | Fidel Castro with General Eva Burrows and other officers.

ANTIGUA

THE SALVATION ARMY
ANTIGUA & ST. KITTS
REGIONAL HOME LEAGUE
**CORPS EFFICIENCY
AWARD BANNER**
ST. JOHNS CITADEL   1996-1997
ST. JOHNS CITADEL   1997-1998

1998 | 95th Annual Congress.

JAMAICA

2002 | Territorial Executive Congress, Kingston.

1989 | United Timbrelists at Youth Councils, Nassau.

2008 | School for the blind.

2010 | Salvation Army aid workers after the earthquake in Haiti.

several components: a home for women and children under 10 years of age, a large farm for youth from 10-20 years old, a larger farm for married couples or families willing to take up farming that allowed each family to have their own home and eight acres of land to cultivate, and a home for the aged and handicapped. The camp was located at Tiscornia, an immigration area opposite the harbor for Havana.[254]

Police accompanied Salvation Army officers as they combed the streets looking for homeless people that might benefit from the services offered. The Army's frugality pleased the government officials when they found that their funds were able to care for twice as many people as they had budgeted.[255] The Salvation Army had a capacity of 741 to care for in these facilities.[256]

Soon after, the territorial commander, Colonel Herbert S. Hodgson, approached the international committee of the YMCA to inquire about the use of their building in downtown Havana, since they had closed operations in Cuba. They agreed to rent it to the Army with the Army taking possession of it in July 1937. It was a facility like none the Army had ever occupied. Hodgson shared what was included in the building and some of the proposed uses: "A men's department, complete with gymnasium, electric friction machines; Turkish, electric and sun baths; cold and hot showers, and on the roof there are eight large courts for Squash racket and handball games. In the rear of this floor is a large hall, previously used for basketball. Arrangements have been made to transform this into a night shelter for homeless men, where they can reside at a small charge, and next morning, before they turn out into the streets, receive hot coffee and bread. One hundred street boys are also entertained to free breakfast."[257]

Ermyn Ellrington

BELIZE | LT. COLONEL E. KENNY

—⊷⊶—

There came a young woman to the Mercy Seat, the Corps Sergeant Major (Sister Stanford) knew and spoke to her; later I learned she was dumb and had lost her speech through a dog bite. However, during the week following, Ermyn Ellrington, for such was her name, had been praying that if God would restore her speech, then Ermyn would be willing to leave home, become a candidate for officership, if God so willed.

Well, on the next Sunday evening, Ermyn came forward to the Mercy Seat, still unable to speak. But she rose and stood before the congregation, who were in prayer; then as they sat up and watched the congregation heard her speak . . . it was a miracle! And how we all rejoiced and praised the Lord.

Ermyn kept her promise and eventually went to the Training College in Jamaica. My wife and I were also on the move, transferred to Trinidad. Later it was a thrill and joy to join the welcome to Trinidad of Lt. Ermyn Ellrington to the Port of Spain Central Corps as second officer (with Adjutant Atwell) and together watched the wonderful way God used Ermyn Ellrington to sing, (with guitar) and speak and the crowds were blessed; and we marvelled at the miracle and healing power of God which we rejoiced and witnessed.

In a surprising throwback to days gone by, the police in Port Antonio, Jamaica ordered the Army to stop holding open-air meetings after they had done so for years at Market Square. Apparently the Portland Parochial Board resurrected an ordinance passed 28 years earlier but never enforced! Popular opinion forced the bylaw back into dormancy.[258]

The Salvation Army continued to be viewed as a resource to various governments when dealing with offenders of the law. In the Bahamas, the Army was appointed to do probation work.[259] But in Trinidad, where the Army had long been at work in this field, a problem arose as to how to designate the Salvation Army officer. The authorities maintained that he should not be called "Salvation Army Chaplain" because there were no Salvationist prisoners. However, they still wanted him to be involved. Someone suggested that he be called "Nonconformist Chaplain" since the Army was neither a part of the Anglican or Roman Catholic Church. The Church of Scotland would not hear of it since they were not Nonconformist. Finally they settled on a title: The Nonconformist and Church of Scotland Chaplain.[260]

One of the youth activities that thrived during the 1930s was a boys' scouting program called Life Saving Scouts. A number of the boys and leaders distinguished themselves with heroic acts worthy of note. In 1937, in Montego Bay, Life Saving Scout William Campbell gave courageous service by carrying women and children across a raging stream. At times the onlookers cheered him for his bravery. When a boy was being washed away, Campbell climbed a telegraph pole to direct others to save him. The boy was finally rescued by someone doing as Campbell instructed.[261] Also in Montego Bay, in 1938, Celeste Longmore and her son were cornered by a man wielding a cutlass. Conrad Kenton, Patrol Leader for the Life Saving Guards, went to their rescue.[262] In Port Antonio, a crowd rushed to see a house fire but in the dark fell into the river. A Mrs. Dexter was among these and it was clear that she was drowning. Life Saving Scout Arnold Smith dived into the water fully clothed and saved her, Mrs. Dexter suffering only from a fearful moment.[263] Another advance among youth was the first Salvation Army athletic team, formed in Montego Bay to play football in the Junior League. The team's name: Armyites.[264]

The School for the Blind moved to a site on Slipe Pen Road in Kingston in 1937, the former home of the Baptist Missionary Society. There were seven buildings that greatly expanded the capacity of the school and served it for over 30 years.[265] That same year in Suriname saw the initial broadcast of a radio program that has continued nonstop to the time of this writing. The aim of Adjutant Govaars was to reach the sick and shut-in who could not get out to church.[266]

As tensions rose between the European powers on the eve of the Second World War, advances were made despite the threatening times. Major Thomas Lynch formed the first Salvation Army Advisory Board in the territory in Costa Rica in 1939 to aid in fund raising.[267] In Trinidad, a Working Lads Hostel in Port-of-Spain was opened as part of the government's Slum Clearance Scheme.[268] In Belize, the government handed the Boys' Industrial Home in Pomona over to the Army to operate.[269]

The Second World War that had been threatening for some time broke when Hitler's armies invaded Poland on September 1, 1939. The Salvation Army had to make major adjustments, even greater than in the First World War. When both the Netherlands and France fell to the Germans, the situation became complicated. Suriname, a Dutch colony, remained loyal to the exile government. For French Guiana, the situation was a bit more difficult. It related to the Nazi collaborationist government of Vichy France. Communication was cut off, then allowed, then cut off again with the rest of The Salvation Army. The work in French Guiana largely had to manage itself while Suriname was able to continue to relate to Army headquarters in Kingston. The Army forces in French Guiana, already facing extreme difficulty being in a penal colony, had to wait and see which way the tide was going from day to day. Occasionally welcome visitors came through and mail managed to get in, but for all intents and purposes, a wall of silence divided the Caribbean.

Where they could be, efforts were made. In Curacao, sailors whose ships had been torpedoed found refuge in the Army's Seamen's Home.[270] Survivors also crowded the Army shelters in Trinidad, where by war's end over 100,000 military personnel from several nations and colonies found a warm greeting and vital services.[271] It was also in Trinidad that a Red Shield Center was opened for African American troops who at the time were segregated from white troops in the USA armed forces.[272] A Red Shield Mobile Canteen was dedicated in 1942, a gift from three local businesses—Alston and Company, Todd Ltd. and McEarney Ltd.

In Suriname, a house was taken over to service Dutch troops with sleeping accommodations and a recreation room.[273] Collections of food and clothing by the Home League and League of Mercy in Jamaica and the Panama Canal Zone were sent to England to alleviate some of the hardships created by the war there.[274] Also in Panama, Red Shield Centers were established to serve military personnel.[275]

Other things were going on during the war years as well. In Guyana in 1940, the Belfield Girls School opened, the result of a committee appointed to "enquire into and report on the advisability of establishing a home for delinquent girls and administered by The Salvation Army with an annual subvention from the government . . . Belfield Girls' School is a residential institution for the education and training of delinquent girls up to the age of 18 years, who are considered by the court to require not only removal from home but also a fairly long period of residential training. The court may commit a juvenile to Belfield Girls School in any of the following circumstances:

a) Found guilty of an offence punishable in the case of an adult with imprisonment.
b) Found wandering and to be in need of protection.
c) Brought before the court by a probation and welfare officer while under supervision."[276]

The school was opened by Major Rosling and assisted by Adjutant Atwell and Captain Worell.[277]

During the war years the first General to visit the Caribbean arrived in the person of General George Carpenter, accompanied by his wife. Even within the island of Jamaica it was difficult to travel around due to the wartime travel restrictions, but it was still a time of great rejoicing.[278]

The war came to an end. A common error after wartime is to think that things will go back to the way they were before hostilities broke out. The world had profoundly changed. The new realities in the world began to affect The Salvation Army in the Caribbean as well.

THE PROMISE OF HAITI

WITH WAR'S END, The Salvation Army turned its attention more fully to the internal problems in the individual colonies and countries. The various governments found in the Army a partner in service as old prejudices began to evaporate.

In Barbados this took the form of entrusting to The Salvation Army the entire probation program for the colony. Begun in 1946, the caseload reached the point where five officers were assigned to the department.[279] In Trinidad the work so expanded that the government asked that the officer in charge be relieved of his other duties so he could fully devote himself to probation work.[280]

Colonel Francis Ham made a bold and controversial decision when he purchased Westerham Farm Estate, just outside of Kingston in what is now the suburb of Havendale. The acquisition of the 44-acre site was made possible by a legacy of £5,000 from Archibald Munro. The possession of the land seemed like the height of folly, earning it the name of "Ham's white elephant." But the purchase was visionary, with the Army reaping the benefits over 70 years later. Immediately the Bethesda Home for delinquent girls was moved.[281] The Nest Children's Home, still serving the children of leper patients, was in deplorable condition. It was replaced by "Tunstall Cottage," named for a British airman who died in the Second World War. The home was opened by Lady Huggins, the younger daughter of the Governor. Quite taken by the children, she promised to send them a puppy as soon as she could find the right one. True to her word, the puppy arrived in the New Year to the delight of the children.[282]

In Belize, the Boys Training Home at Pomona had been under Salvation Army direction for almost twenty years. The home's purpose was to provide intervention for boys who were drifting toward lives of crime. Beginning with farming, the trades taught grew to include furniture making and construction. The numbers of boys continued to grow until 1947, when the government transferred the operation to an abandoned military camp near the Belize airport.

The home was renamed the Listowel Boy's Training Home, named for Lord Listowel, Minister of State for the Colonies, an avid supporter of the work. An advisory board was formed with the Colonial Secretary as chairman.[283] One of the features of the home was an exceptional boys' band that was so good that one boy devoted himself to criminal activity in order to be sent to the school so he could play in the band!

Before the advent of The Salvation Army into Suriname, the Alvarez sisters had opened a small eventide home for 15 "respectable, elderly ladies." But the two remaining sisters, Envoy Henriette and Corps Sergeant-Major Nellie, felt that it was becoming too much for them to manage. They discussed the problem with the Emma Fonds Committee, a group that supported the home, and agreed that Huize Emma (Emma House) should be turned over to The Salvation Army.[284]

Major John de Boer

THE SCHOOL FOR THE BLIND FIFTIETH ANNIVERSARY BOOKLET

—◦✕◦—

On our arrival in 1947, we realised a lot had to be done. We had no experience of blind work, but we were determined to do whatever could be done.

We determined to find blind children at an early age, because that would give them the full benefit of education and training, besides the children we had received were so poor in health that it took almost a year to build them up a little. They were so weak they could hardly stand on their little feet. We suspected that many born blind children died of starvation dependent as they were on what was given to them. Very often we had to feed them every two hours a little because of their weak system. Cod liver oil and food yeast were daily supplied.

We sent circulars to sanitary inspectors, district nurses, the clergy and schools throughout Jamaica urging them to contact us if any blind child could be reported so we travelled far and near to find blind children, sometime we took a party of blind children with us to show what could be done, how they too could learn and be happy in life.

By receiving them we would send them to the eye specialist in Kingston Hospital. They were very cooperative, examining them and if possible at all doing for them whatever could be done, which could be very helpful.

The diamond jubilee of The Salvation Army was marked by the visit of General Albert Orsborn. During his visit he conducted meetings in Jamaica, Trinidad, British Guyana, Panama, Belize and Cuba.[285]

Senior-Major and Mrs. Herbert Tucker, then in charge of the School for the Blind in Kingston, were sent to Panama in 1948. They decided that services for the blind were needed in Panama and set to work. With a room loaned by the Methodist Church, the Tuckers began with two students, the work increasing over time until students were offered courses in sewing, stool-making, belt assembly, rubber mat making, English, Spanish,

145

mathematics, geography and typing.[286] That same year, Major Josephus Govaars gathered together seven blind people at the Grant's Town Corps to give them their first lesson in Braille. Thus was launched the Bahamas School for the Blind.[287]

A pressing need in Kingston was met with the opening of the Evangeline Residence at 53 Orange Street. With accommodations for fifty, the Evangeline provided a safe place for single working women, many of them from outlying areas who had come to Kingston for employment.[288]

On May 22, 1949 a telegram was received from Haiti at The Salvation Army USA National Headquarters for Commissioner Ernest I. Pugmire. *"Desire affillier avec vous avons 350 membres réponse urgent—Carrie Guillaume."* Loosely translated: "We wish to affiliate with you with 350 members. Respond quickly." It was decided in New York that the telegram should be passed to the West Indies Territorial Headquarters where it was received by the territorial commander, Colonel William P. Sansom.[289] What led to this?

Carrie Guillaume had been in ministry for a number of years, drifting from one denomination to another. He finally founded his own mission called "Christ for All" that began at the Bas Fort National in Port-au-Prince. The character of his work prompted one observer to say, "What you have is The Salvation Army." Guillaume responded, "Salvation Army? What is that?" Apparently at the same time, one of the people associated with his mission, Emilia, made contact with The Salvation Army in California. They, too, forwarded her letter to Jamaica.[290]

Colonel Sansom wasted no time following through on the information. He wrote to Guillaume to acknowledge the offer from his mission and to tell him that the matter had to be referred to International Headquarters for approval. He enclosed a copy of the Articles of War and stressed that they had to be willing to accept the structure and principles of The Salvation

Army. A little over two weeks later, a letter was received from Guillaume, saying, "All of us are united together with joy in adopting the content of laws which run ahead of The Salvation Army . . . and our desire is repentance, contribution, conversion, regeneration, sanctification, wisdom, justification and the grace in the love of the Lord."[291]

With that response in hand, Sansom immediately dispatched Brigadier Oliver Dadd, the territorial youth secretary, to go to Haiti and to meet with Guillaume and the people he led. Dadd returned with a glowing report about what he had seen. He then returned to Haiti with news that the territorial commander would arrive on February 2 to hoist the flag of The Salvation Army. Then Brigadier Dadd began holding classes in the five locations (Port-au-Prince, Girard, Bethel, Fond-des-Negres and Lafeonnay) where Guillaume's mission operated for those who wished to be soldiers. The Articles of War were translated into French and hundreds of copies printed in anticipation of the Army's official arrival.

When Colonel Sansom arrived on February 2, he was met by 100 people, all of whom had indicated they wanted to be Salvation Army soldiers. Sansom was surprised and pleased to see the number, some of whom had already prematurely donned Salvation Army uniforms. A band of musicians played and songsters sang in both French and English, "God is good to me," and "I want to live right."

The welcome meeting was held at Bas Fort National, the mission building woefully inadequate for the crowd that packed themselves into the building. During the meeting a tropical downpour made so much noise on the zinc roof sheets that Colonel Sansom was unable to continue speaking. Guillaume went to his knees to ask for the rain to stop—and stop it did. At that meeting the territorial commander enrolled 200 soldiers and commissioned 24 local officers. Within a short time a total of 515 soldiers were on roll.

As the weekend progressed, Colonel Sansom shared slides of the Army's worldwide ministry. But the most thrilling moment came on Sunday with the official raising of The Salvation Army flag promptly at noon at Mile Latortue's School near Camps de Mar. First, the flag of Haiti was raised to the strains of its national anthem. Then, with orchestra and singers leading, the martial words of "Onward Christian Soldiers" were sung in French as the Salvationists gave the Salvation Army salute to the unfurled Army tri-color.[292]

When the territorial commander visited Fond-des-Negres, he saw that Salvationists were worshipping under a grass roofed shelter supported by eight poles. The building had no sides with only a dirt floor. There were some crude benches supplemented by chairs brought by worshipers. Envoy DeLouis Marcelin, a baker by trade, was in charge. In order to help people make uniforms, he gave them the white flour sacks left over from his bakery trade. Unfortunately, the print did not always completely disappear so it was not unusual to see a woman wearing a uniform that said, "50 pounds." After witnessing the dedication and seeing the need, Colonel Sansom promised to provide funds for a proper building—the first to be built in Haiti.[293]

But things started to go wrong almost immediately. Envoy and Mrs. Guillaume were made "envoys-in-charge" until a set of officers could be appointed to take command of the work. They had already been selected: newly married Captain and Mrs. Jacques Egger from Switzerland. The understanding was that when the Eggers arrived, Guillaume would turn the work over to them and then he and his wife would go to Kingston to enter the Training College.

Captain and Mrs. Egger arrived in June 1950 with the transition seeming to go well. But it soon became clear that Envoy Guillaume was struggling with letting go of his authority. It appears that he thought the requirement to go to the Training College might be dropped since he had only a rudimentary knowledge of English whereas his wife was functionally illiterate and could not speak English at all.

Questions were also being raised about the Army's non-practice of baptism and communion. Although The Salvation Army's stance on the sacraments was clearly explained and agreed to by Envoy Guillaume, it was not made clear to those who joined the Army. Envoy Guillaume had told several people that an exception would be made for Haiti to allow baptism.

The issue was a divisive one. At the Port-au-Prince Corps during a Soldier's meeting, it became clear that the Army was not going to make an exception for Haiti. An argument arose between the Corps Sergeant-Major and the Corps Secretary who defended The Salvation Army's position. The Corps Sergeant-Major slapped the Corps Secretary and stormed out with 20 other Salvationists.[294] There was also a large defection from the corps in Bethel, with a splinter group led by the Corps Sergeant-Major actively campaigning against The Salvation Army.[295]

The Guillaumes went to Kingston to be trained, but since no translator was provided for them it resulted in minimal benefit. Lt. Guillaume was appointed as Captain Egger's assistant, returning to Haiti on August 16, 1950. When he returned, Guillaume seemed more determined than ever to undermine Egger's authority and to push the issue of the sacraments.[296]

There were other problems besides doctrinal issues. Captain Egger tried to find people to match the numbers of those said to be on roll but he could not. When he questioned Lt. Guillaume about it he found him to be evasive. Contact with many revealed that some of the people had no idea what they were signing and had come that day out of curiosity with no intention of being Salvationists. Others had already left over the sacrament question, so that the best number that Egger could confirm in June 1950 was 398—far less than the 515 reported to territorial headquarters.[297]

The problems with Lt. Guillaume were such that Colonel Sansom dispatched Lt. Colonel Dadd to meet with him. This was done to rule out that the issue was merely a personality conflict and to confirm the information being shared by Captain Egger. When Dadd met with Guillaume there were very frank discussions concluding with Dadd asking Guillaume to sign a renewal declaration of faithfulness, which he did.[298] They thought that the problems were on their way to being resolved. Guillaume was issued farewell orders to an appointment to Gonaives.

Lt. Guillaume resigned not long after his new appointment. Arriving in Captain Egger's office out of uniform, Guillaume told him that as William Booth was the founder of The Salvation Army in England, he was the founder of The Salvation Army in Haiti. Guillaume then went to the Ministry of Cults (the department of the government that handled all non-Roman Catholic religious work) to inform them he was no longer associated with The Salvation Army.

Egger accepted his resignation effective September 18, 1951 based on three reasons:

1. His willful and determined preaching of doctrines and performing ceremonies that were not in harmony with Salvation Army principles and practices;
2. His refusal to leave Port-au-Prince and proceed to an appointment in Gonaives; and finally,
3. His own action in going to the Ministry of Cults and announcing he was no longer with The Salvation Army.[299]

His next action was to write a letter to the president of Haiti in which he said,

Now Egger has sent me a letter of resignation from the service in the Army. Yes, I accept it as far as the Army from London is concerned. But in my own country, where I could gather 115 members, I am duly a shepherd for the service of the Lord entrusted me with the salvation of souls of my poor compatriots and fellow creatures. Until all these things may be cleared up, I ask the reimbursement of all the expenses I had in connection with the officers from London. I had called for help and strength for the work of God but not for (a) ravening lion drinking to the full blood of my poor, innocent compatriots before a wolf in sheep's clothing. So I hope, Excellence, to find help and protection by you, being the Father- Protector, chosen by ourselves to be a real "luck bringer" for all who are the sons and daughters of the homeland, our Haitian homeland which we inherited through the precious blood of our ancestors. I am expecting your fatherly deliverance in order to liberate us from under the yoke of this wicked man who came to unto us with a real idea of exercising royal authority, and wanting at any cost to lose the salvation of the faithful souls he found in the Church as good and devoted Christians, all working in Heaven. I believe that you will never forget the past history, of the whites against us, the poor black race of the small country Haiti.[300]

It is unknown if the President of Haiti ever read the letter or if it was answered. At any rate, he chose not to involve himself or the government of Haiti in an ecclesiastical affair. Beyond that, The Salvation Army was already at work opening schools and starting on a scheme of social work desperately needed in his impoverished country. The president and members of his government would know that expelling the Army from Haiti would cut off aid that was desperately needed in his country. Guillaume could not garner such international support.

At the airport, Guillaume met two newly commissioned officers arriving from Jamaica for appointments in Haiti. He persuaded both Lt. Rosamond Loiseau and Lt. Edith Icard to immediately resign and follow him. Guillaume formed a church known as the Army of Christ, but beyond its name, there were no similarities to The Salvation Army. He lived into his 90s and, following his separation from the Army, made no further trouble for it.

Captain Egger's problems were hardly over. The abrupt loss of two officers from his small field of command was difficult to overcome. Beyond that, all the difficulties resulted in massive losses to The Salvation Army. By June 1951 he could count only 81 active soldiers out of the 515 that were on roll when he arrived a year earlier.[301] When he reported the situation to territorial headquarters he was told that he could report no less than the 515 that were in the statistics. The territorial commander had made glowing reports to London. Those stories of the auspicious beginnings of the Army in Haiti then went out around the world. He admitted that he did not want to be embarrassed before International Headquarters to report that the field had shrunk by eighty-five percent.[302]

It is part of The Salvation Army's DNA that when difficulties and losses come, the Army presses on. The first of many schools was opened in the village of Coupon under the supervision of Lafeonnay Corps.[303]

Regardless of the wounds he may have taken with the defections and dissent, Captain Jacques Egger soon found himself binding wounds of another kind. While traveling in one of the country areas, Egger noticed a boy who had hurt his foot while tending horses. He looked at the boy's foot and using the supplies from his personal first aid kit, bandaged it up. Seeing this, the people thought he must be a doctor and so they brought him babies, children and adults, all of whom needed medical attention.

Relating this story when he got back to Port-au-Prince to a friend who was a medical doctor, he was given a list of medications, ointments and drugs that were safe to use. Egger sent the list to The Salvation Army in the USA Central Territory which quickly sent a shipment of the needed items. This was the first step taken to provide medical services in Haiti under Salvation Army auspices. His only knowledge to carry on the work was what he had learned as a medic in the Swiss Army where he worked under the supervision of a doctor. Making it even more interesting was his venture into dentistry, limited solely to tooth extraction. Now, he was the medical "expert" armed with these limited medical supplies, his Swiss army knife and his best instincts.[304] In 1959, the Department of Public Health would provide an airplane for the Eggers to take a doctor and dentist to travel to the Central Plateau. Their only problem came when several landings were aborted pending the removal of cows from the runway.[305]

The Suriname government on December 8, 1955 agreed to turn over to The Salvation Army its leprosarium known as *Groot Chatillon*. When The Salvation Army inspected the facility, which was at that point actively caring for leprosy patients, it reported finding the following:

- 798 rats lived in the main building at one time;
- On the first floor 4 inches of filth from bats was found;
- All housing flats were badly maintained and neglected, needing paint;
- The surroundings of the flats were muddy, not attended to, and in many instances covered with wood;
- Loafing men and women were all about the place; others were idling their time away;
- No mosquito nets were seen in use;
- No flowers about;
- The whole showed lack of leadership and supervision;
- No variety in the stock of the shop.

Brother Stallen

SURINAME | *THE WAR CRY* 1960

Brother Stallen is dead! None can believe it, especially the long term patients who 27 years ago witnessed the arrival at the Colony of a young lad of 16, a rebel against God and man.

Before the Army took over Groot Chatillon Leper Colony five years ago our comrade was of all patients the most difficult. His disease took full toll of his body, destroying his hands and feet so that finally he was confined to a wheelchair and gave way to despair.

Parallel with the endeavour to ameliorate the physical condition and improve the material benefits of many hundreds of patients the Salvation Army officers conducted religious services and Home League meetings. The patients of Red Indian and Javanese stock came from the bush of the Guiana Interior and spoke Taki Taki; those from urban areas, Dutch. Many of African origin used English.

Stallen, who spoke Taki-Taki but was still a notorious rebel, was asked to translate in the meetings. Much of his bitterness sprang from frustrated teacher training. Translation appealed to him. It has happened before! The translator was much affected by the message transmitted and responding to his own words of appeal, eventually gave his heart to God.

Under the direction of the major he began to teach, educating the bush patients whose schoolmaster had until then been nature and folkloric tradition. He discovered a gift for poetry and translated English and Dutch songs into Taki Taki, compiling a song book still in use. The Gospels and vital Old Testament sections were rendered into Taki Taki. To see him laboriously using the foreshortened remainder of his hands to propel his pencil was to witness a miracle of faith.

Enrolled as the first Salvation Army soldier and with mental processes reoriented, Brother Stallen fell in love with one of the first Home League members to be converted to the worship of Christ. An Army wedding followed. Their little home was a picture. Next door was the studio wherein he wrote, controlled and fed the radio-diffusion of beautiful music over the large area of the Colony, and received the long stream of fellow patients whose problem he so well understood.

Instrument of Christ the great Physician, Brother Stallen transformed the Leprosarium. His Master called him home. The band and soldiers of Paramaribo Corps travelled the long journey on the crocodile infested river to the semi-peninsular on which Groot Chatillon stands. Full Salvation

Army honours became this humble soldier of Christ whose testimony was ever the same.

The Army reported upon takeover that everything had to be totally reorganized, and since it had stopped the sale of liquor, work therapy groups were now active including gangs to do weeding, cleaning, sanitation, tailoring, carpentry, masonry, painting and laundry.[306]

In 1955, Hurricane Janet smashed into Barbados and Grenada leaving behind widespread ruin. Three Salvation Army buildings were totally destroyed, the comrades carrying on their meetings under trees or between the broken walls of roofless buildings.[307]

The School for the Blind in Jamaica continued to make strides, opening a new hostel and workshop. Attending the Army's annual Christmas program at the school, an amazed reporter from the Star wrote, "Quietly and simply but with impressive results The Salvation Army is doing a grand job with a number of blind children and adults at their Institute on Slipe Pen Road. It was a revelation to watch so-called 'helpless' people help themselves. For nearly two hours I watched these blind children and young people of both sexes carry through a programme of entertainment that would have done credit to some of our more talented amateurs with eyes. There was not the slightest trace of nervousness or hesitancy on their part. They sang in groups and singly: they carried through a 'Keep Fit' exercise to musical accompaniment with rhythm and precision; they recited and played little sketches and capped a fine performance with a tableau of the Nativity and a play. The way in which they walked around the stage and found their positions and made straight for the exits without faltering made me think at times that they were really not blind."[308] That same year the

School for the Blind in the Bahamas received a royal visit from Princess Margaret who accepted a gift of straw mats that had been made for her.[309]

The first former students to meet and then marry from the School for the Blind were Mr. Gilbert Gordon and Miss Jestina Lucinda Clarke. They were married at The Salvation Army Corps at Port Morant.[310]

The first recipient of the Order of Distinguished Service, The Salvation Army's highest award for a non-Salvationist, went to Dr. Harry Eno of Panama in 1956 . He was cited because he "rendered distinguished service during many years and unfailingly served our cause, giving Salvationists the benefit of his medical skill as well as sponsoring and personally supporting our welfare work through practical and generous gifts, including three residences to be converted into a shelter for women."[311]

The Hanbury Home outside Mandeville, was started by two American missionaries, Pat Taylor and Millie Mylam, former students of Jamaica Bible College. In 1959, the founders asked The Salvation Army to rescue the home which, because of financial difficulties, was threatened with shutting down.[312]

Major Bruynis was appointed to take over. She was shocked at what she found: "The former management left immediately and did not wait for me to open the door. We stepped inside and were astonished to find the building stripped of everything. All the furniture, electrical equipment and fixtures were gone. Not even a bed to sleep in, neither a cup to drink from. There was nothing at all, only the ink bottle which stood on the sink in the kitchen which they probably had forgotten to take with them. There was no running water either and out of the two water tanks, one was leaking and the other was filled with at least three feet of mud. The grounds were overgrown with weeds and high grass and I did not know where I should start first. For the time being, two local people cared for the eight small girls who were sleeping in the Girls' House on wooden beds infested with bugs. The hardest part of it all was, that there was no source of income and I had to start collecting in the daytime and to clean and paint in the evenings. Mr. and Mrs. Coke invited me to their home to sleep until I could purchase a bed for myself, and to make accommodation for three young babies who were coming to join us."[313]

It seemed that the life of the Army in the Caribbean had found a steady march forward. But the whole character of the Caribbean was to change when on New Year's Day in 1959 Fidel Castro took control of Cuba.

LOST FROM SIGHT

WHEN FIDEL CASTRO took power in Cuba in 1959, it sent shockwaves throughout the world. Communism previously had been restricted largely to China, North Korea, Eastern Europe and the Soviet Union. It was now on the doorstep of the United States, the country which was taking the lead to try to check the global drive of Marxism. Although when he took power, Castro denied being a communist, he made a quick about face. The United States placed an immediate embargo on the country and then looked with anxiety around the remaining countries of the Caribbean and Latin America, all ripe for revolution because of the poor standard of living in most of them.

Adding to the tensions of the region were two power plays between the United States and Cuba. The first was a disastrous U.S. backed invasion of Cuba at the Bay of Pigs. Although the force was comprised of Cuban exiles, it was clear that the United States was behind every detail. Following this was the effort by the Soviet Union to place missiles in Cuba capable of striking the United States with atomic warheads. It looked to the world as if the faceoff between the United States and the Soviet Union would force the nations to the eve of World War III. But Soviet Premier Nikita Khrushchev backed down, disassembling the missile site. Tensions eased. But for twenty years the threat of communism was a strong undercurrent in nearly all that transpired internationally in the Caribbean and Latin America. The strategy of the United States in the region was to support any government that did not lean toward communism—even if it was headed by another dictator. And U.S. and other Western aid poured into those countries where any leftist elements might ally themselves with world communism.

In the years that followed The Salvation Army in Cuba would undergo tremendous pressure and for a while the outside world thought it had ceased to exist. But it came triumphantly through, always faithful to the Lord and to the Army.

When Castro first seized power, it did not appear that The Salvation Army had a great deal to be concerned about. Political coups were not uncommon in this region of the world and although there was always concern, The Salvation Army continually kept its focus on its mission and rode out whatever storm was blowing. There was also some optimism that things would go well for the Army since The Salvation Army had been kind to Castro when he was a student and minor league baseball player in the United States a few years earlier.

The Salvation Army set to work again during the humanitarian crisis created by Castro's taking power. The Army distributed over four tons of food, clothing and furniture, helping in excess of 25,000 people.[314] But in 1961 the Army found that their social work was being closed down institution by institution, particularly its children's homes. Its evangelical work had not yet been curtailed and the Army happily reported that there were great crowds who attended the open-air meetings with nearly every meeting recording decisions for Christ.[315]

The Salvation Army Year Book (1964) later reported, "The overall picture of the territory is clouded somewhat by the problems and restrictions faced in Cuba. Exemplary tenacity of spirit and loyalty of the divisional commander, Lt. Colonel

Claas Leegstra and his officers and soldiers . . . who maintained their witness in open-air meetings."[316] Further crackdowns were described: "Our social services in Cuba have been reduced and corps operations are now in a 'back-to-the-wall' struggle. The training college curriculum had to be greatly reduced. Two cadets comprise the present session, receiving training on weekends and on some evenings, ordinary daily occupation is vital to merit ration cards and other necessities."[317] In 1965, official communication with Cuba was ended.

Major Doreen Hobbs

CUBA

It was very difficult. Everything was lovely in the garden after the revolution. They turned police stations into schools. Then there came this Saturday when Castro got on the radio. Everyone was instructed to turn on their radio or their television on loud because he was going to speak. He spoke for nine hours. He said, "I am not a communist. I was never a communist. I will never be a communist."

One Sunday morning we got up and overnight we had become a communist state. The first thing they did was nationalise all the banks so money wasn't yours anymore, it belonged to the country. The following Sunday they nationalised all the property. There were no more landowners. Things started to become very difficult after that.

The Army had difficulties as well. But because the Army had been good to Fidel Castro when he was a student in the States we were allowed to operate when some other religions weren't. We had our moments. I was arrested more than once where I had to go to the police station and if you were leading the open-air meeting and they said you weren't supposed to be there, they'd take you in for questioning. But we always got away with it.

They tightened up quite a bit. They fell out with America. A lot of people started fleeing the island while they could still get out. I had to bring forward commissioning in January. Then they said I would get farewell orders because they were getting rid of all the foreign missionaries. I was to go to the Training College in Jamaica but it took me three months to get out of the country. Territorial headquarters sent my fare three times but the government kept confiscating it. I never got the money back because the government officials said each time that they had changed the rules.

It was a very tragic time for everybody. When you went to the airport it was so sad. So many families were being parted from one another. They would only let women and children out. They wouldn't let the men go. You went ever so early for your flight. They put you in a room to wait. People were writing notes and putting it on the glass for their relatives to read on the other side and then the people on the other side would write a note back.

They took my luggage out on the tarmac. We were allowed only one suitcase with one change of clothing. They asked which was mine and then I had to stand in the blazing sun while they searched everything. They were looking for ammunition and weapons or to see if you were taking money. But we didn't earn much money in those days. The little bit that I did have was just a few dollars but all they left me was 35 cents in change. If I hadn't been going to Jamaica where they were sending someone to meet me, I couldn't have gotten into Kingston. I never got my luggage until 18 months later. They had been through my trunks and taken out a lot of my things, replacing them with Spanish newspapers and magazines.

Life still had to go on in the rest of the Caribbean. The territory received gladly its international leaders, General and Mrs. Wilfred Kitching who visited Jamaica, Trinidad and Barbados. While in Barbados, General Kitching received the Freedom of the City. It was a large mahogany key custom-made by prisoners out of admiration for the work of Salvation Army officers over the years.[318]

In 1961, Belize once again was besieged by a monster storm when Hurricane Hattie bore down on the Central America colony. Winds of up to 175 miles per hour and gusts that topped 200 miles per hour raged against all in its path. The historic Presbyterian Church which had survived the 1931 hurricane came crashing down. Several islands off the coast were totally obliterated, their occupants never found. The storm destroyed 70 percent of Belize City.[319] Milton E. Arana described what happened, "The tidal waves came gradually at first but relentlessly until they quickened and, within an hour, the entire city was covered to a height of ten feet. In some places the waters reached fifteen feet. Evidently people who had been trapped by fallen beams or jammed doors now perished and drowned. Those who could made superhuman efforts to escape from the reach of the seeking, searching monster. People stood on top of their tables or climbed into attics or onto their roofs. Parents stood on the highest things they could find and held their children out of the reach of the water."[320]

The Salvation Army shared in the suffering. The Central Corps, a wooden structure, collapsed during the onslaught. What made it worse was that it was also a shelter. People had to go downstairs into the water to escape. A lot of Army documents and the history of what the Army had done in Belize were lost.

But again, notwithstanding its wounds, The Salvation Army set to work. The government was totally compromised since Belize City was then the capital. It had no choice but to work through the various charities. Many people were resettled in a refugee camp that eventually became a town called Hattieville, named after the storm. The Salvation Army worked among these refugees, establishing a Home League that outlasted the storm relief.[321]

In 1963, Hurricane Flora, although not as strong a hurricane as Hurricane Hattie, cut a wide swath across the Caribbean beginning with Haiti and then moving on to the islands of St. Lucia, Tobago, Trinidad, Jamaica, Barbados and Cuba.[322] The work began in Haiti, with the government entrusting food distribution for 60,000 people. In order to reach people in isolated areas, the Army drafted horses, mules and donkeys to form a pack train, sometimes as long as 500 animals, to reach those in need. For their efforts, Captain Leah Davids and Captain Kleivstolen were later decorated by President Francois Duvalier.[323]

A brand new clinic had been built in Fond-des-Negres when the hurricane struck. The storm blew off the roof and wrecked the structure before it could ever be put into use. The corps and the quarters were also badly damaged, forcing Captains Davids and Kleivstolen to sleep in their jeep for the next month.[324]

Hurricane Flora had also wreaked havoc on Tobago. Following the storm, all communications were lost and the harbor so littered with ships that no other ships could get in. Relief workers and supplies had to be disembarked offshore and brought in by lifeboats. The Salvation Army corps building and quarters were badly damaged. The officer, Captain Clinton Burrowes, set immediately to work providing assistance to those who had lost so much in the storm.[325]

But not all was storm and destruction. In 1963, Major Loddes, the officer in Curaçao, noted that a number of ships were due to be in port on Easter morning with their crews aboard. With the merchant navy chaplain and Christians from several churches, he hired a boat equipped with amplifiers and then moved from ship to ship to sing Easter hymns. Song sheets had already been distributed the night before, allowing the services to be conducted in Dutch, Norwegian and English.[326]

The Army's work among youth continued to fill a vital role. In Fond-des-Negres, a young girl fainted in class. When the captain asked why this might happen, she was told that up to 140 children each day rose before dawn and then walked to school without benefit of having breakfast. One child reportedly walked 11 miles each way. A feeding program was begun, underwritten by Christian Children's Fund.[327]

In Belize at the Listowel Farm, a forest fire threatened the Army school. The boys went out to help fight the blaze but the fire grew ever closer. The officers lifted their voices, praying for rain and in a matter of moments there was a downpour.[328] The results weren't so positive in the Bahamas. A newly acquired

Young Men's Hostel and officers' quarters burned to the ground before it could ever be put into use.[329]

The Hanbury Home continued doing vital work among the children of Jamaica. In 1964, they reported on some of their children: "One little girl spent the first year of her life in a cave and had all the attendant bad habits that kind of life produces. A baby who was taken by Major Bruynis from his home was a few hours old; the first sound he heard was the carpenter's hammer making a coffin for his mother. Two little sisters frightened like little birds came to us because of ill treatment by their own mother. They are happy children now because of the love which is given them. Another little boy came in a cardboard box; his mother had also died and he had survived on anything his seven year old sister could produce."[330]

Part of the international centennial observances in 1965 for The Salvation Army was the issuing of two commemorative postage stamps designed by Captain Ian Begley.[331] Having had no experience of preparing four-color artwork for reproduction, Captain Begley set about the challenge with the limited equipment available to him: typing paper, watercolors and India ink. The first six designs were sent off to Jamaica for submission to the authorities, but were stolen from the field secretary's car who was taking them to be photographed.

HISTORY IN THE FIRST PERSON

Major Errol Robateau

BELIZE

⸺◦❍◦⸺

I was only 16 at the time. My mother, having passed through the 1931 hurricane, decided we should not stay home, but go to a shelter. I was working at the St. Catherine's Convent at the time so that is where we went. We stayed in the middle room of the three storey building which was considered the safest. We heard a lot of banging and the wind and all that.

The next morning the wind was still strong but we looked through the window. We saw houses floating down the street in waters about 16, 17 feet high. Cars going down the road. All these things were very different for us. Chairs were floating out of the rooms downstairs.

Belize City was devastated. There were very few buildings left standing. We lost our home which was a new wooden structure. (The yard) was so clean that what I understand about it, the electricity company had some poles stored in the yard and when the water lifted them up they became missiles and they were knocking down houses as they floated by. There were also barges in the river at the time which was used to carry some kind of equipment. These also floated out over the land and knocked down a lot of houses. What the hurricane didn't do the missiles did.

It was very traumatic for me because my mother started crying. "What are we going to do?" I said, "Don't worry, Mama. I'm going to build back a house for you." And I really built back that house at the age of 16. I really marvel at myself because how I learned about it is that after I married my wife and brought her back to Belize my neighbor was telling her, "Errol built that house when he was only 16 years old." And, you know, I check back and it's true.

I became an adult so quickly because of the devastation. My neighbors died, a married couple just two houses away. The father asked them to come to the shelter but they said they were not leaving. Their twins decided to stay so the mother and two daughters all died. The father had gone to the shelter. A lot of people who died were the people who stayed in their homes.

It was very traumatic for me and it still is now. Every time I think about a hurricane I cringe because I know what can happen.

GLIMPSES

The Bride Rode a Donkey

HAITI | *ALL THE WORLD* JULY 1961

In a wholly unexpected way—to the visitor at least—the holiness meeting began with a wedding. Down the fissured roadway stumbled a small donkey bearing the bride in her Salvation Army uniform. Behind, on a horse, came the groom, then the bridesmaid and many friends and relatives. The ceremony was conducted by the Sectional Officer, Senior-Captain Egger, and the wedding party stayed for the meeting which followed.

A request was made at the conclusion of the meeting for the visiting officer, Lt. Colonel Saunders, to lead the bridal procession along the road. Here was fun! Seated upon a white horse (gift to Haiti from the Army in Switzerland), the Colonel, used to traveling on four air-filled wheels, felt far from secure, whilst the horse sensed the apprehension of its "passenger." It refused to move! Behind him at least twenty donkeys and horses, laden with members of the bridal party, waited in mute dignity for the leader. At last laughter had to break out when no amount of pushing, urging or hitting could budge that white charger.

Eventually he began to move on his reluctant way, but looking round now and then as though seeking his owner, whilst the Colonel feared that, in protest, he might suddenly break into a fierce gallop. However, the cavalcade went on its slow and dignified way, with Colonel, bride and groom and all the others in their white uniforms looking like a procession from out of the past.

GLIMPSES

Hartman Sands

THE BAHAMAS | LT. COLONEL AUSTEN, 1961

———◦✕◦———

The conversion in Nassau which affected us most deeply at the time and is still deeply etched on our hearts and minds, was that of Hartman Sands whose aunt was a soldier at Palmetto Point. When still only nineteen he stole a cheque book from a senior member of the local Methodist Church. He forged a number of cheques and misappropriated the proceeds, and when exposure appeared inevitable, he brutally murdered the old gentleman. He was arrested, tried, and condemned to death.

At the request of the family I undertook his care at the Nassau Prison. Until two weeks before his execution he made little response to all attempts to minister to him, until one morning I found him standing behind the barred gate of his cell. His face was aglow. "Major, I've found Jesus," he exclaimed, "and He has forgiven me." This was indeed true and from that day he testified to all with whom he came in contact: family, prison staff and government officials as well.

Ten minutes before I accompanied him to the scaffold he asked for a drink of water which was brought to him by the warden who also belonged to Palmetto Point. He drank the water and touching the warden's arm, he said, "Jack, do you know my Jesus? I wish you did."

Within an hour of his death I had the painful duty of conducting his funeral.

HISTORY IN THE FIRST PERSON

The Saga of The Salvation Army Centennial Stamps

THE SALVATION ARMY YEAR BOOK 1967

I have to confess to being virtually untutored . . . Art in various forms, notably oil painting, has been my hobby. . .

The territorial commander's personal invitation gave me opportunity to submit the designs for the Jamaican commemorative stamps. Nine were prepared, each portraying a distinctive feature of the Army and its work, including a girl reading Braille, against a background of Jamaican and Army flags.

The three penny, with white cap on blue, was inspired by the Swiss stamp issued some years ago . . . The white cap is worn by Salvationists in cities and villages throughout the island, and was therefore the obvious choice. My own cap placed on my desk was the model. The Army colours are seen in the yellow lettering, red trimming on the cap and blue background.

The colour scheme of the 1s. 6d. Stamp carries Jamaica's national colours, green, gold and black with the Army colours in the flag. Action and progress were ideas that had to be expressed, and this was achieved by having the Salvationists marching across the globe. Jamaica is the territorial centre for the Army in the West Indies, and the drum stick is striking the point that would mark the island of Jamaica on the globe. The men in silhouette symbolise any race and colour, as the international Army marches across the world.

From a technical standpoint I hope it will not disappoint art enthusiasts to know I used very ordinary materials . . . duplicating paper, poster paints and a brush from a ten cent store!

For an amateur, it is a thrill to receive mail with his own work on the envelope; the greater satisfaction is to know that the Army has been recognised in this way in the Caribbean and that these stamps have reached all parts of the world, reminding many people of a century of faithfulness to the call of Jesus Christ.

An urgent cable to Nassau requested a duplicate set. Later recalling the incident, Captain Begley said, "I could barely remember the detail on the six designs. I had not kept any rough

168

sketches, so simply started afresh."

The designs were resubmitted and though Captain Begley was not pleased that the paper had warped from the watercolors, the postal authorities liked the effect and reproduced the stamps exactly as submitted.[332]

General Frederick Coutts came to the Caribbean in 1966, conducting the most extensive tour of any Salvation Army General. During his visit a plaque was unveiled at the spot where the Army had its first meeting at the Myrtle Bank Hotel.[333] Among one of the more interesting events for the General was the ride in a motorboat to Groot Chatillon Leper Colony in Suriname.[334] The General also presented seven Braille machines to the School for the Blind in Jamaica, a gift from International Headquarters.[335]

In 1966, Major and Mrs. Raeburn had the honor of being presented to Queen Elizabeth at a Government House reception. The Queen asked several questions about the work of the Army in the Bahamas, taking particular interest in the work being done at the School for the Blind.[336] In Curaçao, Queen Juliana of the Netherlands toured The Salvation Army Seamen's Home.[337]

A rubella epidemic swept Jamaica in 1965 which resulted in the birth of multiple handicapped babies. To meet the needs of these children and their families, the School for the Blind in Jamaica opened a deaf and blind unit so that the children could develop according to their capabilities.[338]

A lighter note from the School for the Blind was struck in 1967 when for the Jamaica anniversary of independence celebration, a colorful float entered the parade highlighting its own rhythm group. The group of boys from the school featured a string bass made from a plywood box and a plastic clothesline. An accordion was borrowed as well as a bongo drum. A cheap set of maracas were added and for the finishing touches, a kitchen grater was borrowed (over the protests of the cook) for special effect. The band was so popular that for the next few weeks they went on a tour through Jamaica, performing to the delight of all.[339]

Major Rosemarie Haefeli

HAITI

---✕✕---

I was 14 years old when Captain and Mrs. Egger went to Haiti to start the work. They had a friend who was a medical doctor in Switzerland going to visit them. When they came back they went around visiting several corps to show the pictures. One of my schoolmates said, "Let's go to The Salvation Army on Saturday afternoon. They have a movie." It was only for children. When the doctor finished the film showing us the poor areas in Haiti, he said, "So children, when you are grownups you are going to learn something good like doctors, nurses and teachers and you can go and help these people."

I had a step-mother who was not very nice to me. She was standing in the garden when I got home. I usually got beaten up for going to The Salvation Army. I said, "I went to The Salvation Army and saw a film. When I grow up I'm going to be a nurse and I'm going to go to Haiti." She said, "Now you're crazy, completely crazy."

My aim was always Haiti from then on. I made everyone crazy because that's all I talked about. They thought I wouldn't do it. When I was 18 I had to break with home. I had to be a domestic for a year before I could go into nurse's training. I went to live with a Salvation Army couple with seven children and helped them with their children before I could go into the hospital for training. I did one year of nursing help to see if I could do it. But I was very practical and they said I could be trained.

I did three years training and then I had to give one year because I had no money so I paid when I was finished. I went to Paris to learn French. Then I went to England to learn the English language. I always ran away from the Army because I didn't want to be an officer. They said I had to be an officer because they were not sending volunteers. The top year for training was 30. The Candidates' Secretary said, "If you want to go to Haiti you must come to Training or you can't go." Haiti was my whole vocation. I said, "Okay, okay, I come to training under one condition. When I am commissioned you send me straight to Haiti."

When I came to Port-au-Prince, there was one teacher. They had 100 children ready to start school. In 1969, I arrived in October. They arranged for me to teach guitar that evening. I had to sing with these people that night in my welcome meeting. I did not speak Creole. I was ready in French. On the platform, Major Townsend said, "I want English so I can understand." I was worse in English.

We had a Swiss volunteer. He was a carpenter. He built two shacks for two classes. We started on Monday morning with the school, College Verena. I had to accept this. Not to be a nurse, to have to stay in Port-au-Prince, it was the Lord's will. I built 41 schools and 8 corps. I built the children's home in '72. We kept adding to the College Verena.

What I regret is that I could have stayed another 10 years. I would do it all again.

A more challenging feat came when six boys from the school accepted the challenge to climb Blue Mountain peak, 2256 meters (7402 feet) high. A mule went with them to carry their packs while the boys used mountain sticks to guide them up the path. In 1969, another group of boys from the school hiked across the island from Kingston to Montego Bay.[340] A further landmark occurred in 1972 when Lt. Meltia Hamilton, a graduate of the School for the Blind, became the first blind cadet in the West Indies and Central America Territory.[341] He was commissioned in 1974.

The School for the Blind had long outgrown its facilities at Slipe Pen Road. But with no funds available there seemed little that could be done. The officer in charge tried to raise funds by sending the children out with collecting cards but this provided only a pittance in comparison to what construction costs would be.[342] The answer came in 1968 with the vision of the territorial commander, Colonel William Chamberlain. He contacted the four USA territories, asking them each to contribute $50,000. That, with the money already collected by the school and a grant from the Jamaican government for $115,000, would be enough to start the construction. At the time, 90 percent of educated blind people in Jamaica came through the School for the Blind.[343] The new facility was completed and dedicated in 1972.

Always trying to find ways to support the work as well as provide meaningful training and work for those at the School for the Blind in the Bahamas, Captain Ian Begley noted that many of the mops sold in the Bahamas came from a blind workshop in Florida. Going to Florida to visit the blind workshop, he came back to the Bahamas, bought the equipment needed and started manufacturing mops at the Bahamas School for the Blind. Having spent money he didn't have, he approached the Lions Club whose members donated funds to replace what had already been invested. He then approached the American Women's Club and received enough money for a second machine.

When the first mops were manufactured, Mrs. Captain Mary Begley took them to a local grocer to ask if he would sell them. He laughed when he heard that they were made by blind people and to prove what he supposed to be shoddy workmanship, he tried to yank the mop head off. After a while he gave up and bought the mops. The Army soon cornered the market for mop sales in the Bahamas.

Seeking to improve productivity, Captain Ian Begley approached Tucker, who had been turning out about a dozen mops a day. Challenging him to do better, Begley promised Tucker he would give him a ten cent per mop bonus. The next day Tucker manufactured 112 mops![344] Begley later approached the Rotary Club about building a two story building for the School for the Blind. They accepted the challenge, conducting a community wide fundraiser and triumphantly turned the building over for the Army's ministry.[345] The new facility would be dedicated in 1971.[346]

The work among the blind extended to Haiti the next year

when a Workshop for the Blind and Handicapped was opened in Port-au-Prince.[347] Sergeant André Sanon, who was blind himself, went to Jamaica to learn skills that he could use when he worked with the blind in Haiti. The workshop eventually employed 44 people, a combination of blind and other handicapped workers, to make woodenware products.[348]

Colonel Walter Morris made history by becoming the first West Indian to both be promoted to the rank of Colonel and to be made Chief Secretary, the second highest position in the territory. Morris had a notable career with the excellence of his service recognized by the Jamaican government when he was presented with "Officer of the Order of Distinction (O.D.) for services in the field of Religion and Social Welfare."[349] Another milestone for the territory was reached when Major Leah Davids became the first woman divisional commander when she was appointed to that position in Haiti in 1972.[350] Colonel Morris would be followed into his appointment by Lt. Colonel Dorothy Purser, the first woman to serve as Chief Secretary, in 1974.[351]

Major changes were made at the Army center in Havendale. The Westerham Boys Training Home was closed because the area, which had once been rural, was now being absorbed by the urban expansion of Kingston. Fifty acres of the site were sold to purchase an 800 acre site in St. James Parish about 10 miles away from Montego Bay. Replacing Westerham was the new Willamsfield Training Centre. This was opened by Prime Minister Hugh Lawson Shearer on June 22, 1969.[352] The property had belonged to the Foster family for more than a hundred years. Originally a sugar plantation that included the ruins of the factory, it still had portions of an aqueduct that carried water more than a mile to power the mill.[353]

Major Leah Davids

HAITI | *ALL THE WORLD* JANUARY 1961

——————

When I traveled with the Sectional Officer, Senior-Captain Jacques Egger, and a territorial headquarters (THQ) furloughing officer, Senior-Major Rollock, to Port-au-Prince, the THQ visitor made a report of the first forty miles of the journey, with the following results: 77 extremely bad patches where it was possible to be bogged; 87 bad patches, five rivers crossed and one lake that had to be driven through.

We were bogged once, had to be pushed twice, had to leave the main road three times and pass through someone's garden. Traveling time was four hours.

Ordinary cars have ceased to work on this road. Only trucks and jeeps are seen. In many places the mud is piled as high as three feet in the middle of the road where some vehicles have been "dug out." This is not a road but a nightmare. The THQ visitor stood in the tracks of the vehicles and the mud banks came up to her waist; she could lean on her elbow on the side. It is only these dried mud banks that keep many of the trucks from turning over. As they roll from side to side they often hit the mud bank and then that rights them.

The Captain removed the fan belt from the jeep to pass through the lake (which has risen above road level) and over the bridge and then through the lake again. For some years this lake has been rising until now the water is about eighteen inches deep over the bridge and two feet deep over the road. The engines stopped before we could reach dry ground. The water was about two inches deep in the back of the jeep and we all had to take off our shoes. We would have loved a photograph but dare not open the door to get out. Several men in the water tried to push us out, but this was no good. Fortunately the engines started again and we got out all right. People have to wade through this water day after day, that is unless they take a boat. Our biggest laugh over this is the fact that there were two rather large rowing boats there, and they were now rowing over the bridge.

———

Windsor Lodge took its place among the essential services to youth in 1972. In explaining the decision to ask the Army to assume control of Windsor Lodge, the Honorable Allan Douglas said, "For two years we planned to open this children's home—and we wondered how we could run the home. We then resolved to approach an organization that already won an award for running the best kept children's home in Jamaica. The Salvation Army!" The home was intended for 20 children between the ages of one and five years old who had been neglected or abandoned.[354]

Then, after years of silence, surprising proof came to light that The Salvation Army was still alive in Cuba.

HIDDEN VICTORY

IN 1973, MAJOR FRANCISCO RAMIREZ traveled to Jamaica to attend the Caribbean Conference of Churches. There, quite unexpectedly, he ran into Colonel John Needham, territorial commander for the West Indies and Central America Territory. Needham thought, as did everyone in the Army world, that the Army had ceased to exist in Cuba. Major Ramirez remembers, "I will never forget his reaction. He saw the Spanish words on my old hat. He looked at me with disbelief but also with gratitude in his eyes. We both thanked God for His faithfulness and asked Him to bless and guide the Army in Cuba." After writing down the names of the existing corps, Ramirez reported that after the Revolution, only a dozen officers remained in Cuba. The government applied great pressure on the Army, slowly taking away what they could. The children's homes were all closed. Open-airs were outlawed. Selling of *The War Cry* was banned. Uniforms were not allowed to be worn. Social work was ended and Salvationists were not allowed to invite people to their meetings. No contact with The Salvation Army anywhere in the world was allowed.[355] There remained, however, a faithful core of Salvationists who pressed on through all the difficulties, praying and believing for a better day. In other communist countries, The Salvation Army had been totally banned. At least in Cuba they were allowed to continue to exist, even if under duress.

Colonel Needham hastily arranged a visit to Cuba to see for himself what was happening. While there he declared three new corps to be opened and enrolled eight soldiers. He was able to report that there remained eight officers, 13 cadets, four Aux/Captains, one envoy and one sergeant. The lone social work program that continued in the Army's hands was the William Booth Home for the Aged, which cared for 60 people.[356] The following November, Colonel Needham returned to Cuba for the commissioning of the 13 cadets of the Soldiers of the Cross session in the Anglican Holy Trinity Cathedral.[357]

Encouraging word also came out of Costa Rica, recently re-opened in 1972 by Major and Mrs. Bernard Smith. Seeing a desperate need in San Jose, Smith opened a center for alcoholics.[358] *All the World* chronicled what was happening in the program:

> Opening last year with "begged and borrowed" furniture which Major (Bernard Smith) painted himself, The Salvation Army project has been rewarded with a 34 percent success rate in alcoholic rehabilitation. The only in-training centre in Costa Rica, the centre is not for "bums and drunks but for alcoholics who want to be rehabilitated," and Major Smith runs it with discipline and determination.
>
> The men work at outside jobs and come home every night to their special sleeping loft, to a hot dinner and whatever communal activity is scheduled for that evening. They are living in security, among friends, and they pay 50 colones a week and contribute what else they can. They stay until they wish to leave.
>
> In what is practically a one-man operation, there is an almost military discipline established. "People don't like the word 'army' or what it implies," Major Smith says, "But we must run this community with unbreakable rules and we reward good behaviour."
>
> No one is evicted without being given a second and third chance. Fifty percent of the men have, at one time or another, left

and then, when they could handle the shame, returned.

In the USA The Salvation Army's success rate is only about 25 percent and the American Medical Association reports a startling one percent success rate in its chemical therapy.[359]

The work in Haiti continued at a quick pace. The Army opened a food depot and food distribution center. Up to 40,000 pounds of food was purchased at any one time. It was then stored and sent as needed. With 17,000 children attending Salvation Army schools in Haiti, feeding programs, children's homes and other centers, the need was constant.[360]

In Suriname, the Ramoth Children's Home was opened on land donated to The Salvation Army by the Alvarez sisters.[361] The home provided landmark service in Paramaribo, taking children from infancy and keeping them, if need be, to adulthood. Because of this and other services of the Army, at the Army's Golden Jubilee celebration the governor of the colony, Mr. J. Ferrier, said, "Everyone knows that when we speak of the Army in Suriname, we mean The Salvation Army."[362]

Concern for what happened with the students once they left the School for the Blind in Jamaica led Colonel Needham to push for a training center for blind adults. A new workshop was opened in 1974 to give vocational training. At the workshop, the men and women worked at re-silvering mirrors and flatware, crafting leather to make items such as wallets, belts and key cases and the refurbishing of hotel furniture.[363]

Not long after this, Jamaica was visited by recording artist Stevie Wonder. At his concert at the National Stadium in Kingston, to the surprise of everyone, Wonder called Captain Gladys Lucario to the stage to present a cheque for $23,000— half of the proceeds from the concert.[364] He then came the next day to the School for the Blind, giving a two-hour private performance to the young people.[365]

Anitredebie Maharban

SURINAME

—◦◦✕◦◦—

I came into the children's home as one of the babies and grew up in it. I don't know the reason why I was placed in that children's home. I did not grow up with my parents. I only know what someone told me. I grew up with different races in that home like brothers and sisters. Different people came to work there so it is not like we always had the same people around who led us there.

At five I started going to The Salvation Army corps. I didn't know much. I liked going to church because there was singing, learning about the Bible.

For me it was different when I went to school to see some parents coming into the home. You always look when you see parents coming seeing the children. It was difficult because no one came for me. I was always sad. I didn't feel good about that. I didn't see my mother until I was 19. My father used to come to pay but I didn't know him. Seeing my mother it was a real hard time when my mother came to look for me. I couldn't call her "Ma" because I wondered, who was that lady? She died three years ago.

There were a lot of children and we were just like one family. A few grew up there like me but some I saw leave. I have stayed in contact with them. Some still come back and visit the home.

I now work with the children in the home as an intern sister. I left there for six years to live three years with someone from the Army and then three years with someone else from the Army. They asked me to come back and work.

Sometimes I remember what it was like to live there as a child. Sometimes you want to place yourself when the children are in different situations. Some know I grew up there. Sometimes when you sit with them you tell them a story from when you were small. They listen. Sometimes they ask me how I feel to be working there. I tell them it is not hard because I love children and even as a child I loved being with the other children.

I always see Ramoth Children's Home as my first home. I say that if it were not for that home I don't know where I would have ended up. I'm glad I am in The Salvation Army now. I say that Ramoth is a blessed place. In that home it is like a Christian home where you can learn about Jesus and the Bible. And we try to take very good care of the children. If I leave Ramoth, I will still never leave The Salvation Army.

The Salvation Army did a lot of things for me.

In 1975 Hurricane Fifi ploughed into Honduras leaving 6,000 dead and over 30,000 homeless. There was no Salvation Army work at the time but the Army responded nonetheless. Major Hortense Townsend and Major Bernard Smith went in immediately to assess the damage and to offer The Salvation Army's help.[366] In addition to providing over $2 million in food, clothing, medicine and vehicles, the Army set up a 200-bed field hospital that had been donated by the USA state of Alabama. Although the Army withdrew in a few months, the hospital remained, serving a community of 85,000 and permanently named "The Salvation Army Hospital."[367]

The work of the Army continued to expand, now in Venezuela. Urgent calls went out to expand the work after a visit from the territorial commander merited a civic function where over 1,000 were on hand to express appreciation for the Army's work.[368] The solid growth in St. Vincent was evidenced by a new feeding center that provided over 400 meals a day to school children.[369]

HISTORY IN THE FIRST PERSON

Major Stanley Griffin

NEVIS

—◦|◉|◦—

There is no Salvation Army in my homeland of Nevis. The way I met it was through an American couple, Majors Henry and Lily Russell who were serving in the Caribbean. They came to Nevis on vacation where they visited the church where my father was the pastor. They struck up an immediate friendship with my parents that lasted over the years.

The Russells arranged for us to receive the Caribbean *War Cry*. I did not know anything about The Salvation Army so when I responded to an advertisement for officers, I thought it would be a great opportunity to join the regular army. I had no idea it was recruiting people for the ministry.

The Salvation Army headquarters in Antigua responded to my application and sent me a one way ticket to Antigua to join "the Army."

It was only after I arrived that I discovered I had applied for ministry in

The Salvation Army. I wanted to go back home but they told me that I would have to pay for my own ticket. So I stayed and got involved. That was in December 1975.

In 1977, I entered the training college and despite the strange beginning I had, I have felt God's blessing on me, the only officer to have ever come from the island of Nevis.

Although there had been a couple of short-lived efforts to form Advisory Boards in the territory, this vital function of Salvation Army life became firmly rooted across the Caribbean, starting in the Bahamas in 1976. The *Nassau Guardian* reported:

Brigadier Lawrence K. Pickering, Acting Regional Commander, has announced the formation of a Salvation Army Advisory Board for the Commonwealth of the Bahamas, as provided for in the organization of The Salvation Army. "The purpose of the Advisory Board," Brigadier Pickering explained, "is purely advisory. It is not a separate legal entity, nor has it any executive or administrative authority.

"On the other hand, we feel that the Board can be of incalculable help to The Salvation Army, assisting us in the conduct of our various activities by being familiar with all phases of the operations of The Salvation Army in the Bahamas. We will ask the Board to formulate plans for the improvement of our facilities and programme, and to make recommendations with respect to widening our services to the community, fund raising, public relations and expenditures."[370]

On February 1, 1976 an earthquake leveled Guatemala. Although The Salvation Army had been at work in that country years before, a new government had banned it. However, in the present crisis, a desperate country was pleased to have any available assistance. The Salvation Army responded with Major Bernard Smith taking the lead on the ground. Over 30 Spanish speaking officers and soldiers from Mexico, Central America, the United States and Jamaica rushed to Guatemala.[371] The government asked the Army to take responsibility for reconstructing the town of Tecpán in the south central part of the country. Cadets Donald Faulkner and David Mothershed, the former with a degree in engineering, the latter with architectural experience, were co-opted from the USA Southern Territory to head the project. Tasked with building 200 homes, there existed no manufacturing capability. A complete cement block was imported, with local people employed to start making concrete blocks. A simple earthquake-proof home was designed and rushed into production to try to complete the project before rainy season began.[372]

HISTORY IN THE FIRST PERSON

Captain Marcel Pierre

HAITI | *ALL THE WORLD* JANUARY 1962

—◦◦✕◦◦—

I work in Haiti, a beautiful little island in the West Indies, the name of which means high land, and I am responsible for two corps and five outposts. This is what is involved in a visit to one of them—Couillot, for instance. It will be a day in the mountains.

I rise at four in the morning, saddle my horse and fasten on the bags, all packed and prepared with foods and medicines the previous night. Then I set off. As I jog along I am thinking of the people and the things I must do; for there is the clinic, the school and the corps. After riding for about four hours, I come to the river, where I dismount, have a wash, take my breakfast and I have a few moments of rest.

As the sun by this time is blazing down, I proceed up the narrow rugged mountain pathway. By eleven o'clock I am in sight of my corps, where many people have anxiously gathered to receive medical treatment and food. There are no doctors or nurses available to tend to the needs of the people, and consequently there are many diseases, and much malnutrition.

After lunch I open the clinic, giving injections and various medical treatments to all who are in need. Then I inspect the school and the work of the children.

In the evening I hold a meeting, and many people come from all parts of the mountain. There are those who kneel to seek God in every meeting and the corps is getting bigger. This, I feel, is the seal of God upon my consecration. God is prospering the Army work on the mountainside. Although I am very tired after such a day, I am happy in the knowledge that He is a rewarder of faith. I was not brought up in the Army but God called me, and I am day by day striving to do His will, finding in it my supreme happiness and joy.

Included in the construction of Tecpán was a corps building in the center of town that doubled as a multi-purpose center. A grateful country readmitted The Salvation Army with another corps opened in Guatemala City. When the project was finished, it was dedicated by the president of Guatemala who was effusive in his praise for the work of The Salvation Army, not just in Tecpán but in the whole country.

The Williamsfield Training Center that had only opened a few years ago was closed in 1976. It represented a lost opportunity and an example of poor management on the part of The Salvation Army. The beginning was extremely promising, with 800 acres of prime farmland that included one of the purest springs of water in the whole country of Jamaica. The main problems centered around officers being sent as administrators who had no knowledge of farming, a lack of adequate investment to guarantee a return and a failure to understand how to relate to the surrounding community, all vital to the farm's success. Even when the property was sold it was handled poorly because the local Advisory Board was ignored, resulting in the property being sold for a fraction of its worth.[373]

On October 1, 1976 a reorganization of the work in Central and South America and the Caribbean resulted in the creation of a new territory called the Mexico and Central America Territory. Transferred from the West Indies and Central America Territory were the countries of Venezuela, Panama, Costa Rica and the embryonic work in Guatemala. The remaining portion of the old territory was renamed the Caribbean Territory.[374]

HISTORY IN THE FIRST PERSON

Major Ivy Staine

JAMAICA

I tossed and turned throughout the night because I had said, "No." But what else could I have said? I'd been asked to take in a three-day-old baby! What could I do with a three-day-old baby? We already had 62 children in the home!

A newly born infant needs a lot of time and attention—more than we could give it with our small staff. I told myself I had done the right thing in saying "No," rolled over and tried to go to sleep again. But I tossed and turned!

It was only a few days off Christmas. I had been out on the streets with Salvationists from all over town collecting for the Christmas Kettle appeal, which would give us some much-needed dollars. It was Christmas and I had said, "No" to a little baby! . . . "No" to Jesus: or rather, to Mary and Joseph; under the circumstances that was the same thing. I told myself, "Now here was I saying 'No' to a little baby, and Jesus had said that what we do to anyone belonging to Him we do to Him."

So next day we added a four-day-old baby to our family.

HISTORY IN THE FIRST PERSON

Lt. Colonel Henry Rostett

HAITI | *ALL THE WORLD* APRIL 1976 | MRS. MAJOR JANET PARKES

When two young officers arrived to extend the work, the Colonel gladly accepted Captain Egger's invitation to accompany him when he took the two officers to their appointment. The heavily laden jeep heaved and groaned its way over 80 miles of treacherous road—the journey took nearly 12 hours. When the officers arrived in Fond-des-Negres they found a small hall and their quarters—a small wooden and zinc house with no electricity or running water. There was little to cheer them. The needs of the people were overwhelming, funds were limited; the young officers knew they would be isolated . . .

As Lt. Colonel Rostett made the return journey to Port-au-Prince he was strangely quiet. To the accompaniment of the noise of the jeep's engine and the conversation with Captain Egger, he was thinking of the vast needs and opportunities he had seen and of the tremendous help that was required. Perhaps he could help—but how? Moved as he was by the dedication of the officers, he was unprepared for the challenging request of Captain Egger who, saying good-bye to the visitor at the airport said, "Why not come back and help us, Colonel?" So, six years after retirement Lt. Colonel Rostett stretched out his hand to shake Captain Egger's hand in farewell. "Yes," he said, "I'll come back and help you with the work."

How little the Colonel knew then what opportunities for service in Haiti would open up to him. He has been "going back" to Haiti for 14 years now, spending from two to seven months working amongst "the friendly and beautiful people," as he calls Haitians. The months spent each year in Haiti entail conducting meetings and also helping to build and repair halls and quarters and constructing hall benches. The Colonel is quite an expert in using carpentry tools—and he is still a deft hand at painting a hall. His work has been a labour of love, for he has received no remuneration; in fact, he has provided his own travelling costs and other expenses. His annual visit had been a source of inspiration to all Salvationists, for it has entailed hours in the saddle visiting mountain corps or bouncing in a jeep over hazardous roads.

Back home in the USA the Colonel spends the remainder of the year still working for Haiti. Through lectures and slides he tells the story of the Army's remarkable work in that country and what possibilities there are for expanding that work. It is a point of principle with Lt. Colonel Rostett never to ask for any money for Haiti, but he prays that God will touch the hearts of his listeners, and during the past 14 years he has received between $80,000 and $90,000 (much of it coming from non-Salvationists) for the Army's work in Haiti. No expenses whatsoever are deducted from gifts— the Colonel himself pays all postage and travelling costs. Every year Lt. Colonel Rostett obtains paid employment from the Army—standing a Christmas kettle on the streets of Miami—but he never sees a cent of his remuneration for, at this specific request, the money is sent directly to Haiti.

Meeting this tall and sprightly retired officer with his genial personality, one finds him reticent to talk about anything he has done for Haiti, but he

talks readily of the wonderful Haitian Salvationists. He is still saddened by
the tremendous needs in the country, but alive to the opportunities that
present themselves to the Army daily. He loves the country and its people.
As he says, "I have Haiti on my heart."

In Antigua, the first basic school in that country was opened
by Mrs. Major Hazel Pyle at the St. John's Corps. Recalling what
was involved in getting it running, she said, "We began in April
1977 with three children. The following week more came until
we had 130 children coming to the school. One of the things
that amazed me is that when other schools opened we would
hear them advertising to have students come to them. We never
advertised but we were always full. Even after I retired, people
would stop me on the street and say, 'Mrs. Pyle, your boy is
doing well in the States,' or some beautiful lady will come up to
me and tell me she was a student in our school and now she is
enrolling her child."[375]

In June, 1978 the Barbados government approached The
Salvation Army which agreed to take over a feeding program it
had begun among the homeless, supplemented by the delivery
of meals to indigent people who were housebound.[376]

In 1980, after an absence of nearly 30 years, The Salvation
Army flag once again flew in French Guiana. A small group of
Haitian Salvationists moved to French Guiana. With no Salvation Army present they tried to join other churches. But they
missed the Army and on their own, started meeting together
under the leadership of a soldier named Michel Christel. Writing a letter to the divisional commander of Haiti, Major Alfred
Pierre, he requested Salvation Army materials and affiliation
with the Army. Pierre sent the materials but advised him that
he was not authorized to allow affiliation as this was the provi-
dence of territorial headquarters. One of the matters that had

to be resolved before moving forward was that French Guiana was a colony of France and because the work that existed there before was part of the France Territory, there needed to be a release to allow the Caribbean Territory to assume responsibility. This was readily given by the France Territory, clearing the way to move forward with development.

Territorial leaders Colonel and Mrs. Orval Taylor, were accompanied by Major Alfred Pierre, who acted as their translator, as they set off to see for themselves what this exciting opportunity offered. At the airport the party was greeted with Salvationists waving Army flags and shouts of "Hallelujah!" A weekend of meetings was scheduled during which 14 senior soldiers and two junior soldiers were enrolled.[377] Six months later on October 1, 1980 with International Headquarters' approval, the work was opened and the first officers were appointed.[378] The opening ceremony was televised with a march that, though missing the familiar drum, tambourine or any other musical instrument, proceeded with the jubilant singing of Salvationists.[379]

The changes in Cuba could be seen in 1981 when General and Mrs. Arnold Brown visited, welcomed not only by Salvationists but by religious leaders and diplomats. Conditions had slowly improved for The Salvation Army as restrictions were eased over time. Uniforms were allowed once more and more freedom given for the Army to carry on its activities. There was still great pressure on The Salvation Army, the Salvationists never knowing when things might change or when a bureaucrat might decide it was time to crack down on them again.[380] Colonel and Mrs. Edward Read, while serving as territorial leaders, visited the island and upon entry had their Bibles and Song Books confiscated on the grounds that they were "seditious literature."[381]

Major Voyans Morancy

In 1978 and 1979 some Haitians came here looking for work: Michel Christel, Edel Hyacinth, Silva Servant. They saw that their numbers were growing. Christel was Salvationist from Aquin. He rounded up Salvationists and started meetings because he did not feel welcome in other churches. They met in one of the quarters on Sunday mornings.

Evangelical churches were not easy to find, only two or three at that time. When Major Jonchal came there were only 12-15 people meeting in a sitting room. He launched out and so the Army began to grow. They looked for a place to rent. People were not pleased the Army was coming in so we had to move. Eventually he found a place and spent about 15 years there.

I was attending a church called Christian Mission. I looked for the Army but couldn't find them. Then Christel came to one of our meetings and I asked him where they were meeting. I was there the next Sunday and that was that. I was the first Soldier to be sworn in and then the first Candidate.

Genevieve Evans

BAHAMAS | *NASSAU GUARDIAN* MAY 9, 1981

One fateful day acid was thrown in her face, and it literally sizzled away one of her most precious gifts—the gift of sight.

My sister wanted to slaughter the man. And my mother died without ever speaking to him again. I told them they had to learn to forgive. My children took it calmly. It wasn't done on purpose. Just in the heat of the moment. He was pretty sorry afterwards. I had a big adjustment to make, and I was in the hospital for almost two months. Dr. Steele-Perkins told me one day that I wouldn't ever see again, and I accepted it right away. I simply placed my life in the Lord's hand and asked Him to accept me. He did.

I was very worried about how I'd support my three children. The Family and Childcare Division came in and took my two girls, who were two and three years at the time. My son, who was born totally deaf, was 12 years at the time and I kept him with me. I have the girls now . . . they were only there for two years. The eldest one came out when she was 5 years, and

189

the social worker used to come by every month to see if I was capable of coping. I also began getting a disability cheque from the government and The Salvation Army was paying me a small salary—that's how I managed. I haven't seen the Family and Childcare people for quite a while but they told me if I ever need help, to call.

After learning Braille at the Army school for two years she was approached by Mrs. Captain John Fisk. Mrs. Fisk asked me if I would like to teach the subject. I started in September. At the time, the Ministry of Education was in need of another teacher and told me if they could find two more subjects to teach, I would be hired. Now I teach Braille, Abacus, English language, vocabulary, math, general science, history and geography. I like teaching very much and hope that when I finish my teachers' studies and get my certificate, I can apply for a government job in one of the public schools and perhaps teach a remedial class—a small one, perhaps.

It was difficult coping with my son at the time I lost my sight. He was aggressive and mischievous, but with the help of The Salvation Army and Dr. Sandra Dean-Patterson, I learned how to handle him. Besides, I know a little sign language and between the two of us, we have a special language, where we use our hands to communicate pretty well.

The Salvation Army was placed in a very embarrassing position by unrest at the School for the Blind in Jamaica. Beginning in 1980, there were a series of public protests at the school involving students and staff masterminded by one of the officers on staff. When she was transferred to the Bahamas, the last of the protests received television, radio and newspaper coverage. The protest failed to have its desired effect, resulting in the officer resigning with no further demonstrations following.[382]

In Guyana, after nearly 40 years of operation by The Salvation Army, the Belfield Girls School was handed back over to a socialist government that preferred social institutions not be handled by private organizations.[383] And in Jamaica, the experiment with the Workshop for the Blind proved to be unsuccessful. It closed quietly in May 1982.[384]

Major Mike Rich, great-grandson of pioneer Colonel Abram

Davey and himself blind, became the administrator of the School for the Blind in Jamaica. Another link to the past came in French Guiana when Commissioner Charles Péan, the officer who headed up the Army's efforts to close down Devil's Island, returned in 1983 for the fiftieth anniversary of his arrival in French Guiana.[385]

In 1983, the United States invaded Grenada, prompted by the Marxist government's construction of an airstrip that could accommodate heavy bombers. During the emergency there was no damage to Army property and in the best Salvation Army tradition, the soldiers assisted Lt. and Mrs. Arthur Richards in distributing food and meeting the needs of the Grenadian people.

The year 1987 was a significant one—the one hundredth anniversary of The Salvation Army in the Caribbean. It was decided that such an auspicious milestone deserved a special celebration culminating in a congress being planned. Colonel David Baxendale, the territorial commander, was confronted with the problem of how to have a Caribbean congress when money was in short supply. He recalls, "I went to the local travel agency and got airfares for 14 countries and added in the two Jamaica divisions, so I even included Bahamas! It came to $92,000! This included the printing of the programs and our THQ staff at the hotel, etc. I wrote and told this to (Commissioner) Bill Roberts and then prayed a lot. You can't imagine the surprise I felt and the thrill to open his letter saying that the Chancellor and he had discussed this along with a check for $92,000! Praise the Lord! I wrote and told each division to send their leaders and corps officers and possibly two candidates or more. Bermuda, which used to be a part of the territory, was sending some folks as was Panama, which also had formerly been a part of the Caribbean. We ended up having over 2,000 come and we stayed in a government hotel, which donated a suite for General Burrows as well as a full-time cook and eating area. We had several former territorial commanders or widows of former territorial commanders like Mrs. Commissioner Ethel Chamberlain, and Mrs. Commissioner Needham, and Mrs. Saunders, as well as Commissioner and Mrs. Orval Taylor. All the meetings were held in the same hotel and in the same big ballroom."[386] Special guest for the event was General Eva Burrows accompanied by the International Secretary for the Americas and the Caribbean, Commissioner and Mrs. William H. Roberts. The General presented a special centenary Salvation Army flag to the territory and presented the Certificate of Exceptional Service to Mary Beryl Browning of Suriname, Major Rosa Marie Haefeli of Haiti, Annie Wallace of Jamaica and Bandmaster Alfred Lewis of Antigua.[387]

When Prime Minister Edward Seaga greeted the General at his private residence, he told her that he had been born in a Salvation Army hospital in New York. He told her, "There is no other institution which ministers to the poor and the disadvantaged in the way The Salvation Army does, and I want to thank you. We in Jamaica find comfort in the fact that you engage in this ministry, for in my opinion, this is the essence of what the Church is all about."[388]

Other efforts to mark the centennial year included the publication of the Caribbean Territory's first history book, *Jewels of the Caribbean* by Major Doreen Hobbs.[389] In Suriname, commemorative stamps were issue.[390]

Colonel and Mrs. Baxendale traveled to Cuba to share with the comrades there. Since the plane only came once a week, a week's worth of activities was planned. The territorial leaders did a round of inspections and held a number of meetings. Baxendale recalls one unforgettable sight, "The last meeting on Sunday night was a real climax and unusual. Six teenage girls were going to do a timbrel drill but they had no uniforms. However, Air Jamaica had donated flight attendants' uniforms which they wore. They had no music so they played a tape of Herp Albert's Tijuana Brass, which was the jazziest number we have ever heard a timbrel drill done to."[391] When it was time to depart, the Baxendales gathered in a secluded spot at the airport so they could have prayer with the Cuban officers that came. In the semi-darkness they prayed and wept as they prepared to leave them behind.[392]

In 1986 a flood in St. Ann Parish in Jamaica was met with the usual emergency response by the Army. But the territorial commander, Colonel David Baxendale, was concerned that each time there was a disaster the Army had to scramble to find supplies. Consequently, a disaster warehouse was built and dedicated in early 1988. No one at the time could know how timely that construction was. Hardly had the paint dried when Hurricane Gilbert ravaged Jamaica.

ADULTHOOD ATTAINED

HURRICANE GILBERT was nothing short of an epic storm. On September 12, 1988, it crashed into Jamaica as a Category 3 storm, the second largest in diameter of any hurricane recorded. Before it had blown out it reached Category 5, the highest ranking for a hurricane. For nine days it terrorized the Caribbean and the Gulf of Mexico. So fearsome was this storm that the USA National Weather Service retired the name, never to be used for a hurricane again. When it finished, 433 people were dead with property damage in excess of US$7.1 billion, a staggering amount in an area of the world filled with impoverished nations.[393]

The most affected island was Jamaica where it came ashore at Morant Bay, tracking westward until it exited at Negril. Had a path been designed it could not have wreaked more damage. When it left Jamaica, 200,000 people were homeless, nearly 10 percent of the total population. Three out of every five homes were at least partially damaged. For some parts of the island it was months before electricity, water and telephone service could be restored.

The hurricane provided a terrible spectacle to those who were in it. Major Keith Graham recalls watching the roof on the Francis Ham Home for the Elderly "roll back like a page in a book."[394] The Salvation Army sustained heavy damage to 70 of its buildings, the worst being the Morant Bay Corps and School where nothing was left but the concrete slab the buildings stood on. The School for the Blind lost half of its roof, while throughout the duration of the storm the children and staff huddled in terror. The Francis Ham Home for the Elderly was effectively destroyed. At Hanbury Home for Children, the boys' section lost it entire roof while at Windsor Lodge the roof lifted off and some of the walls blew down. Children had to be evacuated in the height of the storm. Territorial headquarters was also badly damaged. Massive destruction was done to Army buildings in Lucea, Cave Mountain, Port Maria, Buff Bay, St. Ann's Bay, Lime Hall, Linstead, Montego Bay and Falmouth. Added to that were losses of furnishings and equipment.[395]

Before it even knew the full extent of damage, the Army leapt into action. Within 24 hours of the storm's passing, the Army had taken over the National Arena, serving 6,000 meals to storm survivors the first day. During the weeks that followed, shelters scattered across the island served over 12,000 people a day.[396] The Army then moved to other aid. In the first two months following the hurricane it recorded staggering statistics: food distribution serving 73,032 parcels containing rice, flour, sugar, corn meal, corned beef, sausages, sardines as well as other food that was donated and available. Clothing was distributed to 21, 813 families. Another 1,934 families received beds, mattresses and stoves, complete with a cylinder of gas.

What makes these numbers even more impressive is that not only did so many of the Army properties suffer damage, making distribution all the more challenging, but even before the storm 60 percent of the corps had no telephone service and 80 percent had no vehicle.[397]

While the storm raged, territorial commander Colonel David Baxendale was in California attending a Salvation Army

International Conference of Leaders. As word came, he had an impromptu meeting called by Chief of the Staff Commissioner Ron Cox with Salvation Army representatives from the developed world. Already major corporations as well as individual donors were sending financial contributions to alleviate the suffering of the Jamaican people, but none of those funds could be used to replace lost or damaged Salvation Army properties. What could be done to help repair and rebuild The Salvation Army in Jamaica? After hearing the problem they all agreed to do what they could to help. The four USA territories each initiated financial campaigns, eventually raising over $2 million. The money enabled the Army to effect repairs on 75 of the damaged buildings.[398]

The most moving story of efforts on behalf of Jamaica was word from Commissioner Varampettan Sughanantham of the India South Eastern Territory, one of the world's poorest areas, that a "Jamaica Sunday" had been held in the corps, raising 3,000 rupees (US equivalent: $212) to help the poor in Jamaica.[399]

There was wonderful response to the need internationally. The Kiwanis Club of Kingston channelled 19 containers of supplies from Canada to the Army. The Philip Morris Company, owners of General Foods, flew down 80,000 pounds of food supplies which were distributed within four days. USA Ambassador Michael Sotihhos arranged for Galaxy transport planes to bring in 150,000 pounds of building materials and other necessities to help the storm victims. Hess Stores donated US$1.5 million in new clothing. The Dorothy Burns Charitable Trust allocated £50,000 to help western Jamaica .

With all the wonderful assistance, there were some things that were not so helpful. Among the donations sent to Jamaica for the victims were heavy coats, snow boots, fur coats and children's sleds. One American corps officer told the story of a call he received. The voice on the other end originated from a veteran's organization, relating that they just had a dinner and now were able to give the Army 1,000 "slightly used tea bags!"[400]

Lt. Colonel Clinton Burrowes, reflecting on what happened, said, "The Salvation Army responded to every nook and cranny. The government believed in us. We had a system where people registered and were interviewed after the initial response. We had a sheet on every centre. When the government auditors came they were amazed. They listed The Salvation Army as the best organized agency."[401]

The emergency disaster building that had been built at territorial headquarters allowed The Salvation Army to quickly respond. Having proved its worth, a second such building was constructed in Montego Bay to serve the western part of the island in the months following Hurricane Gilbert.[402]

GLIMPSES

Mr. Townsend

LT. COLONEL LINDSAY ROWE

Mr. Townsend has been blind from birth. He sees only colours from the bright sunlight. He is a graduate of The Salvation Army's School for the Blind in Kingston, Jamaica. Because of the training he received at the school, Mr. Townsend lives a fairly independent life, able to live alone in a small apartment, do much of his own cooking and walk for forty-five minutes to get to the Army twice on Sunday. Mr. Townsend has only this year started to attend the Army corps on a regular basis. While he was at one time a Corps Cadet and quite involved in the corps, he lost interest and did not frequent the Army for some time. In recent days, however, I think mostly because of our efforts to assist his mentally handicapped brother and aging mother, he has come back to the Army.

I have only heard Mr. Townsend testify twice. Each time has been a source of rich blessing to me. He gave his second testimony in the meeting last night. Because of his blindness, Mr. Townsend has difficulty singing along with the songs and choruses in the meetings. I suggested that a young girl in our corps might be of assistance to him by repeating the words for him before the congregation sang each line. She was hesitant, thinking that she could not do the job well, but decided that she would try. Says Mr. Townsend, "I discouraged her from the beginning by reminding her she could not play her tambourine or sing if she did that." But the little girl persisted. She came to me one Sunday saying that she was too short and that something would have to be done so that she could get closer to Mr. Townsend's ear. It was at that time that we decided to bring a footstool into the Citadel and place it where he usually sits. Commenting on the footstool in his testimony, Mr. Townsend said, "I told her not to bother, that she should concentrate on enjoying the meeting." Without ever being rude or impolite to the girl, he did all he could to discourage her every effort to help him.

Yesterday the little girl made a mistake. She forgot to bring the footstool. "Mr. Townsend," she said, "There is only one thing to do. I shall have to stand on the seat." "No!" said Mr. Townsend, "We will not turn the service into a circus." Reflecting on the incident in his testimony last night, Mr. Townsend recalled, "There I was trying my best to discourage her. There she was refusing to be discouraged. There I was blind, unable to see the congregation, worrying that they thought me some sort of freak. There she was, able to see the congregation but couldn't care less what they thought as long as she could help me. Where else could this happen," he asked, "but in The Salvation Army? I wonder how many other churches would really care?"

I thank God for Mr. Townsend, for his faith, his love and his friendship. I also thank God for that little girl. You see, she is my daughter, Cheryl Lynn.

In 1990, Colonels David and Doreen Edwards were summoned to General Eva Burrows' office. When they left her office they had in hand their farewell orders from International Headquarters to take command of the Caribbean Territory,[403] the first Caribbean officers to assume those positions since the work began 103 years earlier.[404] The news was greeted around the Caribbean Territory with triumphant joy. The news was printed in every major newspaper in the Caribbean as well as being shared on the radio and television. One officer wrote, "We could now hold our heads high and show the world that we, too, could lead."[405] Later in 1997, with the rank of commissioner, the Edwards would be groundbreaking leaders as territorial commanders of the USA Western Territory, the first ethnic African leaders in any United States territory.[406]

General Eva Burrows made a second trip to Jamaica in 1990. Although she attended to all the meetings and responsibilities that were hers as General, she also came on a personal pilgrimage. Traveling to the St. Ann Bethany Baptist Church in Alexandria, she dedicated a plaque to her great-great-grandfather, the Reverend Henry John Dutton who had founded the church 150 years earlier. She also presented a donation for the rebuilding of the basic school in his memory. Reverend Dutton is buried under the vestry of the church with the plaque General Burrows presented now over his grave.[407]

From Jamaica, General Burrows travelled to Cuba to share in their congress. But her meeting with President Fidel Castro made headlines worldwide. Castro recalled fondly the kindness of the Army showed to him as a youth and expressed special interest in the recent reopening of The Salvation Army in Russia, which had been closed since 1919. When General Burrows asked if those in the government understood the religious nature of The Salvation Army, she was told, "Not only do they know and understand, they admire and respect, as years ago at the time of the Revolution, whereas other missions abandoned the country, the Army remained, notwithstanding trying and limited circumstances for the work."[408]

Trying times came in Trinidad when an attempted coup in Port-of-Spain found the Army in the crosshairs due to the location of its buildings. Captain and Mrs. Onal Castor, who managed the men's hostel, were lying on the floor because of the gunshots and exploding ammunition outside. Across the street from the hostel was the police station. One block further, Red House, the government center, was under siege, with the government ministers held hostage. Major Eriene Hoyte, in charge because the divisional commander was on furlough, called to check on the Castors. Captain Castor crawled to the telephone and told her that so far everyone was all right.

Wesley Noel

HAITI

—◦▷◁◦—

I was sent to the Bethel Clinic by the Haitian government in 1990 to do my social work training. Major Zimmerman explained she had trouble with TB patients. Even with medicine the patients didn't improve. When I visited patients, we sent blood specimens of twenty of them to the national lab in 1990. Seventeen were HIV positive. For us it was an emergency to start the prevention program.

It was a difficult time. In 1991 people in the countryside didn't believe it. For them it was a disease for rich people, for people living in the city but not for them in the countryside, nothing that had come to bother them. Major Zimmerman told me The Salvation Army is very sensitive to this kind of disease. She thought The Salvation Army would encourage an intervention programme like that. So she asked me to put together a proposal to send to The Salvation Army in London. At that time there was a Salvation Army congress in Lausanne. I put together the proposal and sent it for around $20,000. They approved it right away and sent it to us.

Then the World Health Organization sent enough to go far in this work. We sent it in 1991 and they approved for a second year. After that, UNICEF came to see us and they were encouraged by what we were doing. At that time there wasn't any other NGOs working on this problem in Haiti. There was Partners in Health in the central and The Salvation Army in the south. In the countryside in the south it was only The Salvation Army.

After UNICEF in 1993, we sent a proposal to Norway. In 1994 they started funding it for the next 15 years. Then the U.S. government started funding it.

We have helped people understand that HIV/AIDS doesn't care if you are rich or poor, if you live in the city or the countryside. Everyone is vulnerable and everyone needs to act like they are going to get it.

A few blocks away at Port-of-Spain Central Corps, Sister Evelyn and the others there were frightened that the looting which was occurring in the streets would reach the Army. Already many businesses were set on fire, blazing out of control because the fire department could not respond. Standing guard at the entrance of the corps, Sister Evelyn heard one looter say, "The Salvation Army has money." But his partner replied, "No, we may need them one day." [409]

For six days the city was under 24-hour curfew. The government, however, wanted the Army to help with feeding the security personnel. Major Ian Begley ventured out in his Salvation Army vehicle with food but in the dark the shields were not easily seen. As he pulled up to one checkpoint he was suddenly surrounded by military personnel with their guns drawn. He quickly pointed to his Salvation Army cap. The sergeant asked what his business was and Begley shared that he had some food and coffee for them, which was gratefully received. When they were finished, the sergeant asked if Begley needed an escort home. "I wouldn't think of going without you!" was his reply. [410]

In 1991, the men's hostel in Kingston was converted to a drug and alcohol rehabilitation center. The William Chamberlain Center provided a means for men to turn their lives around through work therapy and counseling. [411]

HISTORY IN THE FIRST PERSON

Derrick Mitchell

JAMAICA | *THE WAR CRY* SEPTEMBER 1998

The order of the day was hard drinking, smoking, drugs and nightclubs galore. But that lifestyle proved very expensive. That's when stealing whatever I could from whomever I could came into the picture. I was soon hooked on cocaine and very quickly spent all my earnings to get it. I dropped out of college and eventually lost my job. After writing a bad check on an overdrawn account, the police started their hunt for me. I left home and stayed with friends in an effort to dodge the police. I quickly became an "area leader," orchestrating and leading dozens of robberies in order to support my drug habit. Knowing the police would soon catch up with me, I fled Jamaica for the United States, hoping to start over. There was even a period when I stopped using drugs. But that didn't last long.

It didn't take long to influence me to join a posse, and it didn't take long for me to start selling and using drugs again. A sequence of events led me to start "state hopping" in an attempt to again escape the police. But my efforts proved futile. Law and drug enforcement agencies finally caught up with me. I spent one year in a U.S. jail before being deported to Jamaica.

The only thing that changed when I returned to Jamaica was my location: I was still using drugs and stealing. One unlucky day, I was caught and beaten. The result of that ordeal left me with a broken arm, a smashed leg bone and a fractured skull. If that weren't enough, my captors proceeded to douse me with gasoline. At that moment, even in my semi-conscious stupor, I prayed to God. I was sincere as I could be in telling Him that I would do anything He wanted me to if He saved me from the fiery death to which I was doomed. The sound of footsteps made me think someone was coming to my rescue. But it was only one of my captors with more gasoline. Suddenly, the strangest sensation came over me and oddly, I felt a kind of calm envelop me. The gasoline container fell from the hand of the carrier, and its contents poured into the streets. The wail of a siren and the sight of a police jeep were, for the first time in my life, more than welcomed by me. I was delivered from sure death. God "kept" His part of the "deal." Now, I had to keep mine.

After spending some time in the hospital, I was admitted to The Salvation Army Adult Rehabilitation Centre in downtown Kingston. While there I got a chance to know a little more about this God who saved me. He helped me understand just how much He loved and cared for me, and for the first time, my life had a purpose. Sadly though, it would be just a matter of months before I would go into relapse and renege on my commitment to God.

A few years later, after backsliding and a roller coaster ride through hell, I hit rock bottom, and God allowed me to stare at death in the face again. I remembered my promise. Helpless and hopeless, I went back to The Salvation Army Rehabilitation Centre, but most importantly, I came back to God. His grace was enough to give me a second chance. I certainly did not deserve His love and mercy, but He willingly gave it to me anyway. I am now a sins-forgiven, past-redeemed, blood-washed Christian, and a member (soldier) of The Salvation Army. I am enjoying a living relationship with the One who knows me best and loves me most. God has since called me to be an officer in The Salvation Army, and with His leading I will gladly follow so that others may know and experience the precious gift of His salvation.

A few blocks away the Evangeline Residence established a training program for young women that included courses in catering, commercial sewing and design, secretarial and computer skills.[412] In Antigua in 1992, the Sunshine Home for Girls was opened by Major Joycelyn Jonas, the first Antiguan to be appointed as regional commander, to meet the needs of at risk teen girls.[413] And in 1993, the Elizabeth Estates Children's Home was established in the Bahamas.[414]

When The Salvation Army reopened its corps in Bartica, Guyana, it went in with a total approach to community need, providing worship and fellowship, day care for small children, life skills training for mothers and fathers, simple skills training and pastoral care. The envoy acquired a boat for outreach to outlying communities up the river, naming it *The General*.[415]

In 1994, Angelita Rosario, a *dominicana* who became a soldier while in the USA, returned to her hometown of Cotui in the Dominican Republic. She sorely missed The Salvation Army, and as had been done in several countries where the Army opened in the Caribbean, she started holding meetings in her home. In October 1994 she sent a letter to the territorial commander, Colonel David Edwards, saying she could not return to the Catholic Church and would like The Salvation Army to open in the Dominican Republic. She shared that she was holding prayer meetings in her living room but she wanted more.

Lt. Colonel Clinton Burrowes was dispatched to meet with her and explore the possibilities of the Army's opening again in that country. Two previous openings had flourished temporarily in the past but the Army did not last. Burrowes arrived in Santo Domingo and with effort, found the little town of Cotui about 100 kilometers away. When Angelita saw him in his uniform, she jumped up and down and then hugged him.

Vilo Exantus

HAITI | *THE WAR CRY*

⸺◦❘◖◗❘◦⸺

I was born in a heathen family who knew nothing about God's amazing love and the beauty of Christianity. My parents were voodoo worshippers, completely ignorant of the things of God. Voodoo is an African cult imported into the Antilles by the African slaves during the colonization. It is characterized by belief in sorcery and witchcraft. The voodoo worshippers believe in evil spirits, called demons, and adore them as their gods. They believe these evil spirits have power over them if they do not fulfill their duty towards them respectfully and faithfully. Therefore, these voodooists are really enslaved by the devil and need to be freed by the power of the gospel of Christ.

It was such an environment that I came from. For fear of these evil spirits my parents never went to church, neither did they encourage us to go. I was not interested in going to church either. I was more eager than all the other children to go to the devil's temple for worship every week with my mother until one day when I was 13 years of age one of the spirits chose me to be set apart for his priesthood.

Although I used to go to the Obeahman and enjoyed the voodoo ceremonies, I was empty, and I did not have any joy and peace within. There was no love, no sense of happiness and satisfaction among these Haitian voodoo worshippers. They envied, hated and killed one another. It was a real hell for me. But blinded by the devil I could not see my way out. There I was, a 13 year old boy, hopeless, desperate and lost in the world. But while I was there in that pit of destruction, chained up by the devil's fetters, God, my loving Heavenly Father, was thinking of me. He had a wonderful plan for my life and so He opened up a way out for me through some little Christian friends.

These young people invited me to go with them to Sunday school.

Without any resistance and unknown to my mother, I accompanied them. The first Sunday I enjoyed it very much, every Sunday it was more interesting. The more I kept on going and learning about God, the less interest I had in the voodoo business until one day I made the decision to stop going with my mother to the voodoo temple for worship. I started going to the Salvation Army meeting. I can vividly remember that Sunday night when the Lord put His hand upon me. It was after listening to a message and the preacher was singing the appeal song, "Have you any room for Jesus?" that sitting in the pew I felt God's hand heavily resting upon me and I could not resist any longer. I burst into tears and groaning and knelt to pray at the Mercy Seat. There at that sacred place I met with God and experienced something that I never felt before—the presence of the sweet Holy Spirit invading my soul—a sense of extreme joy and happiness, and the wonder of all my life was changed. I was born again through the power of the Holy Spirit. Oh! Glory to God! It was a blessed experience that I never will forget.

The home that Angelita was living in was little more than a shack. She and her husband were very poor but her enthusiasm was contagious. Burrowes was placed into immediate service. One of the couples who worshipped with them was not married because they couldn't afford it. A marriage was quickly arranged with Colonel Burrowes conducting the wedding while Angelita pulled together a lovely little reception for them. (The couple later became soldiers and then officers.)

Burrowes arranged for the Rosarios to come to Jamaica for intensive training as they assisted at the Havendale Corps in Kingston. They then returned in early 1995 to open the corps in Cutio.[416]

A meeting was arranged with Colonel Franklyn Thompson, then the Caribbean territorial commander, to come to officially inaugurate the work. *The War Cry* reported, "In the welcome meeting Sister Angelita Rosario was commissioned as an envoy, her husband and son sworn in as soldiers by Colonel Franklyn Thompson. Having had some weeks of intensive training,

Envoy Angelita Rosario and her family go back to the Dominican Republic (their home) to officially open the work there . . . There are 70 people attending the meetings."[417] Within a year there were four more corps established with 71 soldiers on roll. Official recognition was granted by the government as well.[418] Captains Vilo and Yvrosse Exantus were appointed in August 1996 as the officers in charge.

Alexis Cordova

CUBA | *THE WAR CRY* MAY 1998

I had never heard of God or His Son Jesus Christ. I visited my cousin who was a Salvation Army officer. She invited me to the Army's meeting on Sunday. But I did not like people in uniforms. My cousin tried to explain to me that The Salvation Army is a Christian organization. I did not like Christians, but I could not help thinking about what my cousin told me. She mentioned God's love for every human being, including me. I said to myself, "Maybe one person could be wrong, but not so many during so many years."

I was too embarrassed to ask my cousin for answers so I went to her 8 year old son. "If you look at the flag or the uniforms, you will never find God. It is always a person experience," he said. Then he surprised me with a question. "Do you want to know Christ?" I answered strongly, "No!"

Saturday night I opened the Bible for the first time and started to read God's call to Moses in Exodus. I recognised myself: afraid to speak and take the step of faith." I told God: "If you give me a sign in the meeting tomorrow I will make the decision to follow You." During the meeting "promises of faith" with a Bible text were distributed. The one I received had the text "Now go and believe in Me." And that was it. I believed and God saved me.

Guyana enjoyed a significant development in 1997 with the construction of a men's hostel, remand home for delinquent boys, a drug rehabilitation center and a restaurant to help raise funds. This was made possible with a G$22 million grant from the Guyana government.[419]

In 1999 there was a further realignment of the Caribbean Territory when Cuba and Belize were transferred to the newly formed Latin America North Territory. The territory gathered itself and then countered with further expansion, opening nine new corps in Haiti, four additional corps in the Dominican Republic and the opening of a new country: St. Maarten.[420]

In 1989, a young Haitian Salvationist, Avrius Jean Baptiste, moved to St. Maarten. He found there was no Salvation Army in his new land and began attending another church. But he missed the Army and, like a number of others before him had done in the countries and colonies that comprise the Caribbean Territory, started meetings himself. Finding other Salvationists, he invited them to join him and soon a *de facto* Salvation Army was functioning in St. Maarten.

Lt. Colonel Franck and Eudora Louissaint were sent to investigate what was happening. On the same plane, the territorial leaders, Colonels Dennis and Noella Phillips, were on their way to the 95th anniversary meetings for Antigua. That entailed a three-hour layover in St. Maarten. As the Louissaints greeted the crowd that had gathered, they were as thrilled to see the territorial leaders as they were to see this group of enthusiastic Salvationists. Permission was received to make St. Maarten the 106th country where the Army labored.[421]

Visiting less than two months later, General Paul Rader declared St. Maarten officially opened on January 7, 1999. When the General arrived, there were 30 fully uniformed Salvationists to greet him. Captains Vilece and Joan Thomas were appointed to officially pioneer this now booming Salvation Army enterprise.

While in the Caribbean, General Rader visited Haiti for a congress. A great moment came when he enrolled 401 new senior soldiers. The biggest surprise came in the meeting when Majors Alfred and Charnie Pierre were called to the front and promoted to the rank of Lt. Colonel.

General and Commissioner Rader then went to the Dominican Republic where he enrolled 62 senior soldiers and 45 junior soldiers. Four outposts were upgraded to full corps status as well.[422]

FACING THE FUTURE

As the millennium dawned there was a growing realization that The Salvation Army had undergone significant changes. Where there once had been colonies controlled by distant European powers, with the exception of Haiti, the Dominican Republic and Cuba, there were now a host of very young countries with all the accompanying struggles new nations face. As succeeding colonies received their independence, the first wave of politicians made impossible promises of a heaven on earth for their new countries. In trying to deliver on the promises, the fragile economies suffered. Jamaica provides a prime example. Its dollar, which at its height in the 1970s exchanged at the rate of two American dollars for each Jamaican dollar, fell to an exchange rate of nearly 90 Jamaican dollars to a single American dollar by 2010. The economies left an increasing number of people in desperate circumstances, especially those without marketable skills. It wasn't only the new countries that were suffering. The older republics in the Caribbean suffered as well.

It wasn't just the politicians who were to blame. The agricultural sector that for so many years had been fuelled by the sale of sugar cane, was battered, bruised and nearly broken altogether. Rice, a food staple for the Caribbean people, previously had been almost entirely supplied by the domestic market. But cheap rice from Asia undercut the domestic production. Rice as a cash crop had been virtually abandoned. Pressure from the United States on the Caribbean and Latin American countries to open their markets meant that local farmers could not compete against the subsidized farm products coming from their giant northern neighbor. Increasingly good farm land was left to go uncultivated because it just wasn't worth the effort to work that hard for a loss.

There was growing frustration among young people in the Caribbean as well. Better educated than their ancestors could have ever hoped, their new qualifications were of little help when they tried to find jobs in depressed economies. A "brain drain" resulted as promising young people emigrated from the Caribbean to brighter job markets in Canada, Great Britain and the United States. There they found jobs available paying wages that could not be matched in their various homelands. While almost all sent funds back home to their families in the Caribbean, the loss of this vital resource of human skill and intelligence further crippled the development in the islands and Latin America.

Replacing agriculture as the primary industry today is tourism. This has created tens of thousands of jobs. But the tourist industry is shaped by whatever is happening in the world economy. A downturn in the United States or Europe results in an immediate dip in tourism. Beyond that, most of the resorts are owned and operated by multi-national corporations with few showing more than a token concern for the social issues in the lands where they operate.

These issues have directly affected The Salvation Army. For its vast array of social work, the Army has depended on the generosity of the public as well as the support of various governments. But the reality is that when individuals are not able to sustain themselves or are in fear that their livelihoods are not secure, the charitable gift is the first thing to go. It is the same with governments that have to look to such vital services as highways, security forces and other government functions. As much as they might be sympathetic to the Army or any other charity's work, their budgets are often stretched to the breaking point. As the financial crisis deepened, The Salvation Army found its traditional streams of resources strained.

The growing financial issue was not the only major problem facing the Army. The Salvation Army, especially in the Caribbean, is carried on the backs of its commissioned[z] officers. In the local corps, the soldiers are of vital importance but they look to their officer for leadership and direction. The Caribbean has seen a steady decrease in the number of its officers, a trend that can be traced back fifty years. Sessions[aa] have grown smaller over the years while resignations have remained alarmingly high. This is not surprising given that bright and gifted young people find that being a Salvation Army officer is not only hard work, but there is a strong likelihood that they will not be able to draw their pay many times. They often live in homes in need of major repair and have to oversee not just a single corps congregation and program, but several corps or outposts. The Salvation Army believes that God calls people to be officers and that God sustains the individuals who commit themselves to Him. But in an increasingly self-serving age, the calls of the secular world seem to be louder than in times past.

The one bright spot in recruiting has been a steadily increasing stream of candidates from Haiti. The Army in Haiti has a strong sense of Salvationism and the Haitian candidates for the most part are deeply committed, biblically sound and have a

---

[z] Commissioned is The Salvation Army term for ordained and fully certified officers. A commissioning is an event where officers are publicly ordained and begin their officership as lieutenants.
[aa] A session is a two-year class of cadets. Rather than being known as the "Class of 1976" the Army gives the session names like Overcomers, Faithful Intercessors, etc.

tremendous work ethic. But the needs of the territory go beyond Haiti. The Haitian officer who goes to an English speaking country must not only adapt to a language not his own, but also to a culture that differs markedly from that of Haiti. At one time, 90 percent of officers in the Caribbean were Jamaican. Currently, nearly half the officers in the Caribbean Territory are Haitian, with that proportion climbing. The Salvation Army rejoices that Haiti has not only a vital expression of Salvationism, but that its youth are willing to leave their homes to serve wherever sent. However, the Holy Spirit is not just at work in Haiti. But is anyone else listening?

HISTORY IN THE FIRST PERSON

Major Catherine Pacquette

Whenever I cannot go to the corps for service, I will make a time and go to some of the people passing by or sitting by the way. The soul of everyone is a heavy burden to me. I will try my best.

Sometimes I will take a flower and a little dust, encourage them and talk to them and say, "See this flower. It is beautiful. See this dust. It came from the dust. See how you stand, a beautiful old woman or young man. See how God prepared for you a tree for you to have shade. Because God loves you. The Bible said, 'He that hath the Son has life; he who has not the Son has not life.' There's two ways before you. Heaven and Hell. If you are in Christ, you are in life. If you do not have Christ, you do not have life.

"Sometimes we are in an accident and they rush us to the hospital. They give you blood. If you have blood, you expect to have life. Our soul, after death it is more important that you have Christ, you have the Son. If you haven't got the Son you don't have life. So it is up to you."

So I share with people and some are Christians but some are not and they listen. So this is my life.

This is not to demean the work that has been accomplished and is underway. In fact, given the current circumstances, the work done by the present generation of Salvationists may be the most heroic in its history. And because that history is still being made, the Army is as "determined to conquer" as ever.

Heroes of the faith were recognized in quick succession. In 2000, the first person in Haiti to receive the Order of the Founder was Major Rosemarie Haefeli, soon followed by Major Emma Zimmerman, both Swiss officers who embraced Haiti, working tirelessly on behalf of their adopted countries. Throughout all the political turmoil, they chose to stay and suffer alongside the people they loved. Zimmerman did outstanding work in Fond-des-Negres, expanding the Bethel Clinic into a comprehensive medical treatment center and mobile health clinic with specialties in TB treatment and HIV/AIDS. When she was involved in an accident and could no longer continue her regimen of duties, she opened a children's home.[423] Haefeli began a building program that established nearly 40 schools, erected children's homes and corps buildings across the country.

A second recipient of the Army's highest honor was Major Anne Kristine Harje, a native of Norway. She was cited in 2004 for outstanding missionary service, 16 years of which were spent in Haiti. In presenting her award, it was noted that her service was "characterized by compassion, courage and selfless devotion to the many children and families who have benefitted from her care and have been inspired by her example."[424]

In 2006, Major Catherine Pacquette received the Order of the Founder as well. Originally from the island of Dominica, she was so thoroughly in love with her adopted homeland of Haiti that upon retirement she stayed there. She was an innovative pioneer, giving 56 years of service. A story that represents her work was related by Mrs. Colonel Evangeline Stannard when she and her husband visited Haiti as recorded in *Jewels of the Caribbean:*

Colonel John Stannard, then territorial commander, dedicated a hall provided as a tribute to the faithful ministry of Captain Pacquette. As there was no hall she had taught the village women under the mango tree, using pictures affixed to the bark as she told them about Jesus. When she went away she left them the pictures. A mother of five boys who owned a grocery store was taken ill and the local witchdoctor said he would cure her. Payment was one cow. She was not cured and gradually he deprived her of all her possessions. The village women visited her home, repeating to the sick woman the last few lines of the Lord's Prayer—"For Thine is the Kingdom ... Amen"—taught to them by Captain Pacquette. Derisively the sons chided, "Why are you talking about a no-good god who doesn't even have a temple? He only has a mango tree." The women replied, "Our God made the mango tree!"

When Captain Pacquette returned she saw a great crowd gathered around the mango tree. Thinking there was trouble she hurried over and was amazed to find her pictures pinned to the tree and everyone listening to the gospel message. The sons of the formerly sick woman asked her if they could build a temple. Colonel Stannard counted it a privilege to dedicate to God's glory this temple of bamboo uprights, palm-thatched roof, hand-carved benches and a mercy seat with lilies and flowers of the bush beautifully carved on it.[425]

A totally different kind of honor came to 17 year-old Mary Watkins, who won the title of "Miss Bahamas" in 2000. A resident of The Salvation Army Harmony House since she was 12, Miss Watkins said that as Miss Bahamas, "My primary goal is to make the public aware of Harmony House and the positive things that happen there."[426]

Tragedy struck Trinidad just a week before their Centennial Congress. Preparing for the upcoming meetings, a rehearsal of the musical "Spirit" was being conducted at the Josephine Shaw House. Fluctuating electrical current did not sound any alarms. It wasn't until the cry of "Fire! Fire!" that people realized that something was wrong. Next door desperate efforts were being made to put out a fire at the adjoining hostel. Flames soon engulfed divisional headquarters allowing for those inside to escape with only the barest essentials. Despite the quick response by the fire brigade, the building burned down in what seemed to be an instant. With no materials left for the Congress except the souvenir brochures and some commemorative t-shirts, the immediate question arose: will there still be a congress? The divisional commander, Major Keith Graham, declared, "Fire or no fire, we will have our congress." A victorious celebration was held the next week on schedule.[427]

Recovering lost ground, in 2001 Guyana successfully reopened three corps.[428] Later, in 2004 it was honored with a visit from Prince Andrew who toured the Army's drug rehabilitation center. Following his visit, he gave a substantial donation for the continuing development of the center.[429]

General John and Commissioner Freda Larsson came to Antigua as part of their centennial celebrations in 2002. In commemoration of the Army's beginning, the General unveiled a plaque under the same Tamarind tree where the Army held its first open-air on the island one hundred years earlier.[430]

In 2004 a foursome of hurricanes swept through the Caribbean: Charley, Frances, Ivan and Jeanne. Hardest hit were the Dominican Republic, Haiti, Grenada and Jamaica. First struck was a remote area along the border of the Dominican Republic and Haiti. Severe flooding resulted in a heavy loss of life and extensive property damage.[431] Major Vilo Exantus, regional commander for the Dominican Republic, when bringing aid reported from Jimani, which suffered the worst casualties. Major Exantus relayed that 329 bodies had been found but 300 people were still missing. Crops were destroyed, further imperiling the people.[432]

Both Grenada and Jamaica suffered damage when Hurricane Ivan struck on September 7, 2004. Heavy damage was sustained in Jamaica including the destruction of crops and many resorts key to the tourist industry.[433] In Grenada, the Army teamed with the Mennonites and a work team from the Bermuda Division to construct 150 homes in the St. Andrew's Parish.[434] Later, the Army distributed 73 school uniforms to children who had been affected by Hurricane Ivan.[435] In February 2006 the Grenada prime minister as well as other government officials joined in the dedication of the homes by Colonels John and Betty Matear, territorial leaders.[436]

In December 2004 rains started falling in Guyana in the area around Georgetown. They continued to fall until by January 15 the Demerara River had overflowed its banks. Not only was the ground saturated, but garbage clogged the drains which further complicated the situation. The city of Georgetown was completely covered with water. One third of Guyana's population was affected, causing local people to say, "Nature has lost its mind."[437] Besides the actual damage from the polluted water, a condition called leptospirosis broke out.[438, bb] The infection was highly toxic, killing 21 people and causing injury to hundreds more. There were further concerns about the increase of other diseases such as dengue fever, spread by mosquitoes.

At the divisional headquarters where the Army normally carries on a feeding program, the kitchen was in operation 24 hours a day preparing meals and then sending them out by boat to people stranded in their homes. As the waters receded the Army continued to respond with food parcels, clothing and mattresses. Because of its response during the flood, for the first time the Army was invited as part of the president's committee on disaster relief.[439]

[bb]Leptospirosis is a bacterial infection that occurs in tropical countries when fresh water is contaminated by animal urine.

Jean Dover

GUYANA

—⟶✦⟵—

I was working downstairs at the kitchen at divisional headquarters. When we went out to help people we had to go in some water, which was dangerous. We gave food, clothes and sheltered people. We went to Boxton. Plenty work we did.

I remember a man by the name of Desmond Murray. His wife was in hospital and he had a stroke and was bedridden. So his door had to be opened by someone else. I had to jump in the water to get upstairs to him. He couldn't come down. It was very painful. He had the use of just one hand. I had to take my time. The doors were open day and night so I had to run up and down to take his food to him so I could go somewhere to take care of the rest of the people. It was very painful.

But God is good, you know. Because everybody needs somebody. He can't come down so I have to go up to him to help him. That is something I'll never, never forget. We had long boots but the water went in because the water was very, very high. He just was saying, "Thank you. Thank you. I know that you really love people." So that was very good.

People felt a lot of pain because people had no food, they had no clothes but The Salvation Army was taking that to them. The Salvation Army was there with rations. The Salvation Army worked wholeheartedly. We were working night and day just so people had something to eat. People put their beds on the roof and children were sleeping in trees. It was really painful. Really, really painful. People said, "Thank God for The Salvation Army."

I want to thank God for The Salvation Army. If it were not for The Salvation Army, I want to know, where would I be?

Teresa

ANTIGUA | MAJOR CARMEN ROSE MOTT

—⟶✦⟵—

One of the most memorable things that happened when I was at the Sunshine School for Girls was with a 12 year-old girl named Teresa who had eye problems. We knew she could get help but we had no way to pay for it.

Students from the Antigua American University came to the home and during that time met her. When we explained what she needed and our financial problems they raised the funds for Teresa to go to Jamaica to see Dr. Vaughn to have the surgery she needed. It made a huge difference in her sight.

Two weeks later we travelled back to Antigua. When we arrived at the airport, there was the press, university students, girls and former girls from the home to welcome Teresa back. There were balloons and banners and just everything. Fortunately, I had just bought her new shoes and clothes.

It was so moving. Before, Teresa could barely see. Now, when she first saw Antigua clearly it was with a crowd of people welcoming her home.

It was perfect.

The year 2005 brought word that International Headquarters had decided on a further realignment of the Caribbean Territory. Both Cuba and the Dominican Republic were added to the Latin America North Territory because they shared a common language. Belize, an English speaking country, was brought back to the Caribbean Territory once more.[440]

Barbados opened the General Arnold Brown Youth Center to "empower disadvantaged youth in the inner city and its environs" in 2005.[441] With specialized teaching, efforts were made to help slow learners, teach computer literacy and provide homework assistance.[442] The division also opened a new feeding center and hostel for homeless people.[443]

In Antigua, the Sunshine School for Girls was honored by a visit from Prince Edward who toured the center and enjoyed a beautiful presentation of "I Know My Redeemer Lives."[444]

The territory launched a new initiative with the first Caribbean Advisory Organizations Conference held in Nassau, Bahamas. Spearheaded by Major Ward Matthews, Secretary for Business Administration, the conference gave impetus to advisory boards around the territory. The territorial commander, Commissioner Raymond Houghton, presented the Bahamas Advisory Board with the inaugural "High Performance Board of the Year."[445] The next year, the initial Soldiers' College was held at the Training College. Led by Lt. Colonel Devon Haughton, the Soldiers' College sought to "build doctrinally sound and biblically knowledgeable soldiers in the territory and to stimulate and train Salvationists in Christian discipleship principles and practices."[446]

Pioneering work spread to the Turks and Caicos Islands when in July 2008, Captains Matthew and Rebecca Trayler arrived to open the work.

This was far from the unplanned openings elsewhere in the Caribbean. An advisory board member, Mr. Frank Crothers from Nassau, who also had business interests in the Turks and Caicos Islands, was extremely interested in the Army opening there. A study was done by the divisional commander, Major Lester Ferguson, and a past regional commander, Mr. Henry Arrowood.[447] The study concluded that the time was ripe for the Army's opening in the British colony.

After Captains Trayler arrived, rather than starting in the accustomed manner with religious services, they began to build a local advisory board and started social work. After two years the first public religious service was held, quickly followed by the official opening of the colony for Salvation Army work. Several mission teams had visited to prepare the way for this beginning, helped by a local lawyer who offered premises where Sunday meetings could be held. The opening ceremony was conducted by the territorial commander, Colonel Onal Castor, ably assisted by the chief secretary, Lt. Colonel Lindsay Rowe and the personnel secretary, Lt. Colonel Sydney McKenzie. The Florida (USA) Divisional Band added to the occasion with their music and open-air efforts. General Shaw Clifton declared the work officially open, making the Turks and Caicos Islands the 122nd country to fly the Army flag on January 1, 2011.[448]

On behalf of The Salvation Army, Commissioner Houghton

received the Freedom of the City of Kingston in November 2008.[449] The award proves how far the relationship between the city and The Salvation Army has come since the first days when the mayor refused to rent the town hall to the Army for meetings!

Captain Nana Boakye-Agyemang
THE WAR CRY FEBRUARY 2008

From the time we arrived in Savanna-la-Mar, we discovered that there was limited space. My wife and I pledged ourselves to work with all our skills, talents and energies because of our love for God. God gave us a vision for Sav. We needed a revolution that would change the way our people perceived their responsibilities to God and His ministry both in the church and the community.

It took us about three and a half years to communicate the vision. We used our platform as the sensitizing ground to share the need and plans. Special meetings were called to discuss ideas and concepts, view plans and make specific recommendations. Prayer has remained the main component in all this. There has not been a meeting where "Operation Glory" was not been prayed about or spoken about. We decided to build the corps building as a reflection of the glory of God, hence the name "Operation Glory." We wanted a place that would attract people to worship God, a building that reflects God's glory, His beauty and His holiness, a building whereby just looking at it, one would be drawn to God.

My natural being knew it was more than too big. But my faith declared that if God says, "I will provide for my temple," then all I had to do was believe. I did not know how or where we would get the money but I just knew it would work out. It's like this: I cannot explain how God saved me but He did and I was convinced that He would do the same about this project. The contractor we hired to give cost estimates told us that the demolishing stage alone would take more than we had. Some people laughed at us and said we could not buy chicken feed with what we had on hand. Faith allowed us to trust God.

It is up to us in the Caribbean to curb the mentality that whenever we need anything, we have to call on our "godparents" overseas because they have money and we do not. We as Caribbean people need to begin to look at the present resources we have in order to meet our responsibilities.

Faith is accomplishing something that seems unattainable. Everyday God is performing new miracles, providing what we need. I would say what I have been saying all the time. This is not the time to back up; it's time to work and realize the vision. It is a time for self-denial, to make sure the work of the Lord is completed.

A remarkable building project was completed in 2010 in Savanna-la-Mar. The commanding officer, Captain Nana Boakye-Agyemang, challenged the people of the corps not to rely on outside sources of funding but to take the initiative to raise the needed funds themselves. Although at first encountering resistance, eventually the people caught the vision and, as funds were available, the building went up. At one point, the old building was surrounded by the walls of the new building so that they could continue to meet with minimum disruption. Then, when the roof went on, the old building was demolished. Their faith and work were rewarded when the building was dedicated in March 2010.

The year 2010 had dawned quietly. But on January 12, the earth shook in long-suffering Haiti.

14

⚬⚬-)◉(-⚬⚬

HAITI RESURRECTION

ON JANUARY 12 at 4:53 p.m. the earth trembled underneath Haiti for 35 seconds in a 7.1-magnitude earthquake. Within two hours, aftershocks shook the ground six more times; within 24 hours, 26 major aftershocks were recorded, 12 of which were of magnitude 5.0 or greater. Port-au-Prince, Jacmel, Petit-Goâve, and Carrefour, as well as surrounding areas, collapsed in dusty heaps.[450]

Arriving a few days after the quake, Major Cedric Hills, past director of The Salvation Army International Headquarters' disaster relief office in London, quickly surveyed the damage. A veteran of relief efforts from war zones including Bosnia, Kosovo, Albania, Iraq, Afghanistan, and the Republic of Georgia, he had also served in places blighted by natural disaster, including the famine in Kenya, the floods in Mozambique, and the Asian tsunami. Hills commented, "This is the worst I've seen. With the [Asian] tsunami as bad as that was, it affected an area of coast possibly one mile in but beyond that was all the infrastructure of transport, industry, employment, retail—all of it working as normal. But here the earthquake devastated everything. The United Nations, which normally coordinates these efforts, was itself severely damaged so that just when you need coordination the most, those who do it are incapacitated."

Sister Marie Ange Pierrelouis

VOICES FROM HAITI

I was on visitation, visiting some people in the neighborhood, and we had come back to the church and were singing. The pastor had just opened his Bible to Psalms, 121. He started to read, and then I saw the church moving—moving that side, and moving the other side, and we just stayed inside the church and didn't go out. After that the shaking happened three times, and after that it stopped.

We went outside and saw the houses in the street and they were falling down. We said, "This is an earthquake."

I walked to my house and when I arrived I thought about my 91-year-old mother and my daughter. I thought of my mother dying in the house, but then I went back and saw her with other people, and I praised God.

When the earthquake came my daughter was in my brother's house. She did not run away from the house, and she was still inside when the house was falling down. There was no emergency phone calling, no ambulance, there was nothing because the world was broken. People could not walk. We saw people dying, people dying on the road. About midnight we tried to see if my daughter was alive. We found her inside the house; we moved her and we saw an iron bar inside her. She died in the earthquake. The earthquake happened Tuesday. Wednesday would have been her 23rd birthday.

My house has some cracks, but it has not fallen down. Houses close by are falling. I'm afraid to go back . . . afraid to go back. I'm living in the compound in the Salvation Army headquarters, in the yard. I am not accustomed to living in a tent, but I am obliged to accept it. God will deliver me. I am just waiting for the government to say that it's safe, that everyone who has a house can go back.

You see all the houses falling down, but the trees are still standing up. I feel that God is talking to us, to the Haitian people. God put everybody outside—those people who are rich, those people who are poor, He put them together. We all lie down on the ground and see that God is a God of power.

Bob Poff, The Salvation Army's disaster director for Haiti, described what it looked like the moment the quake hit. "I was driving . . . Our truck was being tossed around to and fro like a toy, and when it stopped I looked outside to see buildings pancaking down. Thousands of people poured out into the streets, crying, carrying bloody bodies, looking for anyone who could help."[451]

Over 50 percent of the buildings in Port-au-Prince fell or were damaged so badly that they could not be entered. Houses built on the slopes of the hills surrounding Port-au-Prince tumbled down, often on top of others built further down the hillside, forming a cascade of death and destruction. Damage to Haiti was estimated by the Inter-American Development Bank to be valued up to $13 billion—twice Haiti's annual income. The report called the earthquake "the most destructive natural disaster a country has ever experienced when measuring in terms of people killed as a share of the population."[452]

The Haitian government counted over 318,000 dead, acknowledging that its count was inaccurate and lower than the actual numbers. The tragedy unfolded on every street and neighborhood. Those who escaped with their lives wondered how they had. But there was no time to reflect. Survivors immediately began pulling others out of the wreckage, using little more than their bare hands and crude tools against heavy, unforgiving concrete. Where back loaders were needed, sledgehammers were used. Where cranes could have lifted slabs of concrete, instead bands of neighbors strained to move them aside. From beneath the rubble, desperate survivors used cell phones to send text messages to try to guide someone, anyone, to where they were. But most of the cell phones were not operating because the networks were damaged. And what networks did work were quickly overwhelmed by the volume of those frantically trying to reach their loved ones.

Because of overcrowded schools, tens of thousands of students had been attending afternoon split sessions. Schools became crypts as crumbling floors trapped students, many of whom had no warning or opportunity to flee. The tiny bodies of children, wearing what had been crisply pressed school uniforms, lined the sidewalks. Parents searched hysterically among them for their missing sons and daughters. A parent's worst nightmare was acted out repeatedly upon discovery of a child's body. Others were left to wonder if their child had somehow escaped and was now wandering the streets, or if instead their child's body was crushed and unreachable under tons of twisted metal and broken concrete.[453]

The small Salvation Army clinic in Delmas 2, one of Port-au-Prince's poorest neighborhoods, had been designed to help mothers and children. But on this day, as hundreds streamed into its compound, it dealt with every conceivable medical emergency. Dr. Danielle Prosper, supported by a handful of volunteers, would work for the next week with no other trained medical help delivering babies, stopping bleeding, stabilizing the wounded, diagnosing crush injuries, performing amputations, and doing whatever else was required. She and the volunteers were reduced eventually to using shredded undergarments for bandages and children's medicine for pain. The courtyard became a triage and every able-bodied person a stretcher bearer.[454]

Major Tom Louden

VOICES FROM HAITI

After hearing the news of the earthquake on the radio, Major Tom Louden, area commander of The Salvation Army in Broward County, Florida, fell into a troubled sleep that night. He was awakened at 5:30 a.m. by a telephone call from a Salvationist pilot, Art Stephenson, who urged him to charter a plane to Haiti immediately. Hastily obtaining permission, Louden crowded into the small twin-engine plane with four other passengers, sharing their space with as many supplies as they could take. As the plane approached the Toussaint Louverture International Airport in Port-au-Prince, the U.S. Federal Aviation Authority, then in charge of Haiti's air-space, ordered them into a holding pattern. Unable to communicate directly with the military forces on the ground that were operating the airport, aircraft of all types were left to circle the field, awaiting permission to land. But none came.

Realizing that their fuel was running out, the pilot told Louden they had to land somewhere or turn back to the United States. A small airport was still operating within Haiti in the northern town of Cap-Haïtien. They de-cided to land there and try to reach Port-au-Prince over land. Securing two rented SUVs, the passengers loaded the supplies into the vehicles and headed south. The true poverty of Haiti was visible from the first. "At first I thought that Cap-Haïtien was also hit by the earthquake," Louden recalled, "but we quickly realized that while being spared the quake, the poverty made the countryside look like a disaster area." The driving time to Port-au-Prince was normally six hours. But because of the increasing damage to the roads, the bridges that were out, and the need to maneu-ver around traffic coming out of the city, it was almost 24 hours later be-fore they arrived in the capital.

The streets were choked with debris, and men, women and children wandered about aimlessly. Louden realized that they had to keep moving because people desperate for food and water were eyeing their vehicles, noticing that they were traveling without any armed escort. When they finally reached The Salvation Army's compound, the full measure of the disaster shook them to the core. The survivors and workers inside the compound were heartened by two things: supplies had arrived, and they had not been forgotten. The supplies were quickly offloaded and plans to distribute them were speedily drawn up. The elderly, the small children, and the sick would get the first precious food and bottles of water.

Louden recognized that the supplies he had brought were no more than the proverbial drop in the bucket. Taking some Haitian Salvationists with him, he once again worked his way through the cluttered and blocked streets to the airport. There he found the U.S. military in complete control but not a single plane landing or taking off. Louden met with the com-manding officer, who explained that the range of their transmitter was only three miles—well under the distance covered by the airplanes in their holding patterns. A more powerful transmitter was being set up, but that would take a few more hours.

Louden realized that if he could somehow get word to the four cargo planes that The Salvation Army had loaded and was ready to take off in the Turks and Caicos Islands, they could land immediately. After confirming that his planes could indeed land, Louden used a satellite telephone to contact the pilot leading the relief squadron. "I told them to come and to land regardless of what the FAA told them. The military said it was okay and they were to do it." When Louden was questioned by Stephenson as to how sure he was about that, he replied, "I'm not sure at all. You'll just have to trust me like I'm trusting the officer here." Within an hour, four Salvation Army planes landed in Haiti, and the first measurable vital supplies were en route to the victims of the earthquake.

After 24 hours the need to feed so many homeless and displaced people became critical. The Salvation Army employed its experience in mass feeding and caring for large populations. The efforts were lauded by WORLD magazine:

The UN estimates that as many as 1 million people are homeless, and UN emergency coordinator John Holmes acknowledged that aid delivery remains painfully slow. But in other parts of town, private aid groups are quietly getting the work done. [The Salvation Army distributed] an estimated 552,000 meals in less than four hours. . . While the UN grapples with the maddening conditions of delivering aid to Haiti, groups like The Salvation Army are proving a point: some of the best aid is coming from the groups with long standing connections on the ground . . . Despite the damage, within days Salvation Army staffers formed a plan to be the lead group providing care for nearly 20,000 people near their compound. At a UN meeting last Monday, The Salvation Army was one of just five nongovernmental organizations with a concrete plan for managing a camp.[455]

Rescuers worked past the time that survivors could reasonably be expected to live. In so doing they saved over 130 people. The last to be freed alive was a 28-year-old rice vendor named Evans Monsigrace, who was found alive after being buried 27 days. When the earthquake occurred he was selling rice in a flea market. The quake brought the building down around him, trapping him in the debris. Fortunately he had some food and water near him. When some men were working to clear the rubble of the flea market, Monsigrace heard their voices outside and began shouting. The startled men dug furiously until they reached him, and then rushed him to the nearest medical facility—the Salvation Army clinic. Although the medical staff tried to give him some water and did what they could to stabilize him, they very quickly determined that he needed more intensive medical treatment. Salvation Army workers rushed him to the University of Miami field hospital near the airport. Monsigrace was delirious and so emaciated and dehydrated that the medical personnel were unable at first to get an intravenous line into him.[456]

Finally he was stabilized enough for treatment to begin. Monsigrace was the last person found alive in the rubble. As relief supplies began pouring in, life assumed a strange rhythm to it, almost appearing normal. Street vendors soon reappeared and traffic moved up and down the streets. Some of the first to find a reprieve from the overwhelming situation were the children. The presence of a constant breeze was all that was needed for another return to normal life: children at play. Lt. Colonel Danny Morrow of The Salvation Army relates how children combined ingenuity with the spirit of play to while away an afternoon.

> Richard Deris and Wasnel Samuel Guirand are living temporarily in a tent outside the Salvation Army Haiti divisional headquarters in Port-au-Prince. It's breezy in Port-au-Prince, and it's boring "living temporarily in a tent." But for centuries a breeze anywhere in the world has attracted children and their kites. Richard and Wasnel had no kite, and they have no money with which to buy one. So they made their own. Using a discarded garbage bag, strips of

cloth salvaged from the nearby trash canal, and stripping the middle spine of a coconut palm leaf, they fashioned small kites which catch the wind and provide hours of play and relief from the boredom of their present circumstances. "Go fly a kite" is no statement of dismissal in Haiti; it's a call to have fun because the sun is out and the breeze is blowing.[457]

The Salvation Army itself sustained serious loss. Corps buildings and quarters were damaged across southern Haiti but none more than in Port-au-Prince. All but one building was declared unsafe. Although none had collapsed, all bore huge cracks that, with the right aftershock, were in danger of tumbling down. The one building that was considered safe was later declared unsalvageable. Still, the Haitian Salvationists found there was no place they should be on a Sunday morning other than the Army.[458]

At the Salvation Army compound, although its own church building was unsafe to enter, more than 1,000 people gathered in an open-air worship service. Amazingly, despite all that had happened, Salvation Army soldiers showed up in clean and freshly pressed white uniforms. Colonels Onal and Edmane Castor, territorial leaders for The Salvation Army's Caribbean Territory, themselves Haitian, were deeply moved by what they saw and experienced. Colonel Onal Castor said,

> Here I stood in the land of my birth, where I was raised, went to school, and served as a Salvation Army officer. And all around, all that I knew was in ruins. But the Salvation Army spirit was not diminished. God was alive in our people, and amid all the sadness there was a beautiful sense of triumph. We do not know how we will rebuild or what the future holds, but we are confident that God will make a way. The meeting that morning was an assurance that we are not abandoned by God and we will come through victoriously through Him.[459]

Major Lucien Lamartiniere

VOICES FROM HAITI

———◦)◦(◦———

I had an officers' meeting early in the day. After the meeting my wife and I were on our way home. I dropped her off to run errands and then I continued home; I forgot I had meant to buy some juice at the nearby supermarket. At that moment I felt the earthquake. I immediately knew what it was, and I ran out of my house. The supermarket, where I would have gone to buy juice, was completely destroyed. If I had gone there on the way home, as planned, I would be dead.

I couldn't drive through the streets, so I walked to where my wife was. At the same time she was walking back to our house, and we didn't meet up. When she got home, she saw the house was gone, destroyed. She saw my car. But she didn't see me. She thought that I was in there, in the house. She begged the neighbors to help her get into the house, but they told her, "No, this is not the time. It is not safe; you cannot do that." After ten minutes I got back home. When she saw me she began to cry, she was so happy.

Now in Haiti, people need food immediately. This is the rainy season, and people can't sleep without something to cover them. They need shelter. There are some who lost even their clothes. We are still in an emergency. The schools cannot run, even in the western part of the country, where they are accommodating many schools that collapsed in the city. Our National Palace was destroyed. The Parliament office, destroyed. The Palace of Justice, destroyed. Everything that was the symbol of Haiti was destroyed. Someone told me, it seems that the Lord wants to teach us something. I tell people, now is the time to approach the Lord, to be closer to Him.

An unexpected development was the increased attendances at Salvation Army corps across the country, but particularly in the areas most affected by the earthquake. Divisional commander Major Lucien Lamartiniere explained, "People thought the end of the world came so many, many were converted. Just in Port-au-Prince, in the year after the quake, 84 people were enrolled as senior soldiers, almost all of them new to the Army since the earthquake."[460]

For a long time the Army was fully occupied with emergency care, especially to the 20,000 refugees who had camped out in The Salvation Army compound and adjoining football field. Substantial feeding efforts continued in Port-au-Prince, Jacmel and Petit Goâve.

Almost immediately, The Salvation Army began to formulate a long term strategic plan. The chief secretary, Lt. Colonel Lindsay Rowe, was given little more than two weeks to formulate a plan for the next five years while the full extent of the damage was not yet fully known. The document called, "Initial Project Assessment Team (Haiti) Survey," was presented at a special conference called by International Headquarters in London April 7-15, 2010. The following priorities were outlined:

- The desire to "build back better" in Haiti post-earthquake
- The response should include elements to support the holistic mission of The Salvation Army; considering ways to meet the spiritual, emotional and physical needs of the people of Haiti
- The response should seek to strengthen the current ministry, program and structures of The Salvation Army in Haiti
- Support should not be entirely focused on Port-au-Prince but should rather be decentralized and impact on the Haiti Division[461]

Reported also to the conference was that there were at that time 17,000 people still in the camp being run by The Salvation Army—some had already left to go back to their homes in the countryside. It was also discovered that some of the families in the rural areas had doubled or tripled in size as people fled the Port-au-Prince area.[462]

The Salvation Army decided that a separate department should be created at the Haiti Divisional Headquarters which was ultimately named the Haiti Recovery and Development

Office. One of the tasks given to it was a transitional housing project that, with adequate funding, would build 10,000 houses in two phases.[463]

Vision for the Future

INITIAL PROJECT ASSESSMENT TEAM (HAITI) SURVEY

The Salvation Army in Haiti will continue to develop and increase its influence by drawing on our knowledge and past experiences. We will continue to see exponential growth through the continued development of our community programmes and will continue to see God saving people through our ministries.

Our ministries provide both culturally relevant/sensitive and scripturally accurate teachings to the Haitian community. By committing ourselves to addressing the needs of the community we will inspire new friends and supporters and enhance the image and profile of the Army in Haiti.

The recovery effort will need to provide Haitians with homes, hospitals and offices that can at least resist mid-power quakes like this one and which could provide protection from the island's many other natural threats: floods, hurricanes and mudslides. And it has to be affordable—in the short term, at least, Haiti will only become poorer.

The recovery effort must build up, not supplant, the Haitian government and civil society, starting with putting Haitian authorities at the centre of a single, clearly defined plan to rebuild Port-au-Prince and its environs in a far studier form.

It was further proposed that all the Army buildings at Delmas 2, which included the corps, divisional headquarters, the College Verena School, the nursing home and clinic, should be demolished and the space reallocated. The new master plan included a major expansion of the health clinic with an accompanying extension of its mission to provide a wider scope of services with additional staff. The old corps building was to be replaced with a new one that would seat 3,000 people, making it the largest corps building in the Caribbean and the Americas. The children's home was to be rebuilt to house solely orphans, the number of whom skyrocketed because of the tens of thousands of parents and caregivers killed in the quake. Previously the home had also been taking in children whose families were disadvantaged. Concern was expressed for the many amputees, particularly children. Rather than setting up specific schools to meet their needs, it was proposed that Salvation Army schools be made "amputee friendly" so that those who have lost limbs would not be isolated but rather mainstreamed in the community at large where they would eventually have to function anyway.[464]

General Shaw Clifton attended the closing session of the conference. Thanking the direct service providers to the Haitian people and those who were there to support the mammoth efforts that the recovery of Haiti represents, he then said,

> If we find ourselves under pressure from donors or other sources to take a particular course of action or to adopt some strategy that is not consistent with the needs, vision, aspirations or protocols of the host territory, then we shall not take that course. At the same time, the host territory will consistently respect the high personal cost and the very significant degree of input that will continue to emerge from the territories represented goals and the synchronizing of actions will be the key.
>
> James 1:27 says, "Religion that God our Father accepts as pure and faultless is this: to look after orphans and widows in their distress and to keep oneself from being polluted by the world."
>
> Genuine religion has a practical aspect to it. It gets revealed in helping others in distress. It is revealed also in being free from the corruption of worldly things and standards. I see our efforts in Haiti in this light. We are doing practical work, getting our hands dirty. That is good and God will honour it. What is even better is that this work is being done by people who know the blessing of a clean heart and are uncorrupted by the world. Therefore, I salute each one and I ask Almighty God to bless you richly for the task ahead.[465]

Major Ron Busroe

I flew in two days after the earthquake. The international team flew in a day after the quake. But they were diverted to Cap-Haïtien. I was on the second flight.

I found a place to stay which wasn't easy because so much was damaged. We began organizing incident command structure. Dr. Prosper had set up clinic in the open air, serving people with horrendous injuries. A few days later a team of doctors from Tulsa came to help. The clinic moved to the College Verena building because it was structurally sound. They kept operating there until school started operating a couple of months later.

The first week we were approached by the territorial commander, Colonel Onal Castor. He realized it was going to take years and a system had to be in place. But we didn't hear anything until the end of June when International Headquarters called.

Lt. Colonel Rowe, the chief secretary, put together a strategic plan the first week in March. I worked with him on it from Atlanta, including organizational structure within the Haiti Division.

When some of the international relief workers came in as well as some of The Salvation Army support personnel, they initially were bypassing the Haiti Division and with it, the Caribbean Territory. While they might have been well meaning and were trying to get work done under very arduous circumstances, their attitude marginalized Major Lamartiniere, the divisional commander.

Our efforts changed it so that it was set up where we were answerable to divisional commander.

Following the conference it was decided to appoint Majors Ron and Carol Busroe to head the Haiti Recovery and Development Office (HRD). In recent years, the Busroes had served two consecutive terms as the divisional leaders in Haiti and knew well both the country and the people.

Major Ron Busroe outlined the goals set by the HRD as follows:

1. To organize and implement long term recovery efforts by the Haiti Division. US$49 million has been raised by The Salvation Army. It is important that the money be invested wisely in serving suffering humanity. There needs to be a means of helping the people to recover. That includes counseling, vocational training or other efforts as may become apparent. It should be remembered that Haiti had a 70 percent unemployment rate *before* the earthquake.
2. The Salvation Army infrastructure needs to be rebuilt, especially in Port-au-Prince.
3. There needs to be a long term commitment to create a larger Salvation Army in Haiti. That means more social services beyond schools and medical clinics. It will mean working with families through micro-credit, vocational training and other means. The Haiti Division will have to increase the number of programs past the five years envisioned for the existence of the HRD. There will need to be an office of social affairs, increased staffing in accounting and property departments.
4. If there is an expatriate assisting in the recovery effort, it will mean that a Haitian national will need to be assisting so that he/she can take over the position when the expatriate leaves. Haiti needs Haitians. Whatever transpires must be what Haiti feels it needs, not what someone outside thinks it needs.[466]

Never has the Caribbean Territory shown itself truer to the principles of Scripture or to the ideals of The Salvation Army than it did in its work in Haiti since the earthquake. As soon as the earthquake hit, Salvation Army officers and soldiers supplemented by hundreds of non-Salvationist volunteers, freely offered themselves to go to the prostrate country in order to help it to find its feet again. Salvation Army officers from across the Caribbean Territory left their present duties and their families to work to the point of exhaustion on behalf of the great sea of suffering people in their near neighbor, Haiti. The giving was open-handed, neither looking for a reward nor waiting for an expression of appreciation. It was this spirit that caused those in need during the crisis to often throng the person in Salvation Army uniform. These people, they believed, would do something to help them. And they did.

The same fault line that Haiti sits on stretches across the Caribbean to Jamaica where it sank Port Royal during the days of the pirates and destroyed Kingston in 1907. Fault lines do not stay in place, guaranteeing that more earthquakes will affect the region. In the Caribbean, when it is not the earth moving, it is the skies that angrily knock down homes and destroy crops every hurricane season or heavy rains that swell rivers, washing away people, their homes and their dreams. The nature of the region is that disasters will be followed by more disasters, suffering will be followed by more suffering.

What makes it bearable is that the Caribbean people have learned to help each other. In The Salvation Army that spirit is married with the spirit of Christlike service that not only kneels to bandage wounds but reaches to the soul of the sufferer with the hope of eternal salvation. It creates a channel of blessing, a strong gentleness, a commitment to claw through concrete to seek for the lost and hurting.

It is that spirit that has made The Salvation Army in the Caribbean determined to conquer.

ENDNOTES

Chapter 1

Hobbs, Doreen. *Jewels of the Caribbean*. The Salvation Army, London: 1984: 2
The War Cry, October 1899:10
Phillips, Raglan. "Mrs. Adjutant Phillips of Jamaica, W.I." *Harbor Lights,* 1899: 174
1885:54
Hobbs: 3
The War Cry, January 2, 1888:4
The War Cry (USA) December 10, 1887:5
The Daily Gleaner, November 14, 1887:11
Gall's Newsletter, December 10:1887
[10] *The War Cry*, January 14, 1888
[11] *The Daily Gleaner,* December 19, 1887
[12] January 2, 1888:9
[13] *The War Cry*, January 1978:4
[14] *The War Cry*, May 26, 1888:10
[15] *The War Cry,* USA, May 5, 1888:11
[16] *All the World,* March 1888:68
[17] *The War Cry,* USA June 2, 1888:14
[18] *The Daily Gleaner,* April 7, 1887: 6
[19] *The War Cry* USA, June 9, 1888:14
[20] *The Jamaica Post,* October 11, 1889
[21] Correspondence from Colonel Davey to Chief of the Staff Mr. Bramwell Booth, October 9, 1888
[22] *Gall's Newsletter,* September 25, 1888 and September 29, 1888
[23] September 29, 1888:3
[24] *The Salvation Army Year Book* 1966:50
[25] October 2, 1888
[26] October 9, 1888
[27] *The Daily Gleaner,* December 11, 1888:2
[28] February 18, 1889
[29] *The Salvation Army Year Book* 1966:51
[30] *All the World,* June 1897:281
[31] *The Salvation Army Year Book,* 1966:51
[32] Hobbs, Doreen. *Jewels of the Caribbean,* 1984:19
[33] *The Salvation Army Year Book,* 1966:51
[34] *All the World,* July 1892:18
[35] *All the World,* September 1892:206
[36] *Conqueror,* 1892:230
[37] *The Salvation Army Year Book,* 1966:51
[38] *All the World,* July 1892:18
[39] *The War Cry* USA, September 9, 1892
[40] *The Daily Gleaner,* May 26, 1893:14; February 8, 1896: August 21, 1897
[41] Ibid.
[42] May 13, 1893:6
[43] *The Daily Gleaner,* June 8, 1891:
[44] *The Daily Gleaner,* August 8, 1893:6
[45] *The Daily Gleaner,* May 18, 1897
[46] Church Army Online website: http://www.churcharmy.org.uk/pub/aboutus/international/Jamaica accessed on 31 March 2011.
[47] *The Daily Gleaner,* September 26, 1892
[48] *The Daily Gleaner,* February 9, 1893
[49] *The Daily Gleaner,* October 20, 1891
[50] *The Daily Gleaner,* December 18, 1892

Chapter 2

[51] *The Daily Gleaner,* February 9, 1892
[52] *The Daily Gleaner,* September 17, 1892
[53] *The Daily Gleaner,* June 21, 1893:7
[54] *The Daily Gleaner,* August 8, 1895
[55] *The Daily Gleaner,* June 5, 1897:9
[56] May 18, 1897
[57] *Conqueror,* 1895:483
[58] *The War Cry,* August 1945:4
[59] *All the World,* August 1895:102
[60] *The War Cry* USA, May 4, 1895:8
[61] The Daily Gleaner, May 6, 1898:4
[62] *All the World,* July 1893:51
[63] *The War Cry,* September 23, 1909:3
[64] July 1893:52

Chapter 3

[65] *All the World,* June 1896; The Officer May 1895:136-137
[66] *The War Cry,* June 8, 1895:6
[67] *All the World,* October 1895:213
[68] *The War Cry,* August 31, 1895:12
[69] *Centennial Congress Brochure,* 1995:28
[70] *The War Cry,* July 13, 1895:5
[71] *All the World,* July 1896:301
[72] Doreen Hobbs, *Jewels of the Caribbean*: 88
[73] *Daily Nation,* April 27, 1998:28A
[74] *A History of Barbados,* 2006:196-197
[75] Ibid., 222
[76] April 24,1898
[77] June 16, 1898
[78] *Barbados Advocate,* May 17, 1898:39
[79] *Barbados 100th Anniversary Brochure*: 13
[80] May 5, 1898:3
[81] May 26:2
[82] *Barbados Advocate,* May 28, 1898:5
[83] *Barbados Advocate,* June 11, 1898:5
[84] *Barbados Advocate,* June 4, 1898:6
[85] *The War Cry,* October 1, 1898:4
[86] *A History of Barbados*: 202, 204-205
[87] *Barbados Anniversary Brochure*: 15
[88] *All the World,* 1899: 207-208
[89] *The Daily Gleaner,* January 13, 1899:12
[90] *Harbor Lights,* 1898:148
[91] *All the World,* May 1895:343
[92] *All the World,* n.d.:570
[93] *All the World,* n.d.:92
[94] *The War Cry,* USA September 16, 1899
[95] *All the World,* June 1897: 281
[96] *The War Cry* USA, August 5, 1899
[97] *Jewels of the Caribbean*: 26
[98] *The Daily Gleaner,* September 20, 1899
[99] *The Officer,* March 1896:72
[100] n.d.: 661

[101] August 24, 1895:7

Chapter 4

[102] *The Daily Gleaner,* February 20, 1900:2
[103] Jewels of the Caribbean: 59
[104] *The Daily Gleaner,* February 20, 1900:2
[105] *The War Cry,* October 5, 1901
[106] July 21, 1900:4
[107] *The Daily Gleaner,* August 8, 1900:7
[108] *The Daily Gleaner,* September 11, 1900:7
[109] *The Daily Gleaner,* June 17, 1900:13
[110] *The Daily Gleaner,* October 27, 1902:2
[111] *All the World:* 448
[112] *Jewels of the Caribbean:* 76, All the World, 1902:111
[113] *The Salvation Army Year Book* 1952:25
[114] *Jewels of the Caribbean:* 78
[115] *All the World,* July 1902
[116] *The Daily Gleaner,* April 9, 1902:7 and May 5, 2002:A2
[117] *The War Cry,* July 1975:3
[118] *Jewels of the Caribbean:* 60
[119] Correspondence from E.M. Richardson, January 6, 1983
[120] *All the World,* n.d.: 600
[121] *All the World:* 1903:36
[122] *The War Cry,* February 13, 1904:5
[123] Coutts, Frederick. *Down in Demerara:* 3-4
[124] *All the World,* n.d.: 152-153
[125] *Down in Demerara:* 3-4
[126] *Ibid.,* 6-8
[127] *All the World,* 1910: 636-638
[128] *Down in Demerara:* 13-14
[129] *The War Cry,* April 11, 1904:6
[130] *The War Cry,* November 12, 1904
[131] *The Daily Gleaner,* September 27, 1907
[132] *The Daily Gleaner,* July 27, 1907:9
[133] *All the World,* 1905:607
[134] *The War Cry,* August 11, 1902:12
[135] *The War Cry,* August 19, 1905:4
[136] *All the World,* 1905:607
[137] *The War Cry,* June 24, 1905:4
[138] February 9, 1907, Quoted in Jewels of the Caribbean: 99
[139] December 15, 1905:6
[140] *The Officer,* n.d: 132
[141] *The Daily Gleaner,* February 9, 1904
[142] *Daily Chronicle,* December 5, 1905
[143] *Jewels of the Caribbean:*55
[144] *The Daily Gleaner,* April 2, 1906:11
[145] *Jewels of the Caribbean:*68
[146] "Disaster – The Earthquake of 1907" Jamaica Gleaner, Internet:
   http://jamaica-gleaner.com/pages/history/story0017.html accessed April 2, 2011
[147] *The War Cry,* March 16, 1907:11
[148] *The War Cry,* February 23, 1907:11
[149] *The War Cry,* January 23, 1907
[150] *The Social Gazette,* February 16, 1907
[151] Quoted in *The War Cry,* February 23, 1907:11

[152] *The War Cry,* February 16, 1907:12
[153] *The Daily Gleaner,* October 26, 1907
[154] *The War Cry* USA, January 26, 1907:8
[155] *The War Cry,* July 1907:5

Chapter 5

[156] *The Daily Gleaner,* April 27, 1909, May 4, 1909, June 5, 1909, June 9, 1909, July 17, 1909, October 27, 1910. There were many more exchanges but these are a sampling. Probably 30-40 letters were written over the course of this time.
[157] *The Daily Gleaner,* July 17,1910
[158] *The Salvation Army Year Book,* 1913:20
[159] *The War Cry,* March 16, 1912:14
[160] *The Daily Gleaner,* January 24, 1912:13
[161] August 30, 1912:1
[162] *The Daily Gleaner,* June 7, 1914
[163] *The Salvation Army Year Book* 1967:22
[164] *The Daily Gleaner,* March 16, 1914
[165] *The Daily Gleaner,* August 18, 1913
[166] *The Daily Gleaner,* November 4, 1914:3
[167] *The Daily Gleaner,* December 29, 1916
[168] *Diamond Jubilee Brochure,* 1947:39
[169] *Jewels of the Caribbean*
[170] *Ibid.,* 108
[171] *Ibid.,* 95-96 and *The War Cry,* October 26, 1916
[172] *The War Cry,* November 25, 1916:3
[173] *The War Cry,* May 31, 1919:3
[174] *The Daily Gleaner,* September 18, 1917
[175] *The Daily Gleaner,* November 7, 1918:5
[176] Jewels of the Caribbean: 115
[177] *All the World,* January 1917:28-29
[178] *Ibid.,* 27
[179] *All the World,* n.d.: 117

Chapter 6

[180] "Devourer of Souls, Extinguisher of the Human Spirit", Henry Ramsager, Internet: http://www.suite101.com/content/devil-s-island-a5890 Accessed April 3, 2011.
[181] *The Officer,* November 1931:194
[182] *The Officer,* November 1936:502
[183] Charles Péan, *The Conquest of Devil's Island:* 56-57
[184] *Ibid.,* 7
[185] *Ibid.,* 10
[186] *Ibid.,* 21
[187] *Ibid.,* 45
[188] *Ibid.,* 56
[189] *Ibid.,* 71
[190] *Ibid.,* 74-75
[191] *Ibid.,* 81
[192] *Ibid.,* 94
[193] *Ibid.,* 97
[194] *Ibid.,* 91
[195] *Ibid.,* 100-101
[196] *Ibid.,* 74-75
[197] *Ibid.,* 103

[198] *Everybody's* July 2, 1949
[199] Correspondence from Lt. Colonel E. Chastagnier to Major Doreen Hobbs, n.d.

Chapter 7

[200] Correspondence from Colonel Orval Taylor March 1, 1982
[201] Correspondence from Walter Shaw, April 9, 1956
[202] *The Salvation Army Year Book* 1952:22 - 23
[203] *Jewels of the Caribbean:* 68
[204] *Ibid.*, 81
[205] *The War Cry,* January 21, 1921:6
[206] Interview with Major Keith Graham, March 10, 2011
[207] Theodore Sealy, *Sealy's Caribbean Leaders:* 38-39
[208] Quoted in *The History of Barbados:*203
[209] *All the World* 1924:114
[210] *The War Cry,* n.d.
[211] *The War Cry,* January 1955:3
[212] *Jewels of the Caribbean:* 128
[213] *The War Cry,* December 18, 1926:4
[214] PR Release 1984:1
[215] *The War Cry,* July 16, 1927
[216] Pg. 13
[217] *The Salvation Army Year Book,* 1951:13
[218] *50th Anniversary Brochure,* School for the Blind:7
[219] *The Salvation Army Year Book,* 1929:112
[220] *The War Cry* December 28, 1928:7
[221] *The Daily Gleaner,* April 4, 1928
[222] *The Daily Gleaner,* September 2, 1927
[223] *Jewels of the Caribbean:* 117, 119
[224] *The Daily Gleaner,* February 2, 1928:3
[225] *The Daily Gleaner,* April 20, 1928:10
[226] *The Daily Gleaner,* May 17, 1928
[227] *The Daily Gleaner,* August 8, 1928:6
[228] *The Daily Gleaner,* June 1, 1929:4
[229] *The Daily Gleaner,* May 17, 1928
[230] *The War Cry,* September 28, 1929:4
[231] *The Daily Gleaner,* May 27, 1929:14
[232] *Antigua Anniversary Brochure,* 1983: 13
[233] *The Salvation Army Year Book,* 1932:103
[234] *All the World*,1928:29
[235] *The Daily Gleaner,* June 17, 1930:16
[236] *Ibid.*

Chapter 8

[237] *Guardian,* May 30, 1931: 4
[238] *Guardian,* June 6, 1931:4
[239] *The Tribune,* May 30, 1931:4
[240] *The Tribune,* June 6, 1931:6
[241] Interview with Carolyn Strachan, June 10, 2010
[242] *The Daily Gleaner,* September 15, 1931
[243] *The Daily Gleaner,* September 15, 1931
[244] *The Daily Gleaner,* September 22, 1931
[245] *The Daily Gleaner,* February 9, 1931:10
[246] *Ibid.*

[247] *The Salvation Army Year Book,* 1933:111
[248] *Ibid.,* 110
[249] *Jewels of the Caribbean:* 83
[250] *All the World,* 1982:141
[251] *The Salvation Army Year Book,* 1934:51
[252] *Jewels of the Caribbean:* 134-135
[253] *Ibid.,* 135
[254] *The Daily Gleaner,* April 12, 1934:19
[255] *The Salvation Army Year Book,* 1936:49-50
[256] *The Salvation Army Year Book,* 1936:52
[257] *The Daily Gleaner,* August 30, 1937:13
[258] *The Daily Gleaner,* March 19, 1936
[259] *The Salvation Army Year Book,* 1939:74
[260] *The Salvation Army Year Book,* 1952:26
[261] *The Daily Gleaner,* November 11, 1937
[262] *The Daily Gleaner,* March 13, 1939:10
[263] *The Daily Gleaner,* September 9, 1940:10
[264] *The Daily Gleaner,* October 25, 1939
[265] *The Daily Gleaner,* April 19, 1937:20
[266] *Jewels of the Caribbean:* 132
[267] *The Daily Gleaner,* April 11, 1939:20
[268] *The Daily Gleaner,* December 21, 1939:20
[269] *The Salvation Army Year Book,* 1941:71
[270] *Diamond Jubilee Brochure,* 1947:4
[271] *Jewels of the Caribbean:* 79, 82
[272] *The Salvation Army Year Book,* 1944:36
[273] Territorial Commander's Report to the Chief of the Staff from Colonel Hodgson, 1940
[274] *The Salvation Army Year Book,* 1941:62
[275] *The Salvation Army Year Book,* 1944:36
[276] *Salvation Army History of Belfield School,* n.d.: 1-2
[277] *The Daily Gleaner,* March 1, 1945:5
[278] *The War Cry,* December 5, 1942

Chapter 9

[279] Reminiscences of Brigadier Thomas H. Brooks, n.d.
[280] *All the World,* October 1947:273
[281] *Ibid.,* and *Jewels of the Caribbean:* 69
[282] *All the World,* July 1949:245
[283] *A Brief Sketch of British Honduras,* A.H. Anderson:43
[284] *All the World,* 1982:142
[285] *Diamond Jubilee Brochure,* 1947:55, 56
[286] *The Salvation Army Year Book,* 1954:19
[287] *Jewels of the Caribbean:* 149
[288] *The Daily Gleaner,* August 17, 1949:49
[289] *All the World,* 1950:98 - 99
[290] Interview with Mrs. Major Emilia Joseph, January 16, 2011
[291] *All the World,* 1950: 98-99
[292] *Ibid.,* and *Jewels of the Caribbean:* 170-171
[293] *Article "First Salvation Army Hall"* n.d.
[294] *Memoirs of Commissioner Jacques Egger,* n.d.
[295] Correspondence of Captain Jacques Egger to Colonel William Sansom, October 3, 1951
[296] Egger, *Memoirs*
[297] Correspondence of Colonel William Sansom to Commissioner J.B. Smith, November 16, 1951

[298] *Ibid.*

[299] *Ibid.*

[300] Correspondence from Carrie Guillaume to the President of Haiti, October 3, 1951 (Translated into English)

[301] Correspondence of Colonel William Sansom to Commissioner J.B. Smith, November 16, 1951

[302] Egger, *Memoirs*

[303] *Jewels of the Caribbean:* 121

[304] "A Child Is Born" *Salvation Army Year Book*, n.d.

[305] *All the World,* July 1959: 232

[306] *The Salvation Army Groot Chatillon Report,* September 17, 1960:3, 5

[307] *The Salvation Army Year Book,* 1957:96

[308] *All the World,* July 1955:224

[309] *Ibid.*

[310] *The Daily Gleaner,* 1959

[311] *The Salvation Army Year Book,* 1957:119

[312] *The War Cry,* September 1960:8

[313] Recollections of Major A. Bruynis

Chapter 10

[314] *Jewels of the Caribbean:* 122

[315] *The Salvation Army Year Book,* 1963:74

[316] Pg. 86

[317] *The Salvation Army Year Book,* 1967: 23-24

[318] *The Salvation Army Year Book,* 1962:75

[319] Leo Bradley, Glimpses of our History 1962:35-36

[320] Milton H. Arana, *Cry Wolf:* 12

[321] Interview with Major Errol Robateau, May 31, 2010

[322] *The Salvation Army Year Book,* 1965:134

[323] *Jewels of the Caribbean:* 176

[324] *Ibid.,* 175-176

[325] *The War Cry,* 1965:5

[326] *The War Cry,* July 1963:3

[327] *Jewels of the Caribbean:* 179

[328] *The War Cry,* July 1964:4

[329] *The War Cry,* November 1964:4

[330] *All the World,* July 1964:80

[331] *The Salvation Army Year Book,* 1967:96

[332] *Salvationist,* August 5, 1995

[333] *The Daily Gleaner,* June 23, 1965: 10

[334] *All the World,* 1965:69

[335] *The Daily Gleaner,* February 5, 1966

[336] *The War Cry,* June 1966:7

[337] *The War Cry,* March 1966:3

[338] *The Salvation Army Year Book,* 1977:24

[339] *The War Cry,* March 1967:5

[340] *The Daily Gleaner,* March 20, 1969:8

[341] *The Salvation Army Year Book:* 95

[342] Interview with Major Gladys Lucario, March 11, 2011

[343] *The Salvation Army School for the Blind 50th Anniversary Brochure:* 19

[344] Interview with Lt. Colonels Ian and Mary Begley, March 21, 2011

[345] *Jewels of the Caribbean:* 149

[346] *The War Cry,* July 1971:3

[347] *The War Cry,* January 1968

348 *The Salvation Army Year Book,* 1975:27
349 *The Daily Gleaner,* June 30, 1971:2
350 *The War Cry,* June 9, 1972
351 *The War Cry,* March 1974:2
352 *The War Cry,* 1969; Williamsfield Training Centre Brochure, n.d.
353 *Ibid.*
354 *The War Cry,* March 1973:2

Chapter 11

355 *The War Cry,* April 1998:5
356 *The War Cry,* August 1974:7
357 *The War Cry,* February 1975:5-6
358 *The Salvation Army Year Book,* 1974:95
359 April 1976: 49-51
360 *All the World,* February 1973:92
361 *The Salvation Army Year Book,* 1976:110
362 *Jewels of the Caribbean:* 133
363 *The School for the Blind 50th Anniversary Brochure:* 30
364 *The Daily Gleaner,* October 7, 1975:4
365 *The War Cry,* November 1975:4
366 *The War Cry,* November 1974:11
367 *The Salvation Army Year Book,* 1976:6
368 *The War Cry,* January 1976:2
369 *The War Cry,* February 1976:7
370 September 29, 1976:11
371 *The Salvation Army Year Book,* 1977:92
372 *The War Cry,* May 1976:5-6
373 Interview with Lt. Colonel Sydney McKenzie, March 11, 2011
374 *The War Cry,* October 1976:3
375 Interview with Mrs. Major Pyles, September 17, 2010
376 *All the World,* April 1981
377 *The War Cry,* September 1980:2
378 *The Salvation Army Year Book,* 1982:106
379 *The Salvation Army Year Book,* 1981:109
380 *The Salvation Army Year Book,* 1982:105
381 Edward Read, *In the Hands of Another:* 174
382 *The Daily Gleaner,* September 12, 1981:18
383 *The Salvation Army Year Book,* 1982:105
384 *The Daily Gleaner,* May 23, 1982:1
385 *Jewels of the Caribbean:* 167
386 David Baxendale, *Reminiscences:*88
387 *The Salvation Army Year Book,* 1989:116
388 *Salvationist,* October 24, 1987:3
389 *The War Cry,* June 1987:3
390 *The Salvation Army Year Book,* 1989:117
391 Baxendale: 85
392 *The Salvation Army Year Book,* 1989:118

Chapter 12

393 "Hurricane Gilbert" Wikipedia. http://en.wikipedia.org/wiki/
    Hurricane_Gilbert Accessed April 6, 2011
394 Interview with Major Keith Graham
395 *The War Cry,* Special Edition 1988:26

[396] *Ibid.,* 7
[397] *Ibid.,* 24
[398] David Baxendale, *Reminiscences:* 93-96
[399] *The War Cry Special Edition:*2
[400] *Ibid.,* 10-11
[401] Interview with Lt. Colonel Clinton Burrowes
[402] *The Salvation Army Year Book,* 1992:82
[403] Questionnaire from Commissioners David and Doreen Edwards, January 2011
[404] *The War Cry,* April 1990:2
[405] *The War Cry,* May 1990:3
[406] *The War Cry,* November 1997:6
[407] *The Salvation Army Year Book,* 1992:81
[408] *The War Cry,* February 1991:3
[409] *The War Cry,* October 1990:3
[410] Begley Interview
[411] *The Salvation Army Year Book,* 1982:82
[412] *The War Cry,* September 1991:8
[413] *Antigua Centennial Brochure:* 28
[414] *The Salvation Army Year Book* 1994:90
[415] *All the World,* July 1992
[416] Interview with Lt. Colonel Clinton Burrows
[417] August 1995:4
[418] *The Salvation Army Year Book,* 1998:86
[419] *The Salvation Army Year Book,* 1998:87
[420] *The Salvation Army Year Book,* 2000:85
[421] *Salvationist,* April 10, 1999
[422] *Ibid.*

Chapter 13

[423] *The War Cry,* April 2000:9
[424] *The Salvation Army Year Book,* 2006:15
[425] Pg. 181
[426] *The War Cry,* April 2000:9
[427] Reminiscences of Major Molvie Graham
[428] *The Salvation Army Year Book,* 2002:83
[429] *The Salvation Army Year Book,* 2005:89
[430] *The War Cry,* March 2003:12
[431] *The Salvation Army Year Book,* 2005:89
[432] *The War Cry,* April 2004:12
[433] *The War Cry,* December 2004:12,14
[434] *The Salvation Army Year Book,* 2006:88
[435] *The War Cry,* March 2005:12
[436] *The Salvation Army Year Book,* 2007:89
[437] Interview with Major Sinuous Theodore
[438] "Leptospirosis" Pub Med Health
http://www.ncbi.nih.gov./pubmedhealth/PMH0002352/ Accessed April 7, 2011
[439] Interview with Major Sinuous Theodore
[440] *The Salvation Army Year Book,* 2007:16
[441] *Barbados 110th Anniversary Brochure:* 18
[442] Barbados *Sunday Sun Extra,* February 13, 2005:4
[443] *The Salvation Army Year Book,* 2006:88
[444] *The Salvation Army Year Book,* 2008:88
[445] *The War Cry,* May 2008:4
[446] *The War Cry,* January 2010:4

[447] Interview with Commissioners Raymond and Judith Houghton

[448] *"Salvation Army Now Working in 122 Countries,"* The Salvation Army International News Release, December 13, 2010

[449] *The Salvation Army Year Book* 2009:89

Chapter 14

[450] Allen Satterlee, *Voices from Haiti:*12

[451] *Ibid.*

[452] *Ibid.,* 13

[453] *Ibid.,* 17-21

[454] *Ibid.,* 25

[455] Quoted in *Voices from Haiti:* 55

[456] *Ibid.,* 72-74

[457] *Ibid.,* 82-84

[458] *Ibid.,* 89

[459] *Ibid.,* 87

[460] Interview with Major Lucien Lamartiniere

[461] Section 2.1:9

[462] Ibid., 35

[463] Ibid., 74

[464] Ibid., 92,93

[465] Ibid., 98

[466] Interview with Major Ron Busroe

All the World, 1885 - 2006

Anderson, A.H., *A Brief Sketch of British Honduras,* unpublished manuscript. 1954

Arana, Milton E. *Cry Wolf.* New York: Vantage Press (1993)

Baxendale, David. *Memoirs,* unpublished. 2008

Beckles, Hilary and Shepherd, Verene (Editors), *Caribbean Freedom: Economy and Society from Emancipation to the Present,* Ian Randle Publishers: Kingston, 1996

Beckles, Hilary, *A History of Barbados,* Cambridge University Press: Cambridge, England, 2006

Bisnauth, Dale A. *History of Religions in the Caribbean,* Kingston Publishers Ltd: Kingston, 1993

Bradley, Leo. *Glimpses of our History.* Unpublished manuscript: Belize City: 1962

Brerton, Bridges (Editor), *General History of the Caribbean, Volume V, The Caribbean in the Twentieth Century.* UNESCO Publishing: Paris, 2004

CARICOM: Our Caribbean Community, Ian Randle Publishers: Kingston, 2005

Compton, Jacques, *The West Indians.* Hansib Publications Ltd: Hertford, Hertfordshire, England, 2009

Coutts, Frederick L. *Down in Demerara: Alexander Alexander,* O.F. Salvationist Publishing and Supplies, Ltd: London, 1944

Egger, Jacques. *Memoirs,* unpublished: n.d.

Ferguson, James. *The Story of the Caribbean People.* Ian Randle Publishing: Kingston, 1998

Payne, Anthony and Sutton, Paul. *Charting Caribbean Development,* Macmillan Education Publishing, Ltd: London, 2001

Read, Edward. *In the Hands of Another,* The Salvation Army: Toronto, 2002

Rogozinski, Jan. *A Brief History of the Caribbean.* Penguin: London, 1999

The Salvation Army Year Book: The Salvation Army International Headquarters: London

Salvationist, The Salvation Army United Kingdom Territory: London

Satterlee, Allen. *Voices from Haiti.* Whitman Publishing: Atlanta, 2010

Sealy, Theodore. *Sealy's Caribbean Leaders.* Eagle Merchant Bank of Jamaica, Ltd., 1991

The War Cry West Indies Territory: Kingston 1887 - 2010

The War Cry USA: New York 1887 - 2010

Anthoine, CSM Itezy
Begley, Lt. Colonels Ian and Mary
Buckley, Major Alice
Buidman, Maureen
Burnside, Garnard
Burrowes, Lt. Colonel Clifton
Busroe, Major Ron
Busroe, Major Carol
Castor, Colonel Onal
Codfried, Georgetina
Conorique, CSM Eustice
Contave, Major Miller
David, Sheldon
Davidson, Stephanie
DeLouis, Marcelin
Derendamie, Mr. and Mrs.
Dover, Jane
Falex, Juan
Fredericks, Marlene
Gaspard, Major Chantel
Graham, Major Keith
Greaves, CSM Useph
Haefli, Major Rose Marie
Haughton, Commissioners
  Raymond and Judith
Hills, Major Cedric
Hiwat, Envoy Virginia
Hobbs, Major Doreen
Hoyt, Major Erly
James, Lillian
James, Marian
Johnson, Valli
Jonas, CSM George T.
Joseph, Major Ezrulia
Joseph, Pierre
Karg, CSM William

King, Edith
Lamartiniere, Major Lucien
Limon, Eric Harold
Louden, Major Tom
Louissaint, Lt. Colonel Franck
Lucario, Major Gladys
Maharban, Anitrdebie
Malone, Barbara
Marshall, Charles
Matear, Commissioners John
  and Betty
McDonald, Emiline
McKenzie, Lt. Colonel Sydney
Morancy, Major Voyons
Mott, Major Carmen Rose
Noel, Wesley
Overman, Major Renia
Pacquett, Major Catherine
Pierre, Lt. Colonel Alfred
Pierrelouis, Marie Ange
Poff, Envoy Bob
Purser, Lt. Colonel Dorothy
Pyles, Mrs. Major Hazel
Roberts, Maylene
Robateau, Major Errol
Rowe, Lt. Colonel Lindsay
Salomon, Majors Lysius and Anine
St. Aime, Major Serge
Seymonson, Envoy Marceline
Small, Elice
Strachan, Carolyn
Sylvester, Monique
Tennyson, Major Hortense
Theodore, Major Sinuous
Townsend, Major Kathleen
Watkins, Major Lynette

Territorial Commanders

1887	Colonel Abram Davey
1889	Captain Derracot
1889–1892	Salvation Army officially closed but was commanded unofficially by Raglan Phillips
1892	Major James J. Cooke
1894	Major Emmanuel Rolfe
1900	Brigadier Thomas Gale
1902	Commissioner Elijah Cadman (pro tem)
	Colonel Josiah Taylor (pro tem)
1903	Lt. Colonel Joseph S. Rauch
1906	Colonel C. Herbert Lindsay
1908	Lt. Colonel Sydney C. Maidment
1911	Colonel Charles Rothwell
1914	Colonel Henry Bullard
1920	Colonel Julius Horskins
1921	Colonel John T. Hillary
1923	Commissioner Henry Bullard
1926	Colonel Thomas Cloud (West Indies Western Territory)
	Colonel Joseph Barr (West Indies Eastern Territory)
1930	Colonel Mary B. Booth (West Indies Western Territory)
	Colonel Wilfred Twilley (West Indies Eastern Territory)
1933	Lt – Commissioner Robert Henry
1936	Colonel Herbert S. Hodgson
1945	Colonel Francis Ham
1949	Colonel William P. Sansom
1953	Lt – Commissioner George Sandells
1956	Lt – Commissioner Francis Ham
1957	Colonel John Stannard
1962	Colonel John Fewster
1967	Colonel William E. Chamberlain
1969	Lt – Commissioner F. Frank Saunders
1971	Colonel Ernest Denham
1973	Colonel John D. Needham
1976	Colonel Arthur R. Pitcher
1979	Colonel Orval Taylor
1982	Colonel J. Edward Read
1986	Colonel David Baxendale
1990	Colonel David Edwards
1995	Colonel Franklyn Thompson
1998	Colonel Dennis Phillips
2001	Colonel John Matear
2006	Commissioner Raymond Haughton
2009	Colonel Onal Castor

Territorial Changes

1900   West Indies Territory formed. Territorial headquarters
in Barbados; moved to Jamaica in 1901

1905   West Indies and Central America Territory
(Panama and Costa Rica added). Work was also begun
in US Virgin Islands and Puerto Rico but these US territories
were soon transferred to the USA Eastern Territory

1926   Territory divided: West Indies Eastern Territory –
Territorial Headquarters in Trinidad
West Indies Western Territory –
Territorial Headquarters in Jamaica. Bermuda taken from
Canada Territory and added to West Indies Western Territory

1933   West Indies Eastern Territory and West Indies Western
Territory combined to form Central America and
West Indies Territory – Territorial Headquarters in Jamaica.
Bermuda transferred back to Canada Territory

1968   Caribbean and Central America Territory

1976   Caribbean Territory – Panama, Costa Rica, Venezuela and
Guatemala removed to become part of the new Mexico and
Central America Territory

1999   Caribbean Territory - Cuba and Belize removed to help
form new Latin America North Territory

2005   Caribbean Territory – Belize returns to Caribbean Territory;
Dominican Republic removed to become part of the Latin
America North Territory

Crest Books

Salvation Army National Publications

Crest Books, a division of The Salvation Army's National Publications department, was established in 1997 so contemporary Salvationist voices could be captured and bound in enduring form for future generations, to serve as witnesses to the continuing force and mission of the Army.

Shaw Clifton, *Never the Same Again: Encouragement for new and not-so-new Christians,* 1997

Compilation, *Christmas Through the Years: A War Cry Treasury,* 1997

William Francis, *Celebrate the Feasts of the Lord: The Christian Heritage of the Sacred Jewish Festivals,* 1998

Marlene Chase, *Pictures from the Word,* 1998

Joe Noland, *A Little Greatness,* 1998

Lyell M. Rader, *Romance & Dynamite: Essays on Science & the Nature of Faith,* 1998

Shaw Clifton, *Who Are These Salvationists? An Analysis for the 21st Century,* 1999

Compilation, *Easter Through the Years: A War Cry Treasury,* 1999

Terry Camsey, *Slightly Off Center! Growth Principles to Thaw Frozen Paradigms,* 2000

Philip Needham, *He Who Laughed First: Delighting in a Holy God,* (in collaboration with Beacon Hill Press, Kansas City), 2000

Henry Gariepy, ed., *A Salvationist Treasury: 365 Devotional Meditations from the Classics to the Contemporary,* 2000

Marlene Chase, *Our God Comes: And Will Not Be Silent,* 2001

A. Kenneth Wilson, *Fractured Parables: And Other Tales to Lighten the Heart and Quicken the Spirit,* 2001

Carroll Ferguson Hunt, *If Two Shall Agree* (in collaboration with Beacon Hill Press, Kansas City), 2001

John C. Izzard, *Pen of Flame: The Life and Poetry of Catherine Baird,* 2002

Henry Gariepy, *Andy Miller: A Legend and a Legacy,* 2002

Compilation, *A Word in Season: A Collection of Short Stories,* 2002

R. David Rightmire, *Sanctified Sanity: The Life and Teaching of Samuel Logan Brengle,* 2003

Chick Yuill, *Leadership on the Axis of Change,* 2003

Compilation, *Living Portraits Speaking Still: A Collection of Bible Studies,* 2004

A. Kenneth Wilson, *The First Dysfunctional Family: A Modern Guide to the Book of Genesis,* 2004

Allen Satterlee, *Turning Points: How The Salvation Army Found a Different Path,* 2004

David Laeger, Shadow and Substance: *The Tabernacle of the Human Heart,* 2005

Check Yee, *Good Morning China,* 2005

Marlene Chase, *Beside Still Waters: Great Prayers of the Bible for Today,* 2005

Roger J. Green, *The Life & Ministry of William Booth* (in collaboration with Abingdon Press, Nashville), 2006

Norman H. Murdoch, *Soldiers of the Cross: Susie Swift and David Lamb*, 2006

Henry Gariepy, *Israel L. Gaither: Man with a Mission*, 2006

R.G. Moyles, ed., *I Knew William Booth*, 2007

John Larsson, *Saying Yes to Life*, 2007

Frank Duracher, *Smoky Mountain High*, 2007

R.G. Moyles, *Come Join Our Army*, 2008

Ken Elliott, *The Girl Who Invaded America: The Odyssey Of Eliza Shirley*, 2008

Ed Forster, *101 Everyday Sayings From the Bible*, 2008

Harry Williams, *An Army Needs An Ambulance Corps: A History of The Salvation Army's Medical Services*, 2009

Judith L. Brown and Christine Poff, eds., *No Longer Missing: Compelling True Stories from The Salvation Army's Missing Persons Ministry*, 2009.

Quotes of the Past & Present, A Compilation from the *War Cry*, 2009

Henry Gariepy and Stephen Court, *Hallmarks of The Salvation Army*, 2010

John Cheydleur and Ed Forster, eds., *Every Sober Day Is a Miracle*, 2010

R.G. Moyles, *William Booth in America: Six Visits 1886 - 1907*, 2010

Shaw Clifton, *Selected Writings, Vol. 1: 1974-1999 and Vol. 2: 2000-2010*, 2011

How I Met The Salvation Army, A Compilation from the War Cry, 2011

A. Kenneth Wilson, *It Seemed Like a Good Idea at the Time: Some of the Best and Worst Decisions in the Bible*, 2011

R.G. Moyles, *Farewell to the Founder*, 2012